Post-war Laos

Post-War Laos

The Politics of Culture, History, and Identity

Vatthana Pholsena

Cornell University Press
Ithaca, New York

First published 2006 by Cornell University Press

Printed in the United States of America

Librarians: Library of Congress Cataloging-in-Publication
Data are available.

ISBN-13: 978-0-8014-4503-3 (cloth : alk. paper)
ISBN-10: 0-8014-4503-5 (cloth : alk. paper)
ISBN-13: 978-0-8014-7320-3 (pbk. : alk. paper)
ISBN-10: 0-8014-7320-9 (pbk. : alk. paper)

Cornell University Press strives to use environmentally
responsible suppliers and materials to the fullest extent
possible in the publishing of its books. Such materials
include vegetable-based, low-VOC inks and acid-free
papers that are recycled, totally chlorine-free, or partly
composed of nonwood fibers. For further information, visit
our website at www.cornellpress.cornell.edu.

Cloth printing   10 9 8 7 6 5 4 3 2 1

Paperback printing   10 9 8 7 6 5 4 3 2 1

To my parents

Contents

Acknowledgements

First and foremost, my deep gratitude goes to my informants and friends in Laos, whose identities must unfortunately remain concealed by pseudonyms throughout this book in view of the sensitive nature of the issues involved. Nevertheless, I should like to thank their warm hospitality and their willingness to talk about very intimate and often highly emotive issues.

This project began thanks to Jean Michaud, my supervisor in the former Centre for South-East Asian Studies at the University of Hull, who persuaded me to embark on this long and, in the end, rewarding journey. I understood and learnt from Clive Christie, my second supervisor, the virtue of expressing complex ideas with clarity and depth. My doctoral research was supported by a Studentship Award from the United Kingdom's Economic and Social Research Council and an Open Scholarship from the University of Hull.

Other researchers on Laos were a source of stimulating discussion and advice. I am most fortunate to have benefited from the invaluable expertise and guidance of Grant Evans, and in particular, Yves Goudineau. I should also warmly thank Vanina Bouté. and Grégoire Schlemmer for all those discussions full of ideas, wit and enthusiasm. Olivier Evrard generously helped me to continue my reflections via email and through meetings back in France. The support I received from Sylvain Sturel of ACF (Action Contre la Faim) in Sekong was very helpful in facilitating my fieldwork in that area. My relatives in Vientiane and Bangkok provided me with support and a family environment that I much appreciated whenever I returned from "the field".

In the latter stage of this project, I was lucky enough to have profited from the excellent working conditions and stimulating academic environment provided by the Asia Research Institute (ARI) at the National University of Singapore, where I enjoyed a most productive time as a postdoctoral fellow for nearly two years. A research grant from ARI allowed me to go back twice to Laos and to carry out complementary fieldwork. During this period, various people in Singapore and elsewhere generously helped me in sharpening my post-PhD cogitations. I should thank in particular Christopher E. Goscha, Andrew Hardy, Khoo Gaik Cheng, Bruce M. Lockhart, and Guillaume Rozenberg for their advice and comments. My gratitude also goes to the Southeast Asian Studies Programme at the National University of Singapore, which I joined in 2004, and especially to Reynaldo C. Ileto, who provided me with a supportive environment wherein I was able to complete the last stages of this project.

I am profoundly thankful to Dayaneetha De Silva, my editor at the Institute of Southeast Asian Studies (ISEAS). Without her unfailing support and generosity, it is unlikely that my manuscript would have left its corner of the bookshelf. I am also very grateful to the three anonymous readers who gave me many insightful comments, and to Triena Ong, the Managing Editor of ISEAS, for her professional help and efforts. Martin Stuart-Fox's encouragement brightened the final stage of this project. I was lucky that Minnie Doron recently arrived in Singapore: the book cover shows her wonderful talent.

I should thank the publishers for permission to reprint here: Chapter 4, adapted from "The Changing Historiographies of Laos: a Focus on the Early Period", *Journal of Southeast Asian Studies* 35, no. 2 (June 2004): 235–59; and Chapter 6, adapted from "Nation/Representation: Ethnic Classification and Mapping Nationhood in Contemporary Laos", *Asian Ethnicity* 3 no. 2 (September 2002): 175–97.

My last words go to my family to whom I should apologise for enduring and indulging my academic endeavours. I should thank in particular three of its members: my brother whose support (especially in computing and logistics!) and sense of humour never faltered. Without Paul, the best critic of my works, this book simply would not exist. Finally, I wish to acknowledge the loving support of my father, to whom I owe the most.

A Note on Transcription, Spelling, and Translation

Transcription and spelling

Since no official system of transcription of Lao script into English exists, I have used one that tries to reproduce as closely as possible the Lao pronunciation with sounds that exist in English. For example, the 'or' in *kan tor su* ການຕໍ່ສູ້ ["struggle"] is pronounced approximately as the 'or' in c<u>or</u>n, while the 'o' in *vìlàsòn* ວິລະສົນ ["hero"] is the short 'o' as in b<u>o</u>ne.

Simple vowels in Lao are either short or long. I have differentiated these two types of vowel by marking the short ones with an acute accent over the letter, thus: 'ò'.

The consonants are generally pronounced as in English. An 'h' following any consonant indicates that it is aspirated. Even though the 'r' may be more appropriate for some words because of their Sanskrit or Pali roots, I have nevertheless preferred 'l' so as to be faithful to my informants' pronunciation.

I have generally kept familiar spellings, such as Vientiane (that strictly-speaking should be transcribed as *Viengchan*), for the sake of clarity. For the names of Lao authors of published works, I have retained the spelling used in the publication.

Finally, I have made no effort to represent the tonal elements of the Lao language. However, by writing key terms and phrases in Lao script as well as in English, I hope I have provided sufficient information for those who wish to draw on my work.

Translation

All the translations from Lao into English or from French into English are mine unless otherwise stated.

LAOS
Provinces

1

Post-war Laos: An Introduction

I have no direct memories of my father's country. Like thousands of Lao, my parents left in the late 1970s after the Communists took power, and settled in France. For a long time, Laos remained a distant country for me. But it was there that I found myself drawn to the issues of ethnicity and nationalism; like many others, I was fascinated by the country's linguistic and cultural mosaic[1] and its turbulent history. Two initial, broad research aims eventually unfolded: first, how might sentiments of national consciousness be created in a complex society (such as Laos)? And, second, which form of "nation" would develop in a non-Western, post-colonial and multi-ethnic country (such as Laos)? My interest was heightened by Laos' turbulent history, especially from the late nineteenth century onwards. Laos, like Vietnam and Cambodia, is a former French colony. The country was entangled in the turmoil of the Second World War and the Japanese occupation of the region, which irremediably damaged the "prestige" of French colonial power. Laos was first declared independent in September 1945 (after the surrender of the Japanese and before the return of the French), an arrangement to be replaced less than a year later, in May 1946, with the status of a unified constitutional monarchy within the French Union.

The newly built Lao polity was, however, subsequently destroyed by the impact of the Cold War and the First and Second Indochinese Wars. From the late 1940s to 1975, a civil war tore the country apart along political, ideological and geographical lines. The conflict opposed the Royal Lao Government (RLG) to the Pathet Lao, i.e. the Lao communists. Both sides were heavily dependent on foreign powers: the United States and the Democratic Republic of Vietnam (and, to a lesser extent, the People's Republic of China), respectively. The country was split into two zones, as if an imaginary (and fluctuating) line, drawn north to south, divided the eastern and western halves of the country. Broadly speaking, the government controlled areas embraced the plains, mostly inhabited by ethnic Lao, while the communists dominated the eastern and mountainous territories, which were mainly populated by ethnic minorities. The civil war has left enduring scars within the Lao collective memory; the present regime still struggles with the process of defining a form of nation as it finds it difficult to come to terms with the country's past. My intention here is to discuss the project of nationhood in post-socialist Laos as engineered by the state and its agents, and perceived by members of ethnic minorities.

"Moment of arrival"

Chatterjee has divided the emergence and development of non-Western nationalist thought into three phases or "moments", namely, "the moments of departure, manoeuvre and arrival". The first stage defines the encounter between Eastern and Western cultures, and the discovery of their intrinsic differences. These dramatic events lead to the formation of nationalist thought based on a combination of the "superior material qualities of Western cultures with the spiritual greatness of the East" (Chatterjee 1993, p. 51). The second "moment" involves the mobilization of popular elements in what has so far been the project of an elite. The final phase (which is my main focus here) is "when nationalist thought attains its fullest development", i.e. once statehood is achieved. The nationalist discourse is now a discourse of legitimation (ibid.).

Before I discuss this crucial "moment of arrival" in the context of post-socialist Laos, it is important first to understand the semi-failure of the "second moment" in the history of Lao nationalism. The proclamation of the Lao People's Democratic Republic (Lao PDR) on 2 December 1975, ended a six-century old monarchy. The power of most influential ethnic Lao right-wing families had been broken, the Royal Lao Army (RLA) neutralized, and no more assistance could be expected from the United States. Consequently, the final seizure of power was a mere formality. Though politically and militarily victorious, the new leadership had to face the immense task of reconstructing a country wracked by bombing[2] and artificially sustained by the millions of U.S. dollars of economic assistance that were poured in during the war.[3] But the challenges were not only socio-economic. The leaders of the Lao People's Revolutionary Party (LPRP) were in effect unknown figures to most Lao when they came to power.[4] The Party's seizure of power had not been preceded by a popular uprising in either the urban areas or in the countryside. The Pathet Lao had not mobilized an exploited peasantry with promises of land reform. The civil war had left a disorientated population for whom communism was little more than a name. In effect, the political revolution took place in a virtual vacuum.

What is more, after the failure of the Lao nationalist movement that emerged after the Second World War (which only promoted ethnic Lao culture and therefore excluded the ethnic minorities from the construction of a Lao national identity), the communists faced the enormous challenge of building another form of nation. The success of the "National Democratic Revolution" in 1975 was indebted to the participation of some highland ethnic groups allied with Pathet Lao and Viet Minh troops during the French and American-North Vietnamese Wars; the new leadership could hardly afford to ignore them in its nationalist project. In the context of guerrilla warfare, the support of the local population was indeed seen as

an essential asset. As David Marr accurately noted for North Vietnam: "...
without the active involvement of some of them [the highland minority
peoples], [Ho Chi Minh's] plan to create and defend one or more liberated
zones in the mountains was doomed to failure" (Marr 1981, p. 403). Some
analysts (like Jean Chesnaux, Bernard B. Fall and John T. McAlister) even
attributed the French defeat at Dien Bien Phu in 1954 to the Viet Minh's
ethnic policy, although recent studies also point to massive Chinese
assistance as a major cause for the Viet Minh victory. The recruitment of
upland people is likewise believed to have significantly contributed to the
Lao communist movement's survival and success. Grant Evans has recently
contested this theory, however, by seriously playing down the ethnic
minority factor in the building-up of the revolutionary forces in Laos and
the latter's ultimate victory (Evans 2002, p. 134). It is fairly safe to argue
that the participation of highland populations on the side of the Lao and
North Vietnamese communists was not the sole factor that contributed to
their triumph. Furthermore, their role has been over-emphasized at times
(and understated at others) in the state-sponsored historiography to
conform with the principle of inter-ethnic solidarity. On the other hand,
especially during the early years of its formation and growth in the eastern
regions after 1946, the young Lao communist movement and their North
Vietnamese counterparts depended on the local population's collaboration,
if not active support, to hide from the French (or to simply not be denounced
to them). The revolutionaries also needed to run logistics networks to
carry messages, weapons and food. Without the help of ethnic minority
villagers in those mountain areas, it is uncertain whether early revolutionary
bases on the Lao-Vietnamese borders could have operated efficiently —
or even survived.[5]

Furthermore, as a socialist movement following the Marxist-Leninist
line of Vietnamese communism, the new government had a completely
different ideological framework that could be seen as constituting an
advantage over the traditionalist and conservative Lao governments that
had preceded it. Indeed, the communists saw their ultimate objective,
namely the creation of "socialist man" in a new society, as entailing the

conquest of all the difficulties related to the issue of ethnicity that permeated Laos. Their nationalism, by emphasizing the necessity of including all the ethnic groups in Lao society with equal rights and opportunities, may therefore be defined as a polyethnic or supra-ethnic ideology "which stresses civil rights rather than shared cultural roots, [...] where no ethnic group openly tries to turn nation-building into an ethnic project on its own behalf" (Eriksen 1993, p. 118).

The objective of creating a "socialist man" has waned over the years as the Lao Communist Party's ideology has changed. In the 2003 Amended Constitution (first promulgated in 1991), the adjective "socialist" is no longer applied to "man"; instead, the only educational goal specified is to produce "good citizens" (Article 22), and a Lao citizen is someone with Lao nationality. Similarly, there is no mention of socialism in the preamble, even as a distant goal; Laos is referred to only as a country of "peace, independence, democracy, unity and prosperity". Nonetheless, some socialist principles are still present in the Constitution, "though they have been tempered by liberal notions to reflect contemporary realities and demands" (Stuart-Fox 1996, p. 216). Thus, the Lao PDR is still defined as a "People's Democratic State" (Article 2), and its organizations "function in accordance with the principle of democratic centralism" (Article 5). On the other hand, the Party's belief in the construction of a polyethnic society is clearly emphasized in the preamble, which opens thus: "The multiethnic Lao people have existed and developed on this beloved land for thousands of years". Throughout the Constitution of the Lao PDR (2003), reference is therefore made to the multiethnicity of the population of Laos. It should be stressed that citizenship is granted to all regardless of ethnicity. Nevertheless, only a single article specifically comments on the ethnic minorities. Article 8 commits the state to promoting "unity and equality" among all ethnic groups, which have the right "to protect, preserve, and promote the fine customs and cultures of their own tribes and of the nation". The state is also committed "to gradually develop and upgrade" the socioeconomic conditions of minority groups and "[a]ll acts of creating division and discrimination among ethnic groups are prohibited". Apart from these provisions, no special constitutional status is granted to ethnic groups with regard to their parliamentary representation. Indeed, the Lao government's minority policy has consistently been not to differentiate between ethnic groups. For example, the creation of national minority zones was neither promised nor realized in Laos, unlike in China; rather, the long-standing principle is that of "unity on the basis of equality" with the integration of the minorities into the political, social and economic life of the country.

My intention in the following chapters is to analyse this very "moment of arrival" in modern Laos, following the economic and ideological failure of the socialist project. In other words, I propose to study the nationalist discourse of the post-socialist Lao state. More precisely, I will be looking at the ways the state is uttering its discourse of legitimation within a context of multiethnicity. Accordingly, my objective is not to discuss the reality of a "nation" in modern Laos; rather, my focus is "nationalism" as a process. Indeed, the fluidity of the definition of "nation" should warn us against any kind of simplification. While the people's adhesion to the nation is a necessary factor, it is also essential to bear in mind the fact that a "nation" may be shaped in different forms. The examination of the Lao terms for "nation" is a good method of encouraging a more subtle analysis.

The most commonly used Lao words for "nation" are *pàthet sat* or *sat*; *pàthet* means "country" and *sat* can mean both "nation" and "race", depending on the context. Thus, the conception of "nation" in the Lao language is closely linked to the metaphors of family, blood, lineage. The formal vocabulary likewise stresses the metaphoric relationship: *pìthùphum* and *matùphum* may respectively be translated as "fatherland" (*pìthù* = father) and "motherland" (*matù* = mother). There are also popular idioms that project the image of a localized identity. *Pathet sat ban meuang* is one of them. *Ban meuang* can be translated as "town" or "country" in the vernacular. Similarly, the popular expression, *ban kert meuang norn* ("the village where one was born, the town where one sleeps") emphasizes the metaphor of a territorialized identity, the image of "home", the idea of a place to which one belongs.

The examination of the nationalist discourse is only half the picture, though; the exploration of the sentiments of nationhood of men and women who belong to an ethnic minority group and who have been involved in the communist war and then the socialist project will form the other side of my study. The French and American-Vietnam Wars abruptly changed their historical and social position: from the "periphery" to the "centre", from being "the savage" (or "the slave") to becoming a "patriot". As far as I am aware, no study has ever been conducted of their views on the national(ist) project of the post-socialist era. Yet, they played a role in the socialist project of nationhood, and more crucially, were socialized by the Revolution and its ideals. I therefore believe that this research will provide some insights into their interpretations of the idea of "nation" in present-day Laos, and significantly contribute to the understanding of the project of nation-defining in the post-Cold War era, particularly in a post-colonial, post-socialist and multiethnic country. In brief, my analysis will be structured around two poles: the state and individuals (i.e. educated members of ethnic minorities); between structure and agency, at the interface of nationalism and ethnicity.

Multi-site, multi-level investigation

I had different sites of investigation. The first one was the headquarters of the Lao Front for National Construction (LFNC) in Vientiane. The LFNC is the country's main mass organization, with offices at every political and administrative level. As a matter of fact, when I told a long-term specialist on Laos of my wish to study nationalism in Laos, he advised me to contact the Director of the LFNC Research Department on Ethnic Groups. I knew — roughly — the profile of the kind of key informant with whom I wished to work, i.e. a member of an ethnic minority, male or female, who holds or has held a position of authority within the state. The Director, a member of an ethnic minority himself, consequently constituted the ideal point of departure for my research. Without a doubt, my initial collaboration with the Director opened some valuable doors for me. On the other hand, my pairing with a high-ranking official also undoubtedly had its disadvantages: I was put in a dominant position almost involuntarily, which certainly affected my fieldwork to some extent.

The researcher is always "a positioned subject" in the field, although I tried to project a de-politicized and de-racialized identity as I undertook my field research. I would describe myself as a young, (then) unmarried woman, French-educated to a high level, with Lao and Thai origins. That is the most neutral description I could possibly give of myself, and naively I thought that people in Laos would see me in these relatively straightforward terms.[6] The common assumption, as Judith Okely notes, is that the female researcher is not "hampered" by her sex because she is treated as an "honorary male" (Okely 1996, p. 32). However, Okely found this status to be an inappropriate description of her position vis-à-vis Gypsy men. In fact, as she writes, she increasingly suspected that "women anthropologists [were] given ambiguous status in the field, not as 'honorary males', but as members of an alien 'race'" (ibid.). I would agree with her. I surely was not considered as a "male"; otherwise, I would have possibly spent most of my fieldwork trying to recover from successive hangovers. Neither was I regarded as a "local female" as I was allowed to interact directly with men without any witnesses. I had to accept that I often appeared as a *farang* ("foreigner", usually from Europe or North America), or more precisely, as a "white Lao".

Outside Vientiane, my fieldwork was conducted entirely in southern Laos where my research sites emerged by chance and by choice. I had decided not to try to cover the north of the country, which has quite a distinct ethno-cultural landscape and history. And, although my study is not situated within the discipline of anthropology, I had little hesitation in choosing ethnography as one of my research methods as it is based upon a lengthy, daily and close — or, as close as possible — interaction with people. One of my research locations was in the capital of Champassak Province, Pakse, where I stayed with a family in which the mother and the father were non-ethnic Lao and prominent members of the two main national mass organizations, the LFNC and the Lao

Women's Union (LWU). Another site of investigation was Ban Paktai, in Sekong province in southeastern Laos, which had received the title of "Heroic Village" for its participation in the revolutionary struggle. In addition, my trips with LFNC officials allowed me to observe them in different social, political and cultural contexts, and to meet their colleagues, friends and relatives in the provinces. They were all not ethnic Lao, and some of them held positions within the various provincial administrations. These various sites of investigation emerged as I progressed in my research. I had a feeling that they were somehow connected; yet, it was not until I had completed my fieldwork and put some distance between them and me that I was able to fully elucidate the logic of their relationships.

One reason for conducting a multi-sited ethnography is because the state and its nationalist discourse are not "things" that are suspended above society, but instead play a crucial role in the formation of "the people". First, the state's power and actions are dispersed throughout society. Second, my informants did not exist in the same socio-cultural context. As George E. Marcus has observed: "For ethnographers interested in contemporary local changes in culture and society, single-sited research can no longer be easily located in a world system perspective. This perspective has become fragmented, indeed, 'local' at its very core" (Marcus 1995, p. 98). I should stress that this is not a comparative study, as such, between homogenous units of study, though my research has comparative elements. My intention was not to compare the lives of these people located in various environments. I went "down" from the capital to attain the village. It was not merely a geographical displacement — I went through the hierarchy of power, from the centre to the periphery. More precisely, I followed these people's journeys in space and time. These educated Lao of ethnic minority origin had gone to live in the capital, province, district or village for different reasons, yet all related to their trajectories within the state's apparatus. By interacting with them, I was able to investigate the manifestation, and limits, of state power in various contexts and at differing levels. Finally, in addition to fieldwork and oral interviews, I used Lao-language documents: books, newspapers, official documents, unpublished manuscripts. The volume of such literature represents a far cry from that which can be found in Vietnam or in Thailand, for example. Their paucity made the discovery of a valuable document all the more exciting for me, as if I was an explorer of lost manuscripts.

Forging nationhood in post-socialist Laos

The most comprehensive and perceptive study[7] so far on nationalism in Laos in the post-socialist era is the book written by Grant Evans, *The Politics of Ritual and Remembrance: Laos since 1975*, published in 1998. As Evans recounts, from 1975 to the late 1980s, the communists instituted measures to demonstrate their will to break with the past and with the abhorred former regime and its most potent symbols, i.e. the monarchy and Buddhism. However, after the collapse of the communist ideological project, the Lao state was in need of new symbols of legitimation. The regime consequently has "embarked on modifying old rituals and symbols and creating new ones" (Evans 1998, p. 14). Evans, an anthropologist and a long-term specialist on Laos, thus explores the present regime's ongoing struggle to impose images of cultural homogeneity and historical continuity in Lao people's minds through the politics of representation and reinterpretation of the past.

Evans' analysis encompasses several realms, such as: commemorative rituals (National Day; the That Luang festival; New Year festivities; the "cult" of Kaysone Phomvihane, the first President of the Lao PDR and portrayed in official hagiographies as the leader of the Lao Revolution); the remembrance of symbols of the old regime, i.e. the monarchy and Buddhism; "national" monuments, such as statues; the re-writing of history books with their rag-bag of remembered and forgotten events; and ethnic minorities and their instrumental role. Evans shows that either the rituals of legitimation initiated after 1975 to mark the change from the old patterns abandoned their triumphalist style (as is the case for National Day celebrations) or merely failed to appeal to the population (like the "cult" of Kaysone, which never managed to attain the level of that of Ho Chi Minh in Vietnam).

The most obvious example of the Lao state's "serious existential crisis" (Evans 1998, p. 10) is the revival of Buddhist practices at both state and popular levels. In post-socialist Laos, economic and social liberalization in the late 1980s certainly favoured an atmosphere of regulatory relaxation that led to the resurgence of Buddhist popular practices.[8] Evans argues that it was primarily the collapse of communism that urged the regime to find a new formulation of Lao nationalism and a new ideology of legitimation, to such an extent that he describes the phenomenon as "a re-Buddhification of the Lao state" (1998, p. 67). His analysis of the relationship between Buddhism and the state is clearly political and instrumentalist; although he seems at times to adopt a somewhat perennialist perspective, as in his conclusion when he states that "with the collapse of socialist ideology an older Buddhist discourse on Lao history has re-emerged to fill its place — a discourse which is centred on righteous kings and was suddenly interrupted by the historical hiatus of 1975" (1998, p. 70). Evans appears to suggest that the 1975 revolution was only an "accident" and that historical continuity has resumed with the return of Buddhism at the core of Lao nationalism.

In this, his view has something in common with Anthony D. Smith's ethno-symbolism and its sense of continuity (Smith 1998). Evans' chapter on the monarchy, entitled "Recalling Royalty", is even more demonstrative of continuing linkages with the past. Despite the forceful suppression of all royal symbols after 1975, the regime still shows some kind of nostalgia for, or at least reminiscence of, an ostensibly distasteful past. Evans' descriptions of the Lao officials' behaviour during the visit of the Thai king and queen and their daughter to Laos (the first for the Thai king) for the opening of the Friendship Bridge in 1994 are rather intriguing, even amusing. He wrote, for example: "What is striking about this occasion [a baci[9] sponsored by the president and the prime minister and their wives for the royal couple and the princess at the presidential palace] is the ease with which the Lao officials and their wives conformed to royal protocol, and the obvious delight they took in moving within the charmed circle of the Thai king" (Evans 1998, p. 113).

Evans' long experience of the country allows him not only to comment on the recent evolution of the state's cultural politics but also to provide insightful views on the older patterns under the RLG or the French. However, what constitutes the major theme of his book also constitutes the main weakness in his argument: although he never quite makes it explicit, his analysis is obviously centred on culture, history and society from the perspective of the ethnic Lao majority. Likewise, the geographical focus of his study is revealing: his case studies are drawn from urban or semi-urban areas; more precisely, from Vientiane and Luang Prabang, both towns with predominantly ethnic Lao populations. Evans only hints at the reactions of the urban-based ethnic Lao population to the state's cultural politics; there is no mention of the minorities' feelings regarding the actions of the state or how they make sense of their worlds and interpret the nationalist discourse. Only one chapter deals with the non-ethnic Lao population ("The minorities in state rituals"). Following Archaimbault's seminal research on Lao religious structures (1973) and Göran Aijmer's subsequent paper (1979), Evans similarly emphasizes the central role of the upland peoples, the *Kha*, in the political and religious rituals, notably surrounding the monarchy, during the pre-1975 period (1998, pp. 143–46). Unsurprisingly, the meaning of these ceremonies was diluted from 1975 to the 1980s by the themes of "multiethnic solidarity and unity", in which the previously symbolic kinship relationships between the ethnic and non-ethnic Lao were lost. However, under the present-day Lao state, ethnic minorities have been turned into neutral items whose main use is to instil ethnic flavour into the "national" culture. Yet, Laos is a complex, multiethnic country. As a result, studies of Lao nationalism should more fully incorporate the "ethnic" factor. The following chapters will be concerned with Laos' "minority" component as much as with the "national" culture itself, in an attempt to redress this imbalance.

To be sure, recent ethnographic studies of the politics of ethnicity and ethnic populations in Laos have been written (Proschan 1997, Trankell 1998). In his study on the Kmhmu,[10] Frank Proschan offers a brilliant example of the extraordinary fluidity and variability of ethnic identities (1997). In a sense, he renews the concept of boundaries by demonstrating that it is possible to have (within the same ethnic group) two competing models of ethnicity and identity coexisting: a primordialist one based on descent and a constructionist one based on behaviour. On the other hand, Trankell argues that external classification, the "official discourse of ethnicity", has led to the process of "laoization" by incorporating some populations within the "Lao Lum" category, despite their self-identifying as not being "Lao". The reason for this arbitrary classification is because they fit even less well into the other two categories, i.e. "Lao Theung" and "Lao Sung" (Trankell 1998, pp. 51–52). However, Proschan's theory is indifferent to the state and neither essay says much about nationalism.

My study of Lao nationalism in the post-socialist era differs from these works in two ways: first, my intention is to analyse the ideology of nationalism as a discourse of power by focusing on the relationships between the One/Majority and the Other/Minorities. Second, I argue that the construction of this cultural, historical and political representation of a nation fails to encompass a section of the Lao population, i.e. educated members of ethnic minorities. My ethnography of a number of individuals' lives reveals a very different representation of the nation, reflected in their narratives of the past and their discourse about their ethnic and national identities.

I have divided this study into six chapters. Chapter 1 provides a historical background on the changing patterns of interactions between lowland and highland populations, starting from the Lan Xang era and extending to incorporate the period of French Indochina (1887–1945), of which the most intriguing episode was arguably the emergence of a modern identity among some highland groups in colonial Laos. I then address the issue of national identity and culture in contemporary Laos through an analysis of the politics of Minority/Majority representation in Chapter 2. It is indeed not sufficient to only unravel the structures of domination and unequal power if one wishes to grasp the complexity of the nature of the Majority (national) and Minority (ethnic) identities. They do not constitute two oppositional entities immutably separated by the binary division of domination and resistance. As Eriksen rightly reminds us, "like other concepts used in the analysis of ethnicity, the twin concepts of minority and majority are *relative* and *relational*" (Eriksen 1993, p. 121, original emphasis).

In order to capture the mechanisms as well as the tensions of the process of nation-defining in post-socialist Laos, it is necessary to deepen the perspective and to take a closer look at the state's technologies of power, their potency as well as their limitations. The nationalist ideology primarily provides the pretext for the control of the state and its resources by one dominant group. The latter dictates the values and the symbols of the society, giving rise to what Brackette F. Williams (who borrows the expression from Gramsci) calls the "transformist hegemonies" that aim at homogenizing heterogeneity. These are fashioned through the assimilation of elements of heterogeneity through appropriations that devalue and deny their link to marginalized others' contributions to the patrimony — i.e. culture and history (Williams 1989, p. 435). In Chapters 3 and 5, I will therefore extend my discussion to the debates concerning the re-writing of history and the ethnic classification of the population.

Post-colonial historiographers share an obsession with origins. Nations need a foundation, a mythical past so as to enforce a *longue durée* — an essential component for consolidating a collective memory and identity. But the past appears seamless because it is constructed as such. The state's representation of the nation, as it is well known, loathes disruptions and discontinuities. In Laos, on the contrary, as I show in Chapter 3, state-endorsed history books and textbooks present three interpretations of the origins of the Lao people, each of them situated in divergent geopolitical, political and ideological perspectives.

In parallel, the formation of a nation within a complex society, once state control is achieved, always depends on two opposite, yet complementary, trends: homogenization — the blending-in process where ethnicity both as a process and as a category is suppressed — and stigmatization — through which ethnicity, by contrast, is enhanced and controlled *outside* the cultural mainstream but *within* the national paradigm. As Marcus Banks remarks, "the nation's defining group, the one that claims the national label as its own [...], is not then simply another "ethnic group", it is very deliberately and self-consciously everything and nothing" (Banks 1997, p. 160). The "transformist hegemony" seeks to create and define both the national (normal) and the ethnic (deviant) identities. As a consequence, those outside the mainstream are now defined as "ethnic" or "minorities", racially differentiated because culturally stigmatized, as opposed to the "non-ethnic" members of the nation sharing a seeming cultural purity. These deviant groups outside the mainstream will not become full members of the ideologically defined nation unless they stop claiming their rights to a self-defined cultural identity. Their sole authorized contribution to the nation's patrimony will then be de-politicized traditions turned into harmless and colourful folk elements. As scrutinized in Chapter 5, in Laos, those two techniques of mapping nationhood — homogenization and stigmatization — are hampered by an inconsistency that reduces their efficacy.

Just as the dominant group is falsely homogenous and hegemonic, the dominated people are not always either submitting or resisting. As a matter of fact, they may themselves belong to the (national) majority in specific socio-cultural contexts. Ralph Litzinger succinctly formulates the dilemma in the introduction of his book on the Yao in modern China (2000). He asks: "What happens when minorities are no longer seen as simply reacting to or always already resisting the Chinese state, but rather as central agents in the cultural politics of the post-Mao nation? What might the anthropology of post-Mao nationalism look like if it refuses to find in the ethnic subject the perfected example of authenticity or resistance?" (Litzinger 2000, p. 20). More generally, the dualistic simplification between hegemony and resistance is giving way to the multiple, politically complex positions of interpretations that contend within the same social spaces of heterogeneous societies. Chapters 4 and 6 will therefore be focused on the multiple voices of those being represented as they reveal their interpretations of, and their response to, the nationalist discourse under different historical, economic, social and political conditions.

To a great extent, theories of ethnicity and nationalism have drawn on Foucault's model of the state and the binary project of individualization and totalization. The state's power creates and defines both the national (normal) and the ethnic (deviant) identities. The very few recent studies on ethnicity *and* nationalism in Laos rest upon this asymmetrical pair, i.e. Majority–Minorities. Thus, non-ethnic Lao peoples, according to these works, are either culturally integrated within the Majority, or modelled as objects to instil a degree of exoticism in the national culture. In both cases, their identities are externally defined. Their own perceptions of their membership of the nation are silenced, either blended in the cultural mainstream or muted under a label. In this book, my specific intention is to go beyond this dichotomy, the apparent immutability of these two oppositional groups, the Majority and the (Ethnic) Minorities, by focusing on a country that battles through a post-colonial era of triumphant capitalism and (still) vibrant nationalism.

Notes

[1] While the 1995 Lao population census shows 47 groupings, another survey revealed 236 ethnic groups (Chamberlain et al. 1995). The ethnic Lao proper, the socio-politically dominant group, does not constitute an overwhelming majority. They are distributed in the lowlands, primarily along the Mekong. Other lowland areas are inhabited by ethnic groups related to the Lao who speak a variety of Tai-Kadai languages. Members of the Austroasiatic family,

generally acknowledged to be the original inhabitants of the country, are found throughout the country in both upland and lowland environments. Tibeto-Burman speakers arrived recently from southwest China, while the Hmong-Mien (Miao-Yao) peoples, likewise recent arrivals, came from southern and southeast China. These latter two families are confined primarily to highland areas in the northern provinces.

2   Laos holds the unfortunate distinction of being the most heavily bombed country on a per capita basis in history. Mennonite Central Committee (MCC) and Mines Advisory Group (MAG), *Summary Description: Unexploded Ordnance Project, Xieng Khuang, Lao PDR* (Vientiane: MCC and MAG, 1994).

3   More than US$500 million flowed into the country between 1964–75 (Stuart-Fox 1997, p. 153).

4   The famous exception was Prince Souphanouvong, member of the Lao royal family and because of that a much-respected figure in the eyes of ethnic Lao. His role was to represent officially the clandestine Communist Party in the wartime negotiations.

5   The history of the hinterlands of Indochina straddling the frontiers between Laos and Vietnam during the First Indochina War, arguably the least researched aspect of this turbulent period, will be the focus of my forthcoming study.

6   The fact was that I already bore a "non-neutral" name — I never fully realized how significant it was until I arrived in Laos. I knew, of course, that one of my uncles (my father's cousin), Kinim Pholsena, had been assassinated in 1963 whilst serving as the Foreign Minister under the Second Coalition government. As such, my family name was already politicized even before I started my fieldwork. Kinim's reputation as a Neutralist was a double-edged factor for me. It all depended on the type of person I was dealing with, and their degree of political radicalism. Overall, however, the reactions were neutral, if not positive, though I encountered suspicion at times.

7   In fact, there is very little literature at all on the topic.

8   The leadership indeed underestimated the structural role of Buddhism within Lao society, especially at the village level. The Lao authorities thought they could replace it by the ideology of "new socialist men", but this ideology largely failed to appeal to those villagers who practised Buddhist rituals (Evans 1993). Accordingly, the Lao authorities were unable to control, let alone suppress, religion in the countryside.

9   A popular ceremony in Laos that is organized to celebrate such events as a
     marriage, a birth, or more simply, the arrival or departure of a guest.
10   I have followed Proschan's spelling.

2

The Awakening of Ethnic Identity in Colonial Laos?

From the fourteenth century, there was already some interaction within the polity of the Lao kingdoms between ethnic Lao lowlanders and the highland peoples of various ethnic origins. The latter were the "others", however, geographically, culturally, politically and symbolically located at the edge of the kingdom. Here, I will discuss the relationship between lowland and highland peoples in historical perspective, from the Lan Xang era to the period of French Indochina (1887–1945). My aim is to show the changing patterns of interactions between these two populations and, more significantly, the disruptive impact of French colonial administration, of which the most intriguing symptom was arguably the emergence of a modern identity among some highland groups in colonial Laos. French policy, especially towards the upland peoples, played a significant part in the rise of rebellions that occurred from the late nineteenth century in Indochina. It also, albeit indirectly and involuntarily, led to the transformation of some of these revolts into modern political claims. In the last section, I will focus on Ong Kommandam's armed resistance in southern Laos as a remarkable example of the emergence of ethnic consciousness in colonial Laos and as an early expression of identity politics before the advent of an independent Laos.

The divinities, the ethnic Lao and the upland people

Geographical and ecological frontiers

The polity of the traditional Lao kingdom, like other pre-modern Southeast Asian states, was based on an ecological and geographical core which was immutable, constituting as it did the "heartland of irrigated rice cultivation" (Leach 1960–61, p. 56). Beyond this heartland, the state could expand or retract since it had no irrevocably fixed boundaries, nor a permanent administrative apparatus. The core of the kingdom, the rice-lands, would remain despite the unstable mode of governance. Consequently, there was a real distinction between the peoples who lived on the plain and the populations who inhabited the mountains. Thus, Edmund Leach contrasted the "Hill peoples" to the "Valley peoples", while Georges Condominas used variations on the term "civilization" to differentiate between the "civilization of mountains and the civilization of the plains" (Condominas 1980, p. 185). The most salient features that distinguished these two groups of peoples from each other were their modes of subsistence (the highland peoples used shifting cultivation to grow dry rice, whereas the lowland peoples were wet rice cultivators) and their religion (Buddhism for the latter and animism for the former).

By the 1970s, this distinction, which overlooks historical inter-ethnic relationships, was becoming an academic cliché, and was then abandoned by anthropologists in favour of the modern concepts of ethnicity, cultural politics or the politics of identity. It is not my purpose in this chapter to debate these issues. These lowland and highland cultural systems are certainly ideal types; nevertheless, there existed a cultural, ecological, political and geographical distance between the ethnic Lao and the upland peoples. In addition, the Lao historian, Savèng Phinit, interestingly remarks that these mountainous and forested regions were perceived by the ethnic

Lao as a sacred and magic place haunted by powerful spirits whose task was to protect the (fuzzy) frontiers of the kingdom (Savèng 1989, p. 194). This would reinforce the hypothesis that, among the ethnic Lao, there existed the perception of an incommensurable gap between those living at or around the centre and the others settled at the "periphery", far away in a sort of mysterious, wild and feared land. This gap was more likely to exist in the case of those upland peoples who lived in remote areas, since assimilation could occur when these people lived among or near their "masters", as Leach showed in the case of ancient Burma (Leach 1960–61, pp. 61–62). However, the ethnic Lao, although they controlled the government, had little interest in assimilating the upland population during the pre-colonial period. Cases of assimilation were not the result of a deliberate policy on the part of the lowlanders (Condominas 1980, p. 275); systematic and institutionalized policies were not enforced to draw the upland peoples into a unitary culture, which would have been that of the ethnic Lao.

Still, the upland groups did not live in strict autarky. Contacts between the ethnic Lao and these upland populations were primarily economic, and studies have demonstrated that there has always been a tradition of interdependence between the various ethnic groups, mostly through exchange (Gunn 1990, p. 72; Walker 1999, p. 39). Peaceful interactions were stimulated by a geographical setting that required people to interact occasionally in order to exchange certain necessities. However, these contacts were largely limited to the border areas of the populations' living environments. Much of the trade took place outside of individual communities, and was either mediated through an agent such as the *lam* (Halpern 1964, p. 94) or was carried out by Chinese traders who brought their goods to the mountain villagers (Lebar, Hickey and Musgrave 1964, p. 215; Walker 1999, p. 32, see also Lefèvre-Pontalis 1902; Forbes 1987). Contact between the peoples living at the periphery and in the lowlands was also limited simply because of the extremely mountainous topography, aggravated by the poor means of communication. Under loose political arrangements, the highland peoples were able to maintain a real autonomy. Unlike the Chinese empire, the Buddhist polities moreover lacked the centralized and bureaucratic organization to control the margins. Furthermore, their rulers never sought to civilize the "savages" living on the frontiers of their empires (Keyes 2002, pp. 1172–73). The frontiers of the kingdom were relatively fluid, their definition and spatial extent depending upon the power of the monarch at the centre.

The mandala politico-religious system

The Lan Xang kingdom (fourteenth to eighteenth century), like the kingdoms of Lan Na and Ayutthaya, was influenced by the political and religious model of the Khmer empire of Angkor that existed between the ninth and the fifteenth century (Condominas 1980, p. 261). The Angkorean kings, claiming to be of divine essence, were the intermediaries who linked this cosmic order to the human world. Their task was to maintain harmony between the empire and the universe. To achieve this aim, they strove to replicate the former in the image of the latter. They were the object of a cult, that of the *devaraja* (the divine king), and placed at the centre of the world on earth (Keyes 1995, p. 73). Despite the decline of the Khmer empire of Angkor in the thirteenth and fourteenth centuries, there remained in the Theravada Buddhist polities of mainland Southeast Asia, including the kingdom of Lan Xang, this conception of the world being centred on a point; hence, the often-quoted Hindu and Buddhist concept of mandala[2] to define the political system that governed the Southeast Asian pre-states. The Tai[3] leaders borrowed the concept and turned it into a political principle to organize and legitimate their rule. Thus, as a religious-cum-political image, the mandala was:

> [...] a particular and often unstable political situation in a vaguely definable geographical area without fixed boundaries and where smaller centres tended to look in all directions for security. *Mandalas* would expand and contract in concertina-like fashion. Each one contained several tributary rulers, some of whom would repudiate their vassal status when the opportunity arose and try to build up their own networks of vassals (Wolters 1999, pp. 27–28).

The mandala system was formed of several "circles of power", the centre of which was dominated by a Buddhist king who ruled by right of (divine) descent and right of merit. He had, it was believed, accumulated enough merit in his previous lives to have deserved to be born as a king. The expansion or contraction of the mandala would depend on his ability to gain the allegiance of smaller political structures and lesser rulers. His power was not in fact measured in terms of territorial gains but rather determined by the size of the ruled population. The power status of the centre was therefore highly variable in accordance with the resources available to the ruler from trade, tribute and manpower, the latter mobilized through military conscription or slavery (Wolters 1999, p. 114).

These conquerors were what Wolters dubbed the "men of prowess", endowed with "the spiritual and leadership resources [...] for mobilizing settlements and *mandalas* in pre- and protohistoric mainland South-East Asia" (Wolters 1999, p. 112). The "men of prowess" were also considered to be "Siva-like figures" for possessing such mighty qualities (ibid.).[4] In effect, the likening to Siva played a crucial role in the development of Southeast Asian conceptions of political authority. The Southeast Asian elite adapted Hindu religious beliefs to develop a personal cult centred on the Siva-like man, through which they could legitimate their rule. This perception is fundamental as it implies that religious ideas legitimate political expansion and order. The earliest law code to have survived from the Lan Xang period, known as the *Law of Khun Bôrom* and written in Xieng Khuang in northeastern "Laos"[5] in 1422, refers in detail to the structure of early Lao society. The latter consisted of four categories: aristocracy, free peasants or commoners (*phai*), slaves (*kha*), and at the bottom, the non-ethnic Lao. As Martin Stuart-Fox explains:

> At the apex stood the king, surrounded by his powerful lords comprising the *Sena Amat* [Council of Nobles]. [...] Below the nobility came the free peasantry who were valued as productive farmers and soldiers, for every able-bodied free man was expected to fight. Other ethnic groups, the Lao Thoeng, abided by their own laws and customs. They stood entirely outside the pale of Tai-Lao society, their status even lower than slaves (*kha*), let alone domestic servants (*khôy*) (Stuart-Fox 1998, p. 47).

In the organization of the Lao mandala, the religious-political order served to legitimize the relations of inequality by providing for the subject population an explanation of their position in the merit-ranked social order. Each individual's position corresponded to a social and political status as well as to a specific position in the production system to which were attached privileges and duties. The hierarchy was also justified by religious principles. Accordingly, the non-Tai peoples were believed to be condemned to the most degrading tasks because of their original exclusion from the religious (Buddhist) mainstream as recounted in the ethnic Lao myth of the origin of mankind (see below).

Myth and cosmology

In his study of Lao religious structures, Charles Archaimbault showed that the unequal relationships between the ethnic Lao and the "indigenous peoples" (*aborigènes*) were inscribed in the ethnic Lao myth of the origin of mankind, known as the myth of Khun Bôrom (Archaimbault 1973). This cosmology divided the world between the descendants of the deities (Khun Bôrom was himself the son of the king of deities), called the *then*, and the human beings who were born to marrows that grew on earth. Originally, inside these vegetables, the ethnic Lao and the "indigenous peoples" were similar, but as soon as they came out, from two different holes, they became distinct from one another. From then on, there were the ethnic Lao on one side and the "Kha", i.e. the non-ethnic Lao, on the other. Archaimbault wrote, thus:

> Or, si au sein des courges régnait l'indistinction, dès la sortie des courges, une dicrimination fut soigneusement établie entre les différents clans et entre les Lao et les aborigènes. Les Khà sortis par un trou spécial foré au fer rouge furent installés sur les montagnes où ils cultivèrent des ray, tandis que les Lao établis dans la plaine s'adjugèrent les rizières (…) (Archaimbault 1973, p. 77).[6]

The role of the myth, among other functions, was to help to give legitimacy to the existing social order by conflating the latter with a putative natural order. It asserted the right of the ethnic Lao to rule over the "indigenous peoples".[1] It also justified the politico-religious order by placing the Buddhist kings in the rank of deities, since they were the descendants of Khun Bôrom whose seven sons went on to establish different kingdoms in the northwestern region of mainland Southeast Asia.[7] Thus, Khun Lô, the eldest son of Khun Bôrom, founded Meuang S'va, which would later become the kingdom of Luang Prabang (Archaimbault 1973, p. 105). On the other hand, Archaimbault also revealed a more complex relationship than the traditional hierarchy placing the king above his rulers and his slaves. He noted that the rites of Luang Prabang were also charged with the right of the aborigines to the soil, as they were its first occupants. He wrote:

> Au combat qui opposa les conquérants lao et les aborigènes, combat qui demeura en dehors des bornes de la culture, fut substitué — du moins selon les textes — un jeu *agonal*[8] chargé de réintroduire momentanément les barbares au sein de la communauté, et de retracer l'évolution d'un droit exclusivement foncier (Archaimbault 1973, p. 79, original stress).[9]

Similarly, Aijmer challenged the common perception of a natural and simplistic politico-religious hierarchy (Aijmer 1979). In so doing, he referred mainly to Archaimbault's works on ethnic Lao culture and religion. He goes even further, however, by claiming that the Kha and the king shared "blood brotherhood" since in the foundation myth of Luang Prabang, the eldest son of the founding king, Khun Lô, was given the name of the dispossessed indigenous chief, in recognition of his former rights to land. For Aijmer, that act established a kinship between the two royal lines, for this transfer of name implies "the sharing of their respective protective spirits and symbols of ancestry" (Aijmer 1979, p. 745). However, the existence of this relationship is exclusive to the Luang Prabang cosmology that, as Archaimbault demonstrated, is a product of the Kingdom's particular history. Aijmer admits, therefore, that "[the] contract [blood brotherhood] which has united the two ethnic groups is a particular solution which has emerged out of a particular historical situation. Outside the domain, the ideology of inequality applies" (Aijmer 1979, p. 745). Nevertheless, these elements of the myth are still revealing of the ambiguities that surrounded the relationships between the conquerors and their subject population.

Inclusion of the highland peoples in the modern world: the French period

In a stimulating and well-documented article, Oscar Salemink argued that the montagnard[10] identity in the Central Highlands of Vietnam under French colonial rule was constructed by the French, who "through a deliberate and carefully planned ethnic policy, supported, protected and exploited this distinct identity for their own purposes" (Salemink 1995, p. 265). Salemink obviously challenged the assumption that there was a primordial montagnard–Vietnamese animosity. Furthermore, he showed that this montagnard identity was built up around an opposition to the Vietnamese identity in "a process of *ethnicization*", which he defined as the relation of a population to a *nation-state*. He then contrasted the process of ethnicization to the process of "tribalization",[11] "which essentially defines upland peoples in relation to *territories*" (Salemink 1995, p. 263, original stress). In other words, the ethnic group is self-perceived and subject whereas the tribe is object and conceived by others. The former is mobile and has awakened to an ethnic political consciousness while the latter is ascribed to a place, with no clear sense of identification with a political unit any broader than the local level. My intention here is to test Salemink's thesis in the case of colonial Laos by asking whether the French were involved in the awakening of ethnic consciousness amongst highland populations in "Laos". An examination of French ethnic policy and the rise of some highlanders' rebellions in eastern "Laos" may point out to an early example of identity politics among those who would become "the minorities" in post-independence Laos.

Colonial writings

The objectification of the "Kha"

The writings of Reinach (1911) and Le Boulanger (1931) on the peoples of "Laos" were fairly typical of their time. According to these French authors, there were two major racial categories: the Tai and the "Kha". However, if the Tai category was justified to a certain extent by linguistic criteria, the "Kha" grouping appears to be much more dubious. The "Kha" were first assigned specific morphological features. Le Boulanger, who based his book on earlier French ethnographic data, described the "Kha" as the "traditional type of savage with their dark skin, straight nose, non-slanting eyes" (Le Boulanger 1931, p. 15).

In fact, the French reappropriated the Lao word *kha* to construct a pseudo-scientific category, whereas the Lao term originally referred to a class and social representation. In other words, the "Kha" were turned into an *objective* ethnic category, in spite of the fact that, amongst themselves, there were significant differences — in languages, rituals, customs, domestic architecture and clothing — which made Reinach note, in contradiction to his own argument: "Scattered, with no links between them, spread out so that they would offer less resistance, speaking different dialects, deprived of common interests, the various Kha tribes appeared before us under a degenerated aspect" (Reinach 1911, p. 126).[12]

In effect, the "Kha" were singled out for their indigenous origins, as well as identified irremediably as "primitive" compared to the more "civilized" Tai peoples, on the basis of so-called scientific works. Their status as the most ancient inhabitants of Laos, as the two authors argued, had been demonstrated by the excavations carried out by the Pavie[13] Mission. Some pre-historical discoveries, such as basic tools and weapons, served also to prove their low level of development as well as to provide an explanation for their rapid subjection by more "evolved" conquerors (Reinach 1911, pp. 125–26). Similarly, the adoption of Buddhism by some "Kha" groups was considered as a sign of evolution. For instance,

Reinach observed that the "moral recovery [of the Kha Khouènes, Khmous and Lemets[14]] had already begun with the practice of Buddhism" (Reinach 1911, p. 128). There were, therefore, some hopes that they would emancipate themselves and eventually dissolve their intrinsic "inferiority" by mixing with "superior" races, such as the Lue, Lao or Thai populations (Reinach 1911, p. 128).[15]

Naming tribes

The French colonial administration's desire to identify and classify its subjects was driven by various purposes, some of them interrelated: scientific enquiry on the part of ethnographers, proselytism in the case of missionaries, administrative requirements for colonial rulers, but also genuine fascination. Ethnographers and colonial rulers were looking for homogeneous units to be used as analytical tools; hence, the common use of "tribe" or "tribal society" to classify people. For Salemink, this process of "tribalisation" progressively corresponded with a "political reality" through the arbitrary linking of the "tribes" to "territories" (Salemink 1995, p. 263). Similarly, in his short essay, Edwin Ardener puts into perspective the significance of contemporary and colonial ethnic labels by showing that they rarely correspond with pre-colonial identities. He also argues that they function in a recursive way: the labels used by colonizers, missionaries and foreign scholars were returned to and appropriated by the people in question (Ardener 1989). In fact, as Salemink observed, the "convergence of ethnography and administration, most notably of linguistics and education and of customary law and policing, resulted in a practical reduction of the number of tribes for administrative purposes" (Salemink 1995, p. 270). In colonial Laos, the "Kha" category became an objective representation, not only through fallacious scientific arguments but also to serve administrative and political purposes. The "Kha" were identified as a category in their own right within the colonial taxation system and were therefore subjected to special requirements, which, in turn, reinforced the process of objectification.

French rule in Indochina

Indochina was a colonial invention. As the name suggests, the territory was first perceived as a geographical space situated between India and China.[16] In the early days of conquest and pacification, Indochina was thus referred to as *Indo-Chine*, with a hyphen reflecting concomitantly its hybrid status and its lack of a specific identity. The French acquisition of these territories that would progressively form the entity eventually named *l'Indochine française*, was less the result of a planned and coherent *politique coloniale* than of an esoteric combination of individual actions, economic interests and imperial rivalry. French intervention in Indochina began in the late seventeenth century supposedly in the name of religious freedom, i.e. the defense of French Catholic missionaries. The French presence in this region of Southeast Asia became, from the mid-nineteenth century, motivated by economic interests and commercial competition with Britain. Indeed, the French hoped that their foothold in Indochina would allow the penetration of the Chinese market via a region from which the British were absent. Many expeditions were subsequently undertaken (including those by the renowned explorers, Ernest Doudart de Lagrée, Francis Garnier and Auguste Pavie) to assess trade routes, and in particular the navigability of the Mekong River, into the interior of China.[17] Opposition from local authorities, rapidly followed by armed conflicts led, however, to heated debates in the metropole pitting politicians pushing for colonial expansion against those opposing further conquests in this area of Asia. Divided views in Paris were to be eventually subsumed by the end of the nineteenth century under a late conceptualization of French imperial policy, driven by a vision of France's grandeur and prestige, bolstered by territorial acquisitions abroad and achieved through military interventions.

The political term *l'Indochine française* was formerly adopted in France in 1887. By suppressing the hyphen and adding the suffix *française*, the influence of Indian and Chinese civilizations was somewhat played down (in a very limited linguistic sense), and the geographical space given a new and uniform identity under French ownership and guidance. The concept of *Indochine* was furthermore superimposed upon artificial political and administrative boundaries that formed *l'Union indochinoise* (widely referred to as French Indochina). The latter was composed of five entities, Laos, Cambodia, Tonkin, Annam and Cochinchina — the last three composing present-day Vietnam — governed by diverse regimes of control and administration: colonies (e.g. Cochinchina, Central and Southern Laos) and protectorates (e.g. Tonkin, Luang Prabang, Cambodia, Annam).

During their administration from 1887 until 1945, the French incessantly pursued the goal of filling the "gap", that is, drawing together the disparate and culturally different peoples and kingdoms of what are today Cambodia, Laos and Vietnam. The act of constructing Indochina was at the same time carried out through concrete, though not entirely successful, policies (e.g. the policy of *mise en valeur*, of which more below), and also via more diffuse routes such as the publication and circulation of glowing articles and colourful reports by the metropolitan press (e.g. *Le Figaro, Le Petit Parisien, Le Tour du Monde, Le Petit Journal Illustré, L'Illustration*, etc.). These vivid accounts popularized the actions of French explorers and adventurers in Indochina, and fed the popular imagination. The French authorities saw these territories as an empty space to colonize, but equally importantly as a lost world once ruled by great civilizations and now pervaded by backwardness, for which they had to design a new and revitalized identity (as Norindr has put it, "one that would conjure up fantasies of colonial life and promote the benevolent role of enlightened France"[18]).

The policy of *mise en valeur*

Two contradictory principles underpinned the French administration of Indochina: on the one hand, colonization had to be "cheap"; on the other, reaping profits from colonies was an equally strong imperative, a strategy known in French as the *mise en valeur*, which required substantial financial investments (Broucheu and Hémery 1994, p. 74). These objectives reflected, in effect, two radically different perspectives in terms of political rule. The "cheap domination" perspective would merely require a type of indirect rule, following the British model in India. Conversely, the *mise en valeur* postulated a strongly interventionist administration (ibid., p. 75). The latter view eventually prevailed when Paul Doumer took up his position as Governor-General of Indochina in 1897. His arrival resulted in the organization of a systematic and bureaucratic centralized administration. A more sophisticated taxation system was one of his first reforms to be implemented. Indochina had to become a self-supporting colony, and tax collection represented the fundamental financial lever to facilitate the transformation of the colonies into profitable markets and producers. One of the impacts of the new system of taxation was to force the transformation of a predominantly subsistence economy into a monetary one, as money progressively replaced barter as a means of exchange.[19]

Colonial system of taxation

Under Doumer, a more sophisticated taxation system was one of the first reforms to be implemented. Personal annual tax — to be paid in cash, not kind — was required from every male between the ages of 18 and 60. In addition, every male between the ages of 18 and 45 was obliged to serve corvée labour annually; the work generally involved the construction of colonial infrastructure, stimulated by the *mise en valeur* policy (Stuart-Fox 1997, p. 32). In effect, as early as 1896, a distinction was drawn within the taxation system between the ethnic Lao and the non-ethnic Lao. For instance, in southern "Laos", a tax differential was established between the ethnic Lao and the population of the Bolovens Plateau, on the basis that the latter were considered more "primitive" and poorer. Consequently, the ethnic Lao paid 2 piasters a year in personal tax against 1.5 piasters for the people living on the Plateau, namely the non-ethnic Lao. Conversely, the number of days of corvée was higher for the latter (15 days a year) than for the ethnic Lao (10 days a year). By 1914, the number of days had increased to 20 and 16 days a year, respectively (Moppert 1978, p. 98). However, corvée labour could be avoided by an additional cash payment. As a matter of fact, the ethnic differentiation would widen down the years, with the ethnic Lao serving fewer days of corvée by redeeming them, while the non-ethnic Lao would be expected to perform more *prestations* (service) as a compensation for a reduced tax rate, or for their incapacity to meet tax demands (Gunn 1990, p. 55).

By 1940, a complex system was in place with five separate categories differentiated along class, landownership, professional and ethnic lines. The last two categories set apart, on the one hand, the "Lao, Vietnamese and 'evolved' montagnards such as the Hmong, Man, Lu, Yao and Kha Loven [sic], who paid 2.5 piasters a year personal tax"; and, on the other hand, "those montagnards such as Kha [sic] and Phoutheng who paid 1.5 piasters per annum personal tax" (Gunn 1990, p. 52).[20] Similarly, the annual corvée labour was fixed by following the reverse order with the "Kha" serving more days than the rest of the population who, furthermore, could afford to take advantage of the redemption mechanism. This practice appeared to be common, with Gunn noting that "[i]n the period from 1909 to 1912, the number of *prestation* days redeemed was increased to a rate almost equal to one half of the total contribution of resources to the budget" (Gunn 1990, p. 50).

A cross-racial and centralized administration

The colonial state system entailed the integration and subordination of the whole Lao political structure. The French authorities simply appointed French officials to the highest positions in the provinces, which had been specifically created to encompass the traditional districts (*tasseng*), grouped into cantons (*meuang*). The French, meanwhile, assumed the right to approve all appointments. The main reason the French maintained the pre-modern Lao system in this form was the financial constraints they faced: the administration of Laos, if not profitable, had at least to be as inexpensive as possible, hence the extremely small number of colonial staff in "Laos" and the reliance on Lao political structures (McCoy 1970, p. 78).[21]

The French instituted a cross-racial administration among the mountain peoples, however. In doing so, they manipulated ethnic relationships so as to ensure a system of indirect rule in areas where direct control would have cost too much in men and *matériel*. In McCoy's words, "[t]he French used traditional racial hierarchies where they were strong, reinforced them where they were weak, and created them where they did not exist" (McCoy 1970, p. 80). This system, combined with the bureaucratic taxation system, ineluctably engendered or exacerbated ethnic conflicts. As an often-quoted example, Izikowitz, in his landmark work on the Lamet of northern Laos, mentioned (albeit briefly) the tensions created by the cross-racial administration between the Lamet and their neighbours, the Lue (Izikowitz 1951, p. 346).

However, the most unpopular elements of the colonial system were, according to many sources (for example, Moppert [1978]), the *lam kha* and the *tasseng*. The former was an individual, usually of ethnic Lao origins, who used to play the traditional role of intermediary (especially for trading) between the mountain peoples and the ethnic Lao. Such individuals were later employed by the French as interpreters and messengers to pass on French orders to the highland villagers. They therefore were an essential link in the administration of the "Kha" regions, and most of them abused their position and were greatly resented by the population (Moppert 1981, p. 50).[22] The *tasseng* were even more despised due to their tax collecting role. They also had the right to ask for corvée and numerous other services from the villages that came within their remit. These "civil servants" serving the French administration, invested with authority by a great power, often behaved as despots in their small "kingdoms". Not surprisingly, they were usually the first victims of the insurrections.

A process of ethnicization in colonial Laos?

In addition to being portrayed as "primitive", the "Kha" were also represented as rebels (*peuple insoumis*), in contrast to the ethnic Lao who complied more readily with the French administration's wishes (partly because they were better treated, in relative terms). Moppert ironically described the myth of the "dangerous land", inhabited by no less dangerous "savages", as the "zone of barbarity [between] the two zones of civilisation

(Lao and Vietnamese). [...] The barbarian is the one who is not like the others. The proof is that he does not want to understand that it is in his interest is to submit" (Moppert 1978, p. 35).[23] For the French authorities, there were only two possible responses (both radical) that could resolve the "problem", i.e. the resistance of some groups of highland peoples: extermination or domestication (*apprivoisement*). Thus transpired the infamous policy of "pacification".

There was a series of highland peoples' rebellions, beginning in 1895,[24] reaching a peak between 1910 and 1916, and finally dying out in the 1930s, all of which expressed resistance to almost every aspect of the French administration. As early as 1901, some Mon-Khmer highland groups led by their chief, Ong Keo, embarked upon armed resistance to the French on the Bolovens Plateau in southern Laos.[25] Ong Keo was eventually killed in 1910 but the struggle was carried on by Kommandam, who had been one of his right-hand men. Kommandam managed to resist the French for almost thirty years (he was eventually killed in 1936) by conducting a guerrilla campaign throughout the highlands. He was not alone in his struggle, though, and through the years he rallied to his cause partisans among the highland populations (Moppert 1981, p. 53).[26]

For Gunn, the "shared montagnard ethnic identity or sense of separateness from outsiders" could explain the insurrections, although he obviously prefers to stress the material causes, such as colonial tax, corvée requirements and the abuses of the *lam kha* (Gunn 1985, p. 59). According to Moppert, the main factor behind the revolts is to be found in the form of the traditional dichotomy between "valley peoples" and "hill peoples". As mentioned above, the hill peoples managed to preserve their political autonomy to a certain extent, due to the topography of the region; hence, there remained amongst them a strong sentiment of independence, which was ferociously defended on the ground, through armed resistance if necessary. The French administration neglected this fundamental attribute of the highland peoples, and had to face the consequences of their ruthless policy (Moppert 1978, p. 227).

One may argue that there existed a "sense of separateness from outsiders" among the highland peoples even before the arrival of the French. Contacts with the Lao population (albeit limited) in the form of trade and tribute to the lowland rulers made possible the fundamental distinction between "us" and "them". A shared montagnard (or whatever label is applied) ethnic identity, as opposed to a Lao identity, did not exist, though. The idea of an ethnic identity that would have gone beyond the level of the village or a cluster of villages appears rather unlikely. The sense of self (as opposed to the "others") was not attached to a political entity any broader than one's immediate environment. Rather, I suggest that the French policy of pacification heightened the highlanders' fierce sense of independence, and *indirectly* fostered ethnic consciousness among some members of the highland population in southeastern "Laos".

Kommandam: the first "Kha" political leader

Kommandam's political programme went further than that of any other rebel ethnic leader. He was not only fighting against the French administration's abuses but also endorsed his claims with a sense of common identity, embodied in the Khom race. Kommandam's strategy to identify his partisans as the Khom was nothing less than remarkable. He appointed himself as *Chao Phraya Khom* (Great Chief of the Khom) and would refer to his movement as "We, the *Khom*". He also invented a Khom writing system as a medium for propaganda and for the coordination of activities between very remote ethnic groups,[27] stirring up resistance among the hill population so that they would not comply with the French authorities' requirements (Moppert 1981, p. 53). By the late 1920s, Kommandam was explicitly claiming a special political status that reflected a clear ethnic consciousness. Moppert wrote:

> In one of his last known letters (22 February 1927), Kommandam, while not challenging the French administration over Laos, makes a condition [for its continued existence]: that is, every member of the Khom race would

be considered as belonging to a distinct race, that would be allowed to live in its own region and, above all, would be cogniscent of the regime under which it would be placed, and for how long.[28]

The origins of the term are not clear but it seems that *Khom* was an old word used by the Tai peoples in ancient times — perhaps before the foundation of the Lan Xang kingdom — to designate the Mon-Khmer speaking population of Laos.[29] Later on, ethnic Lao texts, such as the *Nithan Khun Bôrom* ("the Legend of Khun Bôrom"), would refer to them as *kha kau*, old slaves (Stuart-Fox 1998, p. 164).

Kommandam was perfectly aware of the name's historical meaning when he used it in his political propaganda. Moppert reveals that, in 1927, he refused to pay taxes to the French authorities and instead stated that he would remit them to the Prince of Bassac,[30] in accordance with the ancient political model that supposedly established Bassac authorities as the "rulers of the *Khom* race" (Moppert 1981, p. 54). Given the fact that the Kingdom of Champassak was not formally founded until the early eighteenth century, Kommandam was probably referring to the *meuang* that, having been under Khmer rule, was then loosely incorporated within the mandala of Lan Xang around the fourteenth century. By proclaiming his disciples and himself as "Khom", Kommandam in fact reappropriated the status of original inhabitants of "Laos". His partisans were no longer the French "Kha", confined in an outsider naming. Instead, they became the Khom or ancient "Kha", to whom was, to a certain extent, attached a glorious past, embodied in the Khmer empire and the Lan Xang kingdom. In brief, Kommandam tried to create a primordial identity rooted in a mythical past and bound together with blood ties through common descent.

A shared montagnard ethnic identity in the Bolovens?

In order to present a complete picture, it is also necessary to question the notion of the Bolovens Plateau as a *geographical* entity in order to demonstrate that Kommandam's appeal for the Khom race was the result of a complex combination of factors, rather than merely an isolated phenomenon. The Bolovens Plateau is only one portion of an area known as the High Plateaux which, from the northwest to the southeast and across the Lao-Vietnamese border, comprises the Bolovens Plateau and the Central Highlands of Vietnam (namely, the regions of Kontum, Pleiku and the Da Lac Plateau). The Central Highlands, originally included in French Laos as early as 1893, were later transferred to the region of Annam in 1904 and 1905. The detachment of Stung Treng from "Laos" to "Cambodia" in 1904 also reduced the administrative territory of southern Laos (Stuart-Fox 1997, p. 27). These changes were usually for reasons of administrative convenience, and therefore contributed to the creation of arbitrary *geographical* entities. The Bolovens Plateau was just such an entity: its boundaries remained fuzzy, vaguely delimited in the north by the Sedone valley and in the South by the Attapeu-Champassak provincial border.

Crucially, the Plateau is composed of two terraces, of which the highest (1,200 metres), known as the "Royal Plain", had been seen by the French authorities and entrepreneurs as a new Far Eastern Eldorado (Moppert 1978, p. 17). The authorities and the entrepreneurs had been entertaining the fantasy that the Plateau would be a highly profitable area for growing products such as cardamom, coffee or tobacco. The dreams were still alive under the Protectorate. By the time the French left in 1954, however, none of these great plans had borne fruit. In their attempt to "unblock" and to integrate the country into the Indochinese economy — and consequently to weaken the trade between Laos and Thailand — the French had in mind the idea of an all-weather road (and later on, a railway) through the Annamite mountain chain dividing Laos from Vietnam. However, the local labour force, i.e. the male population living in these remote areas, was generally insufficient to make possible the French authorities' overreaching ambitions. These construction projects, although only partially completed, incurred great costs in time and labour, especially upon those forced by their corvée obligations to work on the projects.

Under the French, the people inhabiting the plateau were dubbed the *Bolovens*. The category was obviously an outsider naming since the people called themselves *Djerou*.[31] Jean-Jacques Dauplay, the French Commissioner of Saravane, listed other "races" living on the "edge and the slopes" of the plateau: there were the "*Souei*, the *Phou Thay*, the *Alak* and the *Nha-Heun*", but he made no mention of other ethnic peoples, such as the *Ngae*, who were living in that area (Dauplay 1929, p. 7). As a matter of fact, the population arbitrarily called the *Bolovens* may well have consisted of more than one ethnic group, but the reification of this invented naming was reinforced by administrative reality. In May 1907, under the threat of further resistance and insurrections, a distinct administrative territory was created with the delineation of a *Boloven* Province, the centre of which was sited on the Plateau. The objective, essentially, was to gather together all the so-called *Boloven* households under a unique authority. Indeed, it was believed that the cause of their anger and frustration lay within the exploitative system of cross-racial administration. Dauplay wrote, thus:

> The then Superior Resident (Mr. G. Mahé) attributed, and his opinion was shared by the majority of the Europeans aware of the current affairs in Lower Laos, the long-lived rebellion to the absence of leadership unity and to discontent as a result of the division of the Boloven into six distinct groups under leaders who are Laotian and, consequently, alien to their race.[32]

Later on, the politics of creating the "Moi" in the Central Highlands of Vietnam would also affect — to a lesser extent, though — the south of Laos. In 1935, a *Commissariat des Confins Moi* (Authority of the Moi Border Regions) was set up, with the establishment of offices in 1936, in Ban Me Thuot in the Central Highlands and on the Lao side of the border in Ban Tampril (where it was called "the Delegation of the Sekong [river]" [Moppert 1978, p. 43]). The *Commissariat* was then replaced in October 1939 by the *Inspection Générale des Pays Moïs* (General Inspectorate of the Moi Regions). As early as the following year, the newly appointed *Haut-Commissaire des pays moïs* (High Commissioner of the Moi Regions), Lieutenant Omer Sarrault, claimed confidently that "the ethnic and geographical unity of the 'Pays Moïs' should include 'the totality of autochthonous populations' both in upland Annam and Cochinchina and in Eastern Cambodia and Southern Laos" (Salemink 1995, p. 273).

Still, there is no evidence that the French deliberately concocted a plan to create an "essential unity of the Montagnards" opposed to the ethnic Lao identity, as they did in "Vietnam". The "Moi" policy was very much focused on the Central Highlands, and was very limited elsewhere in Indochina. The most notable example of this policy was the delineation of a montagnard territory (under French rule), the *Pays Montagnard du Sud-Indochinois* (PMSI) or the Special Administrative Area, in the Central Highlands in 1946. As a matter of fact, the creation of an autonomous montagnard zone was an element of a much broader strategy: the containment of the northern Vietnamese Communists. The First Indochina War effectively began in December 1946. Less than two years later, in March 1948, the French announced the formation of a Tai Federation to include all the Tai-speaking ethnic groups of the northern Vietnamese highlands living on the western bank of the Red River. The montagnards of the PMSI and the highlanders of the Tai Federation were thus expected by the French to oppose, and subsequently to weaken, the Vietnamese state by claiming rights for cultural and political autonomy (Hickey 1982, p. 401).[33]

In "Laos", such a federalist move did not occur. Kommandam's political claims were not a direct consequence of deliberate manoeuvres on the part of the French administration. His demand for an exclusive Khom political status may, however, have been influenced by French ethnic policy, and especially by the creation of a distinct administrative unit on the Bolovens Plateau in 1907. Kommandam demanded, as early as 1910, that the "other races inhabiting the plateau [of the Bolovens] such as the Nha Eun, Souei and Phou Thay were to be driven off" (Gunn 1985, p. 52). Kommandam was the first leader to unify scattered highland groups on such a scale and to give, or try to give, them a sense of common ethnic identity. His request for a separate status for the Khom should be interpreted, however, as a claim for political autonomy under a superior authority (be it ethnic Lao or French) rather than as a demand for self-determination. His struggle never endorsed a national dimension, nor did Kommandam ask for self-determination: the rebellion he led was not a war of national liberation.

I have shown in this section that the French, for their own interests, contributed to the reification of the highland peoples by imposing a name and a territory on them. Yet, the case of Kommandam shows that these peoples were not ineluctably petrified by the process of tribalization. On the other hand, the process of ethnicization, following Salemink's definition, was not fully achieved, though it did begin. Kommandam's insurrection was simply suppressed too early: upon his death in 1936, Laos was still a Protectorate. Nevertheless, his struggle, as well as that of other highland leaders, heralded what was to occur in the French and American Wars, when highland peoples would again be pulled into the mainstream. Though all the minority revolts under French rule failed, they show the fiercely independent character of these people, their self-proclaimed distinction from the lowland population and their early political awakening. These rebellions also starkly reveal the influence of external factors, which would continue to play a determining role in the coming decade.

The highland populations in Laos were soon caught between the propaganda of the French, on the one hand, and that of the Vietnamese and Lao communist movements — the Viet Minh and the Pathet Lao — on the other, both sides being eager to gain their loyalty in the aftermath of the Second World War. The "choice" between the two sides was contingent and, more often than not, guided by survival imperatives.[34] In some cases, the political orientation of some ethnic groups was determined by their leaders. Once their support had been won, the rank and file would follow. Sithon Kommandam was one such leader (as well as Faydang Lobliayao[35]). The son of Ong Kommandam, Sithon enjoyed considerable prestige among the ethnic peoples of southeastern Laos (Gunn 1988, p. 241; Goscha 2004, p. 155). Sentenced to life imprisonment by the French for his participation in his father's rebellion against the colonial authorities, he and his brother, Kamphanh, were released from jail in Phongsaly province in 1945. Sithon then began establishing resistance bases in Phongsaly and in Xieng Khuang in 1947 (Burchett 1957, p. 247). He soon made contact with the Viet Minh leadership in northern Vietnam and the Lao Issara government in Vientiane. In 1948, he led raids on the Bolovens Plateau and, in 1950, he regrouped communist partisans with his son Sang Kham in their home province of Saravane (Gunn 1988, p. 241).

Sithon's fight against the French and the Americans may be regarded as the continuation of his father's struggle. The major difference between the two revolts was the new concept of "struggle for national independence". The ethnic fighters were enrolled in a larger type of war, in which the ideology and objectives were now nationalist in content. Yet, the Kommandams' struggles over most of the twentieth century testify against the view that highland peoples lacked agency and were solely proxies caught between more powerful adversaries. The next chapter moves the discussion of the politics of identity in Laos to the contemporary period. I will take a closer look at the newly independent state's politics of majority and minorities after 1975, which represents another mode of interaction between the lowlanders and highlanders.

Notes

[1] I use the term "indigenous" here in its restricted meaning; that is, in reference to the people regarded as the original inhabitants of one territory.

[2] The word means "disc" in Sanskrit and referred originally to a cosmological symbol. The mandala is thus a complex diagram in circular form that represents an image of the universe, a receptacle for the gods. It is the place where cosmic and psychic energies concentrate. As a sacred place, the mandala is a form of paradise (Rice 1980, p. 246).

[3] By "Tai", I refer to the language family and their speakers. It therefore includes the contemporary Lao, Thai and Shan populations.

[4] This perception originated from the seminal teaching of the "devotional movement" known as *bhakti* by Indian religious teachers to the Southeast

Asian elite. Hindu devolutionism proclaimed that "supreme spiritual power" or "cosmic power (sákti)", that of the creator god Siva, could be attained by means of asceticism (Wolters 1999, p. 111).

5   I use quotation marks here to emphasize the fact that I am referring to colonial Laos as opposed to the present-day Lao polity.

6   "Whereas within the marrows, social distinctions were non-existent, once out of the marrows, a discrimination was carefully established between the different clans and between the Lao and the aborigines. The Kha, who came out from a special hole made by a glowing hot drill, were settled in the mountains where they cultivated *ray* [practised shifting cultivation] while the Lao, settled in the plains, allocated to themselves the paddy fields".

7   The kingdoms of Annam, Nyuen, Siam and P'uon [Phuan], the lattermost corresponding to the present-day province of Xieng Khuang.

8   For the meaning of the game played in Luang Prabang, Archaimbault refers the reader to another of his writings, "Une cérémonie en l'honneur des génies de la mine de sel de Ban Bô", *in La Fête du T'at* (1970) (Archaimbault 1970, p. 87).

9   "The fight that opposed the conquering Lao to the indigenous peoples, which fight remained outside cultural boundaries, was replaced — at least, according to the texts — by an *agonal* game, the function of which was to re-introduce temporarily the barbarians into the community, and to trace back the evolution of an exclusive right on land".

10   French word that has become a common term synonymous with "highlanders" or "highland population".

11   A term that he borrowed from Georges Condominas (1966): "Classes sociales et groupes tribaux au Sud-Vietnam", in *Cahiers Internationaux de Sociologie*, Vol. XL, p. 168.

12   "Disséminées, sans lien entre elles, dispersées pour qu'elles offrissent moins de résistance, parlant des dialectes différents, privées d'intérêts communs, les divers tribus et peuplades khas se présentent à nous sous un aspec dégénéré" (Reinach 1911, p. 126).

13   Auguste Pavie, the first French vice-consul, arrived in Luang Prabang in 1887.

14   Also known as "Lamet".

15   Yet the French sinologist, Henri Maspéro, denied the assumption that grouped the 'Kha' as an ethnic category of its own. Compared to the works of Le

Boulanger and Reinach, his contribution to the study of the peoples of French Indochina was undeniably pioneering. His legacy includes his famous distinction between "hierarchical" and "anarchic" political organisations (Maspéro 1929). This opposition included other variables, such as religion (collectively practised for the former, but an individual or family matter for the latter), family structure (patriarchal for the former; patriarchal or matriarchal for the latter), and language (tonal for the former, mono-tonal for the latter). Different combinations of these criteria formed different cultural types.

[16] The distinguished French scholar, Georges Coedès, referred the geographical space to as "Inde au-delà du Gange" in his seminal book, *Les États hindouisés d'Indochine et d'Indonésie* (Paris: De Boccard, 1989 [2nd ed.]).

[17] For accounts of the French Mekong expeditions in the second half of the nineteenth century, see Francis Garnier, *Voyage d'exploration en Indochine* (Paris: La Découverte, 1985 [1873]); Auguste Pavie, *Exposé des travaux de la mission*, E. Leroux, Paris, 1901–06; and Milton Osborne, *The Mekong: Turbulent Past, Uncertain Future* (St. Leonard's: Allen & Unwin, 2000).

[18] Norindr Panivong *Phantasmatic Indochina: French Colonial Ideology in Architecture, Film, and Literature* (Durham and London: Duke University Press, 1996), p. 5.

[19] This policy was, however, not solely economically orientated, only aiming at an "empty" space that had been waiting for France to fill it. *Mise en valeur* also constituted the ideological mouthpiece (supported by a set of policies) of French colonial action addressed both to the metropole and the rest of the Western world; in other words, the policy (essentially an "ethical colonialism") served as a cover for what was primarily exploitative rule. The concept of *mise en valeur* was multifaceted. As the keystone of French colonial strategy, the ideology and its set of policies must be understood concomitantly as an economic programme, a moral justification for exploitation and a discourse of legitimation for France's so-called protective and benevolent rule in these territories of Southeast Asia.

[20] Quoted, in turn, from the colonial document dated 1940 and entitled, "Devoirs en matière fiscale des autorités provinciales françaises et laotiennes et des autorités cantonales et communales laotiennes", Résidence Supérieure au Laos, Vientiane, p. 19.

[21] In 1914, there were 24 French officials in the whole of upper Laos (Brocheux and Hémery 1994, p. 89). McCoy quotes the case of Saravane Province, which

in 1938 had only three French officials to administer 6 cantons, 36 districts and 596 villages (McCoy 1970, p. 78).

22   The *kouang, lam haou* or *van* has been characterized by the Lao communist leader, Phoumi Vongvichit, as "a ferocious regime of exploitation" (Gunn 1990, p. 49, quoted from Phoumi Vongvichit 1968, p. 36).

23   "Le barbare, c'est celui qui n'est pas comme les autres. La preuve, c'est qu'il ne veut pas comprendre que son intérêt est de se soumettre" (Moppert 1978, p. 35).

24   The first serious violent uprising erupted that year in southern Laos.

25   I shall return to this revolt later.

26   Moppert refers to him as a Nha Heun. However, according to my field notes, he was a Laven. In both cases, he belonged to the Mon-Khmer ethno-linguistic category.

27   There are, in fact, very few sources regarding the extent of Kommandam's support amongst the highland population.

28   "Et dans une de ses dernières lettres connues (22 Février 1927), Kommandam, tout en ne remettant pas en cause l'administration française sur le Laos, y met cependant une condition, à savoir que tous les khoms soient considérés comme une race à part, qu'on les laisse vivre dans leur région et surtout, qu'on leur fasse connaître le régime sous lequel ils seront placés, et pour combien de temps" (Moppert 1981, p. 54).

29   Stuart-Fox (1998, p. 17) quoting Charles F. Keyes, "A Note on the Ancient Towns and Cities of Northeastern Thailand", in *Southeast Asian Studies* 11 (1974): 503.

30   Bassac is the other name for Champassak.

31   They are also known as the *Laven* (or *Loven*) at the present time (Chamberlain 1995, Chazée 2000).

32   "Le Résident Supérieur d'alors, (M.G. Mahé) attribuait, et son opinion était partagée par la majorité des Européens au courant des affaires du Bas Laos, la longue durée de la rébellion à l'absence d'unité de direction et au mécontentement, résultant de la division des Boloven en six groupes séparés, relevant de chefs laotiens et, par conséquent, étrangers à leur race" (Dauplay 1929, p. 42).

33   The situation in the north was even more explosive since the Chinese Communists came to power in January 1949, thereby providing the Viet Minh with a powerful ally controlling the northern border.

[34] For example, in their joint article on Hmong migrations and history (1997), Culas and Michaud describe the conundrum of the Hmong in Laos during the American-North Vietnamese War. According to their estimates, several thousand Hmong participated in the fighting against the Pathet Lao and Viet Minh, while perhaps just as many other Hmong were enrolled in the People's Liberation Army, the Communist armed forces (Culas and Michaud 1997, p. 232). Different causes — briefly explained in the notes below — led to this partisanship. Even those who did not want to get involved in the conflict, in order to survive under extremely difficult material conditions, had to seek help from one side or the other, i.e. the Royal Lao Government/Americans or the Pathet Lao/Viet Minh. If they did not, they would be suspected of sympathizing with the enemy (Culas and Michaud 1997, p. 232).

[35] Faydang's alliance with the Communists was also probably caused by internal feuds between the Hmong clans. In 1935, Faydang became the leader of the Lo clan, which was opposed to another clan, the Ly, which was led by Touby Ly Fong. Touby's father took the position of *kiatong*, or clan leader, in the region of Nong Het in 1938. The station of *kiatong* had previously been held by Faydang's father, Lo Bliayao, and then by Song Tou Lobliayao, Faydang's eldest brother. In 1939 Touby Ly Fong was selected as the new *kiatong* or what was equivalent to a *Chao Tasseng* in the ethnic Lao administrative system. As a result of these events, Faydang, whose clan's honour had now been disgraced, rebelled against the French and began a bitter feud with the Ly clan. Touby's influence in the Royal Lao Government increased rapidly as he was promoted to the position of *Chao Meuang* (district governor) of Xieng Khuang Province as well as being appointed to the central government (Stuart-Fox 1997, pp. 39–40).

3

Cultural Order and Discipline:
The Politics of National Culture

In 1975, the present regime proclaimed a break with a distasteful past and instead promised the beginning of a new socialist era. However, anti-colonialist rhetoric is now no longer appropriate for rallying the population, and symbols of the past are being recalled in a distorted representation that equally fails to have broad appeal. The anxiety of the current Lao authorities over the preservation and strengthening of the country's national identity has many parallels with that of their predecessors (in fact, the newly reformulated national culture in post-socialist Laos borrows heavily from symbols of the former regime), but the perception of threat is no longer focused on hostile neighbours physically violating national boundaries, but rather on the dangers of social and cultural erosion by external forces. From a post-colonial perspective, the nationalist discourse is in search of "a *difference* with the 'modular' forms of the national society propagated by the modern West" (Chatterjee 1993b, p. 5, original stress). In the case of Laos, however, this desire to construct a distinctive model must first be analysed (at least as far as culture and history are concerned) in the light of Laos' relationship with her neighbour, Thailand. This chapter therefore will demonstrate that the processes of inclusion and exclusion — that is, the politics of Majority/Minority representations — are not only induced by the necessity of constructing an encompassing and homogenized national culture, but are also subsumed within a search for cultural particularity.

Modelling Majority/Minority representations

The year 1999 was marked by the promotion of Visit Laos Year 1999–2000. To celebrate the event, a long parade was organized on the opening day of the That Luang festival in November in Vientiane. The procession was led by a group composed of young female and male students wearing their school uniform and waving the national flag. This first group was called "Lao Modern Time and Great Victory to the Century" [sic] (Brochure of the Lao National Tourist Authority, *Opening Ceremony Visit Laos Year 1999–2000*, 18 November 1999 [in English]). Strangely enough, at the tail end of the procession, the closing group, referred to by the nostalgic title, "Long Distance Friendship and the True Dream", represented the past, embodied by men wearing red and green feudal fighters' clothing. Some of them were perched on elephants, symbol of the former regime. The animals were also carrying three young and attractive women dressed up in the so-called "Lao Lum" (lowland Lao), "Lao Theung" (Lao on the mountain slopes) and "Lao Sung" (Lao on the top of the mountains) traditional costumes. Although this terminology is now forbidden in the official texts, it is nevertheless still widely used, even by state newspapers.

The second group, "Sieng Khene Dene Champa: Welcome to Lao PDR", was a digest of the multi-ethnic national culture, in which the traditional Lao musical instrument, the *khene*, was paired with dances performed by students from the School of Arts of Vientiane and the School of Highland Ethnic groups; they were joined by army troops and members of the National Sports Committee. The commercial floats, referred to as "Honesty and Friendship", constituted the next group in which hotels, restaurants and handicraft shops were represented by lavishly decorated floats carefully integrated into the larger picture. The

companies had skilfully crafted their own brands to include a symbol of
the national culture. For example, Beer Lao, the successful national beer
brand, displayed a model of a racing boat, used in the very popular boat
race that takes place during the celebration of the end of the Buddhist
Lent every October.

The fourth group in the parade was by far the largest in size and
variety, the better to embody "Lao Heritage and Culture". Indeed, all the
provinces were represented in an orderly pattern. Three sub-groups
were arrayed along geographical lines: the "Northern Zone" (including
the province of Vientiane — although it is not situated in the North, it
probably had to come first because it includes the capital); the "Central
Zone" and the "Southern Zone". The parade offered, thus, a panoramic
view of countrywide cultural productions, exhibited in a succession of
visual displays. Each province was led by a young woman, holding a
sign indicating the name of the province and dressed in the traditional
clothes of the province's largest ethnic group. The provincial displays,
which reflected some of the provinces' most salient features, had been
designed by the provinces themselves, in collaboration with the
Department of Culture and Information and the Department of Trade
and Commerce. Some provinces, such as Xieng Khuang, Huaphan, Luang
Prabang, Vientiane, Savannakhet and Champassak, had more tourist
attractions. These provinces are not only the largest in terms of population
and area; during the parade, they were also all particularly eager to
display their specific historical and cultural legacies. This metonymic
process provided a series of snapshots for tourist brochures: Xieng Kuang
and the Plain of Jars ("Thong Hai Hin"); Huaphan and the Viengxai
caves; Luang Prabang and the Lao New Year; Vientiane and the Rocket
festival, Savannakhet and the dinosaur fossils; Champassak and Vat
Phu. As a consequence, one could almost observe a dramatic division of
the national space between the historical and "culturally loaded"
provinces and the "culturally poor" provinces, such as the northwestern
province of Bokeo, the southeastern province of Sekong or the
southernmost province of Attapeu. The latter were represented by "their"

ethnic groups, dancing, singing or simply marching, as if these were their sole cultural attractions;[1] these provinces were conspicuous for their lack of "cultural" material. Their dancers in traditional costumes were trailing on foot behind the province of Champassak and its impressive float carrying a model of Vat Phu (inscribed on the UNESCO World Heritage list since 2001). As a result, the cultural demarcation between the southernmost "small" provinces and their prestigious and imposing neighbour (candidate for World Heritage status) was striking.

This balancing act between past and present was not performed by chance; it is part of the ongoing process of crafting a national culture. The parade epitomizes the government's struggles between socialist principles and the country's integration into the capitalist economy. This display of cultural productions for the local population and for the tourists reflects what Trankell (1999, p. 199) calls the "marketing of 'culture'", remarking that "while preserving the cultural heritage, the Lao national identity is at the same time being negotiated and put on stage for commercial purposes".

Moreover, the parade embodies a paradox in that it promotes an ideology of multiethnic culture, yet through a cultural hierarchy. Some authors have argued that the representation of ethnic minorities has more to do with the construction of the majority identity than it does with the minorities themselves. As Dru Gladney puts it, the objectification of the minority "as exotic, colourful and 'primitive'" homogenizes the undefined majority as "united, monoethnic, and modern" (Gladney 1994, p. 93). Explicitly using Edward Said's seminal theoretical framework that places the relationship between power and representation in the context of colonial relations of domination, he calls such a process "oriental orientalism". According to Said, as a style of thought Orientalism is based upon an "ontological and epistemological distinction made between 'the Orient' and (most of the time) 'the Occident'". On this basis, an "enormously systematic discipline" was created "by which European culture was able to manage — and even produce — the Orient politically, sociologically, militarily, ideologically, scientifically, and imaginatively during the post-

Enlightenment period". Thus, Orientalism was a "Western style for dominating, restructuring and having authority over the Orient": Orientalism created the Oriental. What is more, however, "European culture gained in strength and identity by setting itself off against the Orient as a sort of surrogate and even underground self" (Said 1995, pp. 2–3).

The example of an ethnographic study recently published in Laos shows how ethnic minorities are being depicted, to use Schein's expression, as a "reservoir of still-extant authenticity", imbued with flavours of romanticism and desire for wildness (Schein 1997, p. 70). In a booklet (1997) that recounts his ethnographic trip to encounter the Lolo people in Phongsaly, the northernmost province of Laos, Houmphanh Rattanavong, then director of the Institute of Cultural Research in Vientiane, adopts a tone of genuine enthusiasm, if not lyricism. The parallel between nature, landscape and highlanders is recurrent in his narration. He praises the people and imbues them with nostalgic qualities, such as remoteness and authenticity, by using bucolic images:

> Many people may wonder why inhabitants of the mountains like wearing bright and shiny clothes. Perhaps one answer may have to do with the bountiful beauty that nature at these high altitude places offers them. As man opens his eyes, the first thing he sees is the beauty of nature that surrounds him. He may instinctively like to make himself as Mother Nature. [...] Human society in the mountains has its foundation on nature. The mode of production as well as the rest of the way of life depends on nature, which is in its pristine form, adorned with high ranges of mountains covered with all kinds of beautiful vegetation (Houmphanh 1997, pp. 67–68, original translation).

For Houmphanh, the research trip appears to be a quest for the "essence" of these people as much as a personal achievement. It is a space–time journey, to reach an atemporal, "lost world". His foreword is worth quoting, not least for its style:

> It was pointed out to me: "if you don't trek ravines, climb mountains, how could you know for sure how pristine and how magnificent are some remote territories of our country; how magnificent are some remote

territories of our country; how could you claim to have fathomed the hardship or the joy that our people experience in their daily life; how could you really know their hearts' desire". [...] This is true! I feel that each journey which I have made has given me an added sense of worth as a "human being". [...] Once I finally arrived at Oupao village or any other communities, I felt dazed as if I was in a state of dream. It was hard to believe that I physically was among them (Houmphanh 1997; Foreword [no page quoted], original translation).

As elsewhere in the world, ethnic groups in Laos are being subsumed into the national patrimony. They are given the discrete, bound, objective forms of items; in brief, they become commodified (Foster 1991, p. 240). A seminar on the conservation and promotion of the "intangible cultural patrimony" of the minority groups in the Lao PDR was held in Vientiane in October 1996, organized by UNESCO in collaboration with the Lao National Commission for UNESCO and the Ministry of Information and Culture. The concept of "intangible cultural patrimony" is the definition of "culture" used by UNESCO, and applied as the bedrock of the politics of preservation of the country's multiethnic patrimony. According to the final report (1996), though it does not clearly define it, the notion of "intangible culture" seems to refer to the reservoir of knowledge, such as languages, tales, myths and rituals, that cannot be measured. There appear, however, to be two levels in the discourse of preservation. First, the "things" that bound the minority groups' cultures, such as languages, craft, music, oral tales or habitat, must be inventoried and enhanced. Second, these particular cultures are, in turn, inventoried into a generic national culture. As a matter of fact, "tangible" and "intangible" are similarly defined as "things" to collect and to preserve. Nonetheless, the report warns against the dangers of fixing traditions and perpetuating cultural stereotypes (p. 13). It also recommends that members of ethnic groups, especially the youth, should have the choice between one or several "cultures" and decide themselves on the future of their traditions (p. 16).

The so-called international community, through representative organizations, certainly plays a significant role in legitimizing the framework that defines what a culture should be with respect to minority peoples. As a matter of fact, both states and foreign experts tend to view the world as made of "peoples" with distinctive and discrete cultures. This is what Susan Wright calls the "old definition of culture", i.e. fixed, small and ahistorical entities defined by distinctive characteristics and composed of identical individuals, as opposed to the "new idea of culture", that is, continually contested by multiple agents at different places and times. Unlike the "old idea of culture", there is no top-down definition by the "undefined voice" which Wright sharply criticizes (Wright 1998, pp. 8–9). She takes as an example the 1995 report *Our Creative Diversity* by UNESCO, which for decades has been involved in the mission of preserving and promoting the world's cultural patrimony without engaging with the political dimensions of defining "culture". She argues, thus, that the UNESCO report "deploy[s] a disembodied voice, 'we', to authorize a top down definition of 'culture' as if it were common sense or 'natural'. This strategy, like the old anthropological strategy of objectification, tries to mask or erase the politicization of culture" (Wright 1998, p. 12).

Yet Lao nationalism in post-colonial Laos cannot be fully understood as a process internal to national borders; it is not enough to define the consolidation of the national culture through the Majority/Minority internal dichotomy. As Schein has demonstrated the demarcation of Chinese national identity through "multiple contrastive others", i.e. the external West and the internal non-Han peoples (Schein 2000, p. 106), I likewise argue that the politics of culture in the Lao PDR are being shaped both internally and externally. I argue that two dyadic relations shape national identity in post-socialist Laos. The first relation uses the representation of ethnic minorities to strengthen the national culture. The ethnic minorities serve as an oppositional figure to stress the homogeneity of the Majority. The second relation — between Thailand/the West and Laos — is based on an ideological dichotomy: Thailand appears as an anti-model, the core of which is viewed as being contaminated by the ill-effects of capitalism. Laos, by contrast, tries to define itself as a virtuous nation by applying a moral discourse; in other words, by claiming an authenticity lost by Thailand. "Differences between the Thai and Lao identities are exacerbated during conflicts and periods of tensions, because they boost patriotic feelings. In peaceful times, however, Lao youngsters follow the Thai, because they don't have any idols in the country", a Lao journalist explained to me.[2] It is well-known that the influence of the Thai media is a matter of great concern for the Lao authorities. The Lao Women's Union, for instance, has criticized Thai television programmes for encouraging incorrect dress and manners, at the expense of traditional clothing such as the *pha sin* (the Lao sarong). Similarly, some officials have accused the media of playing a significant role in the rise of consumerism, or worse, of crime, in Laos.[3] These official statements often lack substantiation, however. In any case, Thai media (television, radio, newspapers and magazines) is ubiquitous and accessed by every level of society, including the country's leadership, who indeed keep a close eye on Thai television broadcasts and radio programmes. There is no competition between the latter and the local media: 70 per cent to 75 per cent of the population in Laos watch Thai television programmes, compared to 20 per cent to 25 per cent who watch Lao broadcasting (Vipha 2001, p. 179).[4]

Yet, despite the strong appeal of Thai cultural products, their consumption and appropriation have their limits. Thailand's cultural and economic ascendancy over Laos generates ambiguous and deviating effects, oscillating between attraction and repulsion. In a late 1990s survey of Lao youth living in urban areas, a large proportion of positive opinions were expressed by interviewees craving for their neighbouring country's modernity; however, a few respondents, especially female adolescents, gave a much bleaker perception of Thai society. Here are some excerpts of their statements: "We're not going with them [those who go and find work in Thailand]. We're scared that they would take our eyes"; "They have a bad society, with no laws, and people do whatever they want"; "They will sell us as prostitutes, and then the police will catch us and we'll go to prison, and we're scared that someone may rape us."[5] Thailand is what

Laos should never become for some Lao, including the Lao authorities. The Friendship Bridge paradoxically exemplifies this hazy relation whereby proximity functions like an antithesis. Yet, in 1994, the year of its inauguration, there were hopes that the bridge would boost the rapprochement between the two countries and their peoples via the development of trade and tourism. It has become instead, according to a recent study, a symbol of consumerism and materialism in the eyes of many in Laos. The weekend shopping enjoyed by the small, but growing, Lao urban middle class is specially targeted, denounced as "antipatriotic" and those who practice it as "corrupted by Thai capitalism".[6]

In spite of their cultural, linguistic and geographical proximity, the two peoples on the opposite banks of the Mekong River retain this peculiar combination of *closeness* and *strangeness* for one another, as if the relationships between the two countries were mediated through a distorting glass. "The Lao and the Thai peoples share similar culture and traditions, but Laos has managed to preserve her culture". One often hears this type of comment from Thai tourists, who upon their return from Vientiane and Luang Prabang (their favourite destinations in Laos) uphold an image of Laos imbued with nostalgia and bemoan thereafter the "lost authenticity" theme with regard to their own country. Lao society and culture appear in the eyes of those Thai longing for genuineness what Thailand was "before", that is, before the double effects of modernization and globalization.[7] Their visit to the other side of the Mekong River is not merely a trip through space but also, and perhaps above all, a journey through time. In parallel, the Lao authorities via their cultural policies wish to preserve and reinforce their country's "unique" image of authenticity and purity, so as to be distinct enough from Thailand's, by trying to impose a moral order and a cultural discipline on the population, and especially on the younger generation.

In the next section, I will specifically discuss the nationalist discourse and its search for "a *difference* with the 'modular' forms of the national society propagated by the modern West" (Chatterjee 1993b, p. 5, original stress). This search for authenticity retains a dual agenda, between rhetoric and people's agency, that is between the discourse of cultural and moral discipline and the revival of popular Buddhism.

"Culture in the New Era": Socialism with Lao characteristics

"A new socialist man"

After 1975, the new regime believed that transforming the masses was the first and foremost step in the construction of a newly socialist state. Short of capital and of qualified people but with a plentiful supply of physical labour, the government logically emphasized the crucial importance of the human factor amongst the solutions to economic and social problems. The goal was to achieve a social homogeneity which would transcend ethnic identity. In a country where more than 80 per cent of the population live in rural areas and in the absence of a working class, the peasants were bound to be drawn into the socialist revolution. The state was eager to find, or to create, a new social class on which to base the transition to a socialist economy. In 1978, an accelerated programme was launched to collectivize agriculture. However, conceived as well as executed badly, it proved to be a disaster both from the point of view of production and because it stimulated opposition among the Lao peasantry who had previously been sympathetic towards the new regime. The government condemned the refusal of the peasants to cooperate as a threat to national security and therefore attributed a political dimension to the peasants that they had never had before (Taillard 1983, p. 131).

The government assumed that collectivization of the countryside would bring about what every socialist regime hoped for, i.e. objective independence or self-sufficiency and self-reliance, which would prove the superiority of socialist over capitalist modes of production and thus strengthen commitment to the regime. Grant Evans gives two other main reasons for collectivization, one of which was the communists' distrust of the peasantry, whom the former assumed did not form a genuine class of revolutionary elements and would veer towards to capitalism if they were allowed to keep and use the means of production for their private activity. The second reason is also induced by this suspicion of the peasantry: independent peasants, designated as "rich peasants", would disrupt the planned economy through resistance, opposition and rebellion; in contrast, "[a] collectivized peasantry [...] would be integrated into central planning and be unable to resist surplus transfers from agriculture to wherever the state planners saw fit to invest it" (Evans 1995, p. 18).

Collectivization therefore was not only seen as a means to achieve economic security but also as an instrument for political consolidation. This was particularly true of Laos, the goal of which was to become self-sufficient in food over a period of three years. It was hoped in effect that the three-year plan, with its emphasis upon collectivization, would strengthen security by implanting new popular administrative structures through which to promote party control, and by raising living standards, thus generating commitment to the new regime. Collectivization would thus encourage agricultural production and contribute to the internal security of the state by preventing counter-revolution. Finally, it was expected that collectivization would transform the people into "new socialist men". The collectivization planning was, thus, a part of the logic of trying to change society from above, in the name of building socialism in a peasant country.

Politics of cultural and moral discipline

Although the project of building up "new socialist men" has faded away, the state has not abandoned the idea of "renewing" the people, as expressed in the reformulated concept of "culture in the new era". The examination of a colour leaflet produced by the Ministry of Information and Culture in 1998 throws interesting light on the type of society that the state is attempting to mould. The document was distributed to the Ministry's provincial offices and was unambiguously entitled "Criteria/Guidelines for Constructing Life in the New Cultural Era". These guidelines target three social levels, i.e. the village, the family and the individual; and attribute duties to each of them in order to develop a way of life that corresponds to the prescribed "culture". The pictures that illustrate the leaflet leave little doubt about what constitutes "good" culture. For example, on the balcony of a wooden house on stilts, a "traditional" family — the elderly, the children and the parents — is eating sticky rice from a basket, with ethnic Lao-type dishes placed on a low bamboo table. They are using spoons for the soup and fingers for the rice. Each of the two women (looking like the mother and the grandmother) is wearing a *pha sin*, and the grandfather (or the husband) has cotton threads around his wrist (thereby indicating that it is a Buddhist family). However, it is significant that Buddhism is never mentioned as such in the text, an indication of the fact that it is not constitutionally recognized as the privileged state religion (see below for a fuller discussion).[8] The multiethnic family is not forgotten either with another picture of four women dressed in "traditional" ethnic clothes, yet lined up in front of an ethnic Lao-style wooden house on stilts, divided into three distinctive habitats — presumably, the balcony, the central house and the kitchen — with square roofs, proper fences and surrounded by a green and tidy environment. Finally, the That Luang is on the cover of the leaflet, and a picture of a waterfall (implying a wealth of natural resources) closes the text.

The (explicit as well as implicit) objectives revealed in this leaflet interestingly echo cultural changes noticed in relocated upland villages and mentioned in the 1997 Goudineau report. Indeed, one reads that:

> The most obvious signs of cultural rupture caused by relocation are given by the development of houses and the evolution of dress. The adoption of Lao Lum style dwellings (houses on stilts designed to accommodate, on average, one family) is strongly encouraged in the new villages by the local authorities, who provide advisors to explain how to build houses or construct an example house for the village chief. The new habitat, while

having some advantages (in terms of hygiene and light) is often at odds with the architectural and social traditions of the hilltribes who are used, for example, to long houses (able to house up to a hundred people) as some southern Austro-Asiatic groups are (in Sekong, Saravane), or built on the ground houses as are the Miao-Yao of the North. The difference is not merely technical but signifies the loss of an ancient architectural skill or art [...] (Goudineau 1997, p. 35).

In fact, as early as 1976, a campaign of cultural and ideological renewal was launched with the objective of the transformation of the moral, spiritual, cultural and social life of the people and the formation of the "new individual" possessing a high level of revolutionary morality and culture (Kaysone 1980, pp. 208–10). The new culture had to be founded on a love of socialism and patriotism, but also guided by a "moral life". The new socialist man was to be animated by "a spirit of solidarity, be a good father to his family and respect the laws of the state" (Doré 1982, p. 109). As Evans acutely observed, the ideals of the "new socialist man" of the 1970s and early 1980s actually contained conservative values, specifically influenced by ethnic Lao cultural standards:

> Arguably the interpretation given to the morality of the new socialist man by the LPRP was strongly conditioned by the [ethnic] Lao social environment. That influence explains the highly traditional and conservative as well as nationalistic cast of ideology. Reactions against Western fashion, music and decadent morality, exemplified by prostitution or simply the holding of hands in the street, largely reflected the values of elderly people (whose number included the party leadership), who are traditionally guides in such matters, and the sexual conservatism of village culture (Evans 1995, p. 4).

A quarter of a century after the campaign started, the conservative rhetoric that aims to discipline behaviour is still present.[9] The school curriculum, for instance, shows how the discourse of cultural and moral rectitude is promoted as a daily practice from a young age. The difference between the conservative discourses then and now lies, however, in the present-day sense of urgency to recover former cultural and social practices that are being perceived as endangered and weakening. One school text entitled "Lao Culture and Society" caught my attention. Written in 1998 and printed by the Ministry of Education, the manual is directed at trainee teachers and is part of their final year curriculum's reading material. The book underlines three themes that define and sustain the essence of "Lao culture" as perceived and disseminated by the state: the origins (Chapters 1 and 2); the manners (Chapters 3, 4 and 5); and preservation (Chapters 6 and 7).

"Culture" in this manual is conceptualized as "things" that have been shared by the "Lao people", and which have united them and cemented their community:

> ... if we go back in our research to the historical times of Lao race and Lao-ness [*kwam pen lao* ("being Lao")], to their ability to maintain their existence, their uninterrupted development over a long period of time, we clearly perceive the solid cultural links that have united the Lao people within the same community of thought and heart (...). (Ministry of Education 1998, p. 1).

Culture is in this sense functional and perennial. On the other hand, for the sake of "unity in diversity", "Lao culture" is *also* given a modern birth. Because it is necessarily both multiethnic and national, it is said to have emerged with the reign of Chao Fa Ngum in the fourteenth century. The prince is revered in the standard historiography as the father of the Lao nation for having achieved her territorial unification and uniting her people. Chao Fa Ngum led the "Lao multi-ethnic people" to victory and gave them for the first time a territory and a kingdom, Lan Xang, in 1353: the Lao nation was born, and concominantly, the "Lao traditions":

> ... beside the customs practised by the Lao Lum, there also exists Hmong customs and those of other ethnic groups, such as those of the Lao Theung, which we cannot present in details here (p. 2).

The text then concisely describes the Hmong New Year — reduced to a match-making festival, however.[9] Nation and culture from this perspective are two inseparable entities: no culture means the death of the nation;

likewise, the death of a nation removes altogether the *raison d'être* for a culture:

> Culture, tradition and nation are inseparable elements. If the nation happens to be lost, culture would be affected and on the verge of destruction. The ruin of the nation is the death of the culture. If the culture is swallowed up, the nation will no doubt lose her identity (p. 36).

Cultural and national identities are not only interchangeable, they are as well monolithic: an "aggression" against some parts is perceived as a threat against the whole.

> If the Lao culture gets infiltrated by other cultures, if it is being absorbed, insidiously thwarted or violently and openly attacked, then our culture will be soon given away and immediately replaced by other cultures (ibid.).

The defensive discourse of preservation and integrity against dangers of dilution and absorption is not new. What is interesting is not what is said to constitute the cultural/national identity, but how it is produced and sustained. In this textbook, the body takes the central stage. It is indeed through the body that "Lao culture" is expressed externally. More precisely, every aspect of manners in Lao society and culture is reviewed in the manual, whether they are manifested in private, public or professional spaces, in a mundane or official context. The body is strictly constrained through exhaustive codification: very detailed instructions are provided to the students on how they should stand, walk, sit, converse, eat, greet — when they are on their own or with others (in this latter case, social and age hierarchy are particularly stressed), at school, at home, in the *vat* (Buddhist temple), or in the streets.

Norbert Elias's fascinating history of manners from feudal times to the emergence and development of state monarchies in Europe (focusing particularly on state formation in Germany, France and England) reveals in abundant and remarkable detail the historical process that formed "civilized" people in that part of the world. Human beings learnt to behave "properly" and "rationally" (sometimes with unconscious self-restraint) so as to interact with one another in increasingly complex and differentiated societies. To put it differently, social interdependence and interpenetration that were imposed on individuals created and developed social and cultural manners. Social behaviours were not naturally expressed and biologically programmed, but interiorized at a very early age. They were not natural, but became "second nature" (Elias 1982 [1939], p. 325).

The discourse of self-restraint and control, both moral and physical, permeates the Lao textbook. Social discipline runs through every level of the society. For a government that proclaims itself "socialist", the categorization and definition of social groups appear rather heterodox: separate sections prescribe the manners, and in particular moral behaviour, of the *Phu dii* (a term that may be translated as "gentlemanly people", "well-born people", or even "*bourgeois*"); then of the "leadership" and the "leader"; and finally of the "good people" and "population". These instructions render a picture of a society that is not only virtuous and patriotic, but which is also civic (respectful of laws and rules) and individualized (prescriptions are directed at individuals, not at social, ethnic or religious groups or communities). The manual thus goes beyond the standard rhetoric of cultural essentialism to lay down the criteria of a modern society, however deceptively democratic, secular and equal. The leadership must respect the rights of the citizens, who in return are duty-bound to love the former, in the same way as they love their parents, teachers, religious leaders and elderly people. Civic and rationalized behaviour guides people's interactions as much as emotional and (extended) kinship bonds.

There is little doubt that these codes of *savoir-vivre* (how to behave in a society) and *savoir-être* (how to define oneself) outline a stereotypical representation of "good" ethnic Lao people, that is of the majority's culture, despite the authoritative emphasis on the "multiethnic Lao culture". Manners express the cultural-cum-national identity (which

Elias's theory of the civilizing process does not relate to). These teachings on bodily posture and gestures guide a "natural" way of behaving; in a nutshell, they define a marker of primordial identity as it is expressed by a proverb quoted in the book: "Manners indicate the race, behaviour the lineage" (*kiliyaborksat, malayat borktakun*) (Ministry of Education 1998, p. 12). "Lao-ness" becomes visible through these everyday performances and culturally-embodied interactions.

More importantly, manners foster and maintain the group's identity through repetitive, unconscious re-enactment of a cultural and social memory. Pierre Nora calls "real memory" a "dictatorial memory", i.e "unself-conscious, commanding, all-powerful, spontaneously actualizing, a memory without a past that ceaselessly reinvents tradition... [within which] each gesture, down to the most everyday, would be experienced as the ritual repetition of a timeless practice in a primordial identification of act and meaning" (Nora 1989, p. 8). Likewise, some manners as prescribed in this Lao-language manual carry a unique blend of the repetitive and routine and the sacred; they are performed as rituals of identification with, and perpetual recollection of, one's own community of thought, heart and memory. The greeting gesture, the *vai*, a mark of respect and courtesy, epitomizes this "real memory" that performs seemingly unbroken and timeless traditions. The bodily expression normally consists in joining palms together at the chest or nose level. Variants of the *vai* are explained in great detail according to the type of social encounter. The guidelines on how to *vai* the elderly, officials or masters are as follows: "in form of lotus at the mid-level of the chest, the two arms against the body, and bend the head at the same time; the tip of the fingers must touch the middle of the eyebrows or the tip of the nose". The prescriptions are simpler when one meets friends: "Join the two hands as to form a lotus shape at the mid-level of the chest, and brush against the chin with the tip of the fingers"; and when greeting a child: "Join the two hands in form of lotus at the mid-level of the chest".

The *vai* is not only an act of greeting in Lao society, but also and perhaps above all, a quintessential Buddhist gesture, for it is also performed, albeit differently, to pay respect to the Buddha and Buddhist monks. Here are the instructions on how to *vai* before statues of Buddha and Buddhist monks: "is a variant of *vai* that consists in kneeling down, joining and lifting the hands in the form of lotus at the mid-level of the chest: touch the tip of the hair with the tip of the fingers and bend the head to the floor with the hands applied on the floor and the fingers spread, then bow low three times" [24].

It is, however, essential to bear in mind that Lao society has just begun to recover its older cultural practices from the remains of the *ancien régime* (Institute of Cultural Research 1998, p. 29). For more than fifteen years, the communist regime forbade external expressions of the former "reactionary" culture — of which Buddhism and the monarchy were arguably the most potent symbols. This seemingly mundane gesture is not widely performed in everyday life except in the *vat*, and is certainly less widespread than in neighbouring Thailand. This gesture seems in fact to have become somehow outmoded among the younger generation, perhaps as a result of two decades of Marxist-Leninist "political correctness" and secularism. In fact, this Lao-language manual may become a *lieu de mémoire* ("site of memory") itself, for "the most fundamental purpose of the *lieu de mémoire*", as Nora eloquently notes, "is to stop time, to block the work of forgetting, to establish a state of things, to immortalize death, to materialize the immaterial…" [19]. But the "acceleration of history" may prove too great a challenge for textbooks to overcome.

At another level, the consolidation of national culture is accompanied by exhortations to attain economic competitiveness:

> Culture is the force that allows society to expand [so] it will not be embarrassing to stand next to other nations. The development of a nation goes hand-in-hand with cultural development as well as development in all the domains. The raising of people's level of culture is [therefore] an important factor for the country's socio-economic development emphasized the Party at its Fifth Congress in 1994.[11]

Cultural politics in post-socialist Laos thus appear to be ambivalent, caught between the rhetoric of preservation and the desire for modernity, tensions expressed by Houmphanh Rattanavong in his article on "Culture and Lao Culture":

> For our new culture, if we only preserve the old culture by improving what is inadequate, it cannot be a new culture. We must therefore create a more civilised culture that corresponds to the current situation and realities. Meanwhile, we must accept the best in the world to always enhance our culture (Houmphanh 1996, p. 163).

Ann Anagnost shows that the tensions in contemporary China between the construction of a national culture embodied in primordial traits and the necessity of moving towards modernity (symbolized by economic reforms so as to meet the international standards of the capitalist economy) have led the Chinese Communist Party to construct the complex discourse of "civilization" (Anagnost 1997, p. 75). As she explains, that discourse is, above all, a "discourse of lack"; that is, the official recognition of the failure of the Chinese people to match Western criteria of quality, productivity, discipline and civility — in essence, the standards of the modern labour force (Anagnost 1997, p. 76). Concretely, these tensions have given shape to "disciplinary practices", based on a complex combination of conservatism and evolutionism, in an effort to reconcile the essence of the national character and the urge to reach the advanced stage of world-historical development. Accordingly, Anagnost argues, the authoritarian post-Tiananmen state has endorsed a "pedagogical role of raising the quality of people, but […] acts as capitalism's "despotic double", a socialism with "Chinese characteristics" that invites the imposition of capital logic while suppressing any expression of a popular sovereignty" (Anagnost 1997, p. 79).

Since the early 1990s, Laos has been increasingly integrating into the capitalist world market. To be sure, the openness of its economy is not at all comparable to other states in Southeast Asia that have inscribed the culture of capitalism in their societies. Nevertheless, the country still has to confront the harsh effects of its (slow) economic integration into the world market. It is important to bear in mind that Laos remains very dependent on foreign assistance. Since 1990, financial aid from bilateral donors and multilateral funding organizations has amounted to more than US$250 million per year. The author of a recently published book (2002), entitled *Laos within the International Community* (in Lao), is unequivocal with regard to the country's new challenges; he acknowledges, thus:

> … Isolation is no longer possible. Such coexistence is saturated by intellectual competition, though: a country that possesses a better education system, hence more competent people, will have the capacity to economically and socially develop and strengthen, to become prosperous and to build up an international reputation. To the contrary, an incompetent country will be downgraded to the group of poor and backward countries. It is the situation with which Laos is confronted today, and we believe that no Lao feels happy about his or her nation's humiliating position… But we have to accept it, at least temporarily, so as to avoid being removed from the assistance list, in which case we would become even poorer… Let's accept this position, let's not prolong it to the point whereby it would become an endless habit and make us become permanent aid seekers (Bounkhong 2002, p. 157).

The country may have recovered her full membership within the international community, but the growing exposure of the population to the outside world has stimulated the perception among the Lao people that their society is "backward" compared to others in the region and in the world. The discrepancy between the regime and the population has never been so great. Since the end of the socialist economy, development has become the government's national obsession and mouthpiece, while the dominant view among ordinary Lao about their country today may be its "backwardness".

To a certain extent the revival of Buddhism, both at popular and institutional levels, reflects a remarkable evolution in the government's promotion of national identity in post-socialist Laos. Yet, the phenomenon can be interpreted in several ways: as a step backward in the process of building a modern state or, on the contrary, as the regime's attempt to legitimate its rule, or again as a sign of autonomy from the Western model of the nation–state. Reflections on all these three possibilities will constitute my next section.

The search for legitimacy: Buddhism and politics

After the defeat of France in 1940 and the establishment of the French Vichy government, Indochina came under the control of Decoux's Vichy administration. With the rise of Thailand's pan-Thai movement and the apparent willingness of the Japanese to sacrifice French Laos to the expansionist aims of its Bangkok ally, the Vichy government implemented educational and cultural reforms to prevent the loss of Laos from French Indochina, culminating in a *politique indigène* ("native policy") in French Laos (Christie 2001, p. 114). This change in colonial policy was guided by an overall strategy, the objective of which was to reinforce the loyalty of the constituent parts of the colonial empire to the metropolitan power (and, hence, to diminish the risk of implosion in the course of the Second World War) by enhancing their place within the framework of French Indochina. As Ivarsson notes, "for Decoux and the French authorities to build up this specific Lao identity was not viewed as a goal in itself but as a means to integrate Laos further into the Indochinese Federation and make it a more viable member of this entity" (1999, p. 64). Thus, under the leadership of Admiral Decoux, Governor-General of Indochina from 1940 to 1945, a campaign for national renovation was launched within the smaller domains of French Indochina, "Laos" and "Cambodia".

The Lao Renovation Movement was primarily cultural, focusing on the rediscovery and promotion of Lao literature, theatre, music, dance and history as a means of stimulating a sense of Lao identity. The movement's journal, *Lao Nhay* ("Great Laos"), was first published in January 1941,[12] and regular meetings were organized. In brief, this project to restore Lao culture and identity sent a clear message of unity and homogeneity to the population of Laos. However, if it held that the Lao people were encompassed by a common identity, the latter was defined purely in terms of ethnic Lao cultural traits. Both Rochet and Nhouy Abbay's strong emphasis on the role of Buddhism in the restoration of Lao identity illustrates this perspective well.[13] This was reconfirmed in the 1947 Constitution: Buddhism, along with the monarchy, was given a special and linked status — as the key symbols of Lao identity.[14]

The Department of Religion of the LFNC published an intriguing article on Buddhism in the *Lao Sang Sat*, the LFNC's official magazine, in 1998. The text differed from official rhetoric as the authors did not try to demonstrate common ground between the religion and socialist ideals; rather, they stressed the spiritual force of religion in general, and of Buddhism in particular. The article went on to emphasize the role of Buddhism in various areas, such as education and the arts. More surprisingly, it also pointed out the political role of Buddhist monks in the form of kings' advisers, whose kingdoms furthermore were to be ruled by Buddhist principles and commandments. The conclusion is most innovative as it recognizes that progress in science and technology will never undermine religion. On the contrary, society will always need spiritual support and moral values, no matter how developed it is:

> Nowadays, some people believe that religion will disappear when men attain a sufficiently high degree of knowledge in science and technology. However, what happens is the opposite. The more science and technology develop, the more men need to achieve spiritual and moral happiness, i.e. the greater their need of higher moral values, of justice, humankind, civilisation and peace. In brief, as long as religion keeps its role of moral shelter for humankind, we can argue that religious principles and virtues will always stay in men's hearts (Department of Religion 1998, p. 43).[15]

Thus, the concurrence of the parade marking Visit Laos Year with the That Luang festival was not coincidental. The religious monument, which was the centrepiece of a tribute ceremony to royalty under the former regime, has replaced the hammer and sickle as national symbol.[16] Consequently, the That Luang festival has become the locus of the state's representational project of the nation, a crossroads between socialist ideals, Buddhist rituals, exhibition of multiethnic national culture and the politics of opening Laos to the world. The conflation of Buddhism and Socialism is openly celebrated with the support of extensive media coverage.[17] As Trankell observes, "symbolic production of identity is being staged in the state rituals, now managed not by the king, but by the Lao People's Revolutionary Party" (Trankell 1999, p. 199).

Functioning as collective representations, symbols and rituals aim at producing homogeneity from heterogeneity and integrating what is fragmented. Symbols of nationhood are required to engender social cohesion by arousing a deeply felt sense of shared community. They encompass the unique and distinctive values, or at least those that are officially claimed to be unique and distinctive, of the society. As Kertzer puts it, "the nation itself has no palpable existence outside the symbolism through which it is envisioned. [...] Far from being window dressing on the reality that is the nation, symbolism is the stuff of which nations are made" (Kertzer 1988, p. 6). One may therefore argue that the revival of Buddhism is the sign of, in Chatterjee's words, the "[spiritual] 'inner' domain of national culture [...] bearing the 'essential' marks of cultural identity" (Chatterjee 1993b, p. 6). Chatterjee disputes the claim that the Western nation–state is a universal concept, and argues that post-colonial nations of Africa and Asia are constituted on a principle of difference, founded on a construction of their cultural particularity rather than as an adaptation of their form of nation to the universal form. Thought of in this way, the nation situates itself within universal history (as the history of the nation's coming to self-awareness) while preserving its "spiritual essence" as an identification with a primordial (hence timeless) culture that becomes enframed as the national "tradition".

Keyes, Hardacre and Kendall have termed the present declining influence of standard secular nationalism in some Asian states as a "crisis of authority" or "deficit of legitimacy". They define the phenomenon as follows:

It is the experience of having a problematic relationship with the past, of being alienated from traditional certainties in which cosmology reflects community and vice versa, of being offered and often pressured to accept an identity with one particular version of one's heritage rather than another that constitutes what we term the modern crisis of authority (Keyes, Hardacre and Kendall 1994, p. 4).

For them, the new states of Asia have been promoting too long and too uncritically the Western model of the nation–state. In pursuit of their modernizing and nation-building projects, the governments expected thereby to create a secular identity within a rationalized society. However, the modern state has failed to create feelings of belonging while creating new problems, such as social anomie (Keyes, Hardacre and Kendall 1994, pp. 6–7). The authors thus assert that the "crisis of authority" has led to the resurgence of religion because it fulfils people's need for commitment and sharing. Indeed, they suggest that the nation as an imagined community is itself imbued with a "primordial" identity that is, in their definition, the intrinsic feelings of belonging to the same community. That is the "spiritual essence" of the nation, which the Western model of the nation–state cannot produce (Keyes, Hardacre and Kendall 1994, p. 5). Writing about Burma, Thailand, Laos and Cambodia, they argue that these states have, however, been forced to embrace Buddhism, and as such to attempt to control its public manifestations, in order to counteract a popular source of authority that transcends that of the state. Thus, though Southeast Asian expressions of national sentiment may be *different* to those featured in the model propagated by Western historical thought, they have been partially appropriated by the state.

The Lao government, in effect, still keeps the Sangha, the Buddhist clergy, under its control and although the latter has regained its popularity, links with the Party remain close (Stuart-Fox 1998, p. 168). Buddhism may have been granted a new political role,[18] but its newly reformulated function is nowhere near the type of strong alliance with the state that has never ceased to exist in neighbouring Thailand. In fact, while ostensibly displaying respect during Buddhist festivals, the Lao government has also been trying to present a secularized image of Buddhism in order to reconcile the official political ideology and the religion.[19]

Khamphao Phonekèo, in an article published in Vientiane's French language newspaper, *Le Rénovateur* (18 May 2000), argues that religion and ideology are, far from opposing each other, complementary. To begin with, Khamphao criticizes both the old regime and the Pathet Lao, the former for corrupting Buddhism and the latter for misunderstanding it. He then suggests that religion has now been cleansed of its superstitious aspects while the Party has recognized its previous mistakes. Accordingly, in its newly purified form and fully rehabilitated, Buddhism now enjoys an even greater popularity than in the past.

Khamphao then explains that Buddhism, like Marxism, has no ambitions but to change society for the better: neither of them pretends to provide holistic doctrines, which are anyway "useless discourses"; they are not "ideologies"; both simply offer men and women a "recipe" for happiness. The only difference between Buddhism and Marxism, he argues, is merely a question of scale. "Both of them are extremely practical and put practice above everything", Khamphao asserts, "no matter what the pretty arguments, only the end matters; the Marxists prefer calling this result happiness and the Buddhists, end of suffering".[20] Moreover, Buddhist people, he says, are better able to live in a socialist society because a Buddhist person, some may argue, is not a selfish individual in quest of his/her own salvation, but, on the contrary, a person who is more able to feel compassion for others.

The author goes on to argue that Buddhism, like Marxism, promotes socioeconomic development. In doing so, he refutes the commonly held view that the Buddhist concept of renunciation is contradictory to the idea of material well-being. Poverty has been condemned by the Buddha, he writes, as a cause of immorality and crimes; consequently, to eliminate these negative phenomena, the economic conditions of the population first must be improved. Of course, development must not follow market logic, as that will produce the reverse effect: creating a vicious cycle of needs and desires leading to endless suffering. Accordingly, both Buddhism and Marxism reject the capitalist system that enslaves men and women. Therefore, Khamphao happily concludes,

> ... there is nothing surprising in the fact that Buddhism and Marxism get along with each other in Laos. It is not so much a political deal as a very natural alliance. Not only do they not oppose each other (for they belong to different parts of human life) but they are complementary, and in some ways they reinforce each other.[21]

Attempts in the Lao PDR to demonstrate that Buddhism and Marxism are compatible are not new; they go back as far as 1975 when the Pathet Lao came to power. Soon after the communist victory, monks were already being taught in political seminars that the two belief systems held identical principles, i.e. "essential equality of all the people", and aimed at the same basic objective, i.e. "promotion of happiness through elimination of suffering" (Stuart-Fox 1998, p. 161). The government also wanted to turn the monks into educators for the socialist programme, notably in the countryside. The accommodation between the two philosophies did not go so far as to create a doctrine of Buddhist socialism, as in Burma; nor did the Party intend to suppress Buddhism. Rather, in the mid-1970s and early 1980s, the government tried to limit and control the Sangha, through such means as censoring "wasteful" practices (for instance, merit-making donations to the *vat*) or prescribing compulsory political re-education seminars for the monks. In short, the objective was to "bend [the Sangha] to the will of the state" (Evans 1993, p. 135).

The secular promotion of Buddhism by the government is, however, rooted in a great dilemma: a third of the population is, according to the official data, non-Buddhist (Population Census 1995). Lao citizens have the freedom to choose their religion, as long as their choice does not infringe the law. Nevertheless, although Buddhism is no longer the state religion, the Party unambiguously commands ethnic groups to abandon their "backward practices", that is, their "animist" rituals, which "have bad impacts on solidarity, productivity and life of the diverse ethnic groups as well as of the nation" (Lao People Revolutionary Party's Central Committee 1992, p. 14). The Lao authorities hope that the construction of a nation on a foundation of cultural particularity may help the Lao PDR to gain a sense of "unique-ness" in the region. The promotion of Buddhism at the state level in Laos may thus be viewed as one of the manifestations of the tensions between the principles of incorporation and exclusion in defining the national body and its culture. However, the "revival" of the "spiritual essence" of the national community is focused on ethnic Lao culture, thereby highlighting those who are excluded while reinforcing the process of making Lao-ness the characteristic of an invisible majority.

At both state and popular levels since the 1990s, the impact of a revived Buddhism on the Majority–Minority relationship remains uncertain. Pessimistically, the political instrumentalization of Buddhism may well reinforce an illiberal nationalism by restricting access to national membership to those of a particular religion, although, as stated in the country's present Constitution, Buddhism is no longer the official religion and religious freedom is, in principle, guaranteed (Articles 9 and 43 in the 2003 Amended Constitution). Would a clear separation between the state and the Sangha be preferable, so as to ensure a thinner conception of national identity, i.e. based on a shared language and institutions, rather than on religion, ethnicity or race (Kymlicka 2000, p. 197)? Would this measure not infringe on the ideal of authenticity, which Charles Taylor describes as the "original way of being… that cannot be socially derived, but must be inwardly generated" (Taylor 1995, p. 229)? In pursuit of authenticity through a politics of difference, culture-bearing peoples want to be recognized as unique, in terms of their identities. To be sure, it is an ethnic Lao-dominated post-colonial nation that claims to be constituted on a principle of difference by promoting Buddhism. What we have therefore is the challenge for recognition of minority groups in Laos, on the one hand, and the claim to authenticity in the process of nation-differentiation, on the other. The state has yet to find an answer that would give justice to both demands. The next four chapters will unfold, on the one hand, the two main determinants of access to post-colonial nationhood that are being instrumentalized by the state and its agents in contemporary Laos — historiography (Chapter 4) and ethnicity (Chapter 6) — and on the other, some responses and (re)interpretations towards those official narrations of the past (Chapter 5) and state-controlled ethnicities (Chapter 7) by "revolutionaries" of ethnic minority origins in southern Laos.

Notes

[1]   This is a common pattern (of which modern China has been a long-term producer) whereby minority peoples, as Gladney ironically depicts, are shown as "good dancers, singers, and sportsmen, [which] is a feature of this [objectivised] process well known to travellers in China and of the Chinese state's representation of itself as 'multinational'" (Gladney 1994, p. 264).

[2]   Interview in Vientiane, March 2002.

[3]   Worth noting is a study published in 2000 by a Thai academic, Vipha Uttamachant, on the impact of Thai media on Lao society (Vipha Utthamachant, *Phonkratopkhongsanyawitanyoulaethorathatkhamphromdaenrawangthailao* ("The Impacts of the Radio and Television Signals across the Thai-Lao Border"), Bangkok: Chulalongkorn University Press, 2544 [2001]). These are some of her conclusions as reported in the English-language Thai newspaper, *The Nation* (28 January 2001); see also Martin Clutterbuck's short article, "Official enemy: Thai culture", *Far Eastern Economic Review*, 11 February 1993.

[4]   Interesting, thus, were their fierce reactions when a Thai pop singer was accused of having expressed derogatory remarks about Lao people during a TV show. Below is an excerpt of an article in the Lao-language newspaper, *Vientiane Mai*, written by a Lao female, possibly a member of the Lao Women's Union, which illustrates the sense of insult to national pride:

> If Nicole [the Thai singer] lacked the education to be able to make a distinction between what is right or wrong, the Lao people would not bear a grudge for her naivety. But, on the contrary, she has received a good education, has a rather high living standard, as well as a certain degree of fame. So, how could one forgive her for what she said? The only one explanation left is that she intentionally meant to harm Laos' dignity and reputation, which is

unacceptable. If Laos is a small under-developed country, the Lao people, on the contrary, morally and intellectually, are not inferior to any other people (*Vientiane Mai*, 25 April 2000).

5   UNICEF, *Listening to the Voice of Young People*, in collaboration with Lao Youth Union, Lao Women's Union, Department of Education Vientiane Municipality, and Save the Children (UK), Vientiane, 1998.

6   "Friendship Bridge in name only", *The Nation*, 19 January 2002; and interview with a Lao journalist, March 2002, Vientiane.

7   See the stimulating discussion on this issue by the historian Craig J. Reynolds in his chapter: "Globalization and Cultural Nationalism in Modern Thailand", in *Southeast Asian Identities: Culture and the Politics of Representation in Indonesia, Malaysia, Singapore, and Thailand*, edited by Joel S. Kahn, pp. 115–45 (London, New York and Singapore: I.B. Tauris and Institute of Southeast Asian Studies, 1998).

8   However, in the 2003 Amended Constitution, a new article (Article 9) gives more prominence to Buddhism, although it stops short of proclaiming Buddhism the state religion.

9   Another example is a notice issued by the Ministry of Information and Culture (Notice no. 848, 14 October 1999), which attempts to regulate activities in entertainment places. In that notice, it is, for instance, stipulated that it is forbidden to play and to sing foreign songs. They are, however, allowed if foreigners participate in the event; in that case, foreign songs must be limited to 20 per cent of the total music played. Dress is similarly subject to rules. Thus, it is strictly forbidden for men to wear "eccentric" clothes, to have long hair and earrings; as for women, they are not allowed to wear trousers and skirts, or any kind of clothing that is contrary to the Lao traditions. Sexual conservatism also is reflected in instructions which stipulate that entertainment places must be well lit so that people can be clearly visible, for, as it is explained, dim lighting can lead to indecent behaviour.

10 The choice is hardly surprising: the religious and cultural event has become one of the most emblematic Hmong rites researched by Lao anthropologists for the sake of cultural and ethnic diversity, while it is being progressively advertised and commodified as a tourist attraction.

11 "Concerning Cultural Activities in the New Era". Directive of the ninth meeting of the Party Central Committee's Administrative Commission, Fifth Party Congress, October 1994.

[12] See the recent and very informative essay on the newspaper's role in the awakening of a national 'imagining' among the young Lao elite by Søren Ivarsson, "Towards a New Laos…", pp. 61–78.

[13] Ibid., p. 115.

[14] "Constitution du Royaume du Laos, du 11 mai 1947, révisée en 1949 et 1952", in Le Laos. Son évolution politique, sa place dans l'Union française, Katay Don Sasorith (Paris: Éditions Berger-Levrault, 1953), p. 100.

[15] These claims certainly do not really fit the socialist ideals of "industrial men". The Lao communist leaders emphasized training of cadres, and more generally the necessity to educate peoples. Following the Vietnamese political ideology, the government adopted the programme of "the Three Revolutions" and like his Vietnamese comrades, in 1982, Kaysone stressed the key role of technology in rapidly developing the economy :"[i]n Laos, the urgent problem of the bypassing to socialism is how to develop the new production forces and how to increase the efficiency of work. An answer to these questions rests in scientific and technical progress. This is why our Party, in the three revolutions, considers the scientific and technical revolution as the key point" (Kaysone Phomvihane [1982]; quoted, in turn, from Luther [1982, p. 47]).

[16] Grant Evans expertly analyses in one of his books (1998) the reintegration of Buddhist and former nationalist symbols by the regime into its propaganda in the hope of relegitimizing itself.

[17] The example usually quoted is the picture taken of the Party's senior members making merit during major Buddhist festivals. Even the LFNC has put one of these photos on the cover of its magazine (Lao Sang Sat, 1[2], 1998).

[18] Thus, according to the Party's resolution on religion, Buddhism not only "played an important role in the work of national unification in the past" and presently plays a role in "preserving and developing the national culture" as well as educating the people both literally and morally, but the "monks, the nuns and the believers [also] participated in the patriotic movements to fight against the colonialist imperialists and to liberate the country." (The Lao People Revolutionary Party's Central Committee 1992, p. 12).

[19] Trankell's account of the restoration of the former royal palace in Luang Prabang similarly illustrates the authorities' discomfort regarding symbols associated with the former regime. The palace was built by the French in 1914–20 and was turned into a museum under the socialist regime. During the restoration (financed by a foreign development agency), the name of the

palace changed twice. Known as "The Royal Museum" since the king's abdication in 1976, it was renamed the "Grand Palace Museum" in 1993. By 1996, however, it was being referred to simply as the "Museum of Luang Prabang" (Trankell 1999, p. 199).

[20] "[...] tous deux sont extrêmement pratiques et mettent la pratique au-dessus de tout; peu importent les beaux raisonnements, seul compte le résultat; ce résultat, les marxistes l'appellent plutôt bonheur et les bouddhistes, cessation de la souffrance" (Khampao 2000, p. 5).

[21] "Il n'y a donc rien d'étonnant à ce que le bouddhisme et le marxisme fassent bon ménage au Laos. Ce n'est pas point là tellement un compromis politique qu'une alliance fort naturelle. Non seulement ils ne s'opposent pas (car ils appartiennent à des plans différents de l'existence humaine) mais ils se complètent et, d'une certaine manière, se renforcent" (Khampao 2000, p. 5).

4

The Origins of the Lao People: In Search of an Autonomous History

About Writing an Autonomous History (of Laos)

Post-colonial historiographers share an obsession with origins. As Paul Connerton points out, the politics of *tabula rasa* paradoxically engender even greater reference to the past (Connerton 1995, p. 61). Nations need a foundation, a mythical past so as to enforce a *longue durée* — an essential component for consolidating a collective memory and identity. Horizontal homogeneity must be accomplished along an uninterrupted span of time: "we are what you were, we will be what you are" famously wrote once Ernest Renan (Renan 1997 [1982], p. 32). Patricia Pelley remarks likewise with respect to post-1945 Vietnamese historiography that "[o]nly by determining when it began, they [Vietnamese historiographers] reckoned, could they narrate it in a meaningful way. Only after they had a clear sense of origins could they clarify the trajectory of the past and divide it into meaningful segments" (Pelley 2002, p. 8). History textbooks, as is well known, are the main vehicle for disseminating such a history, particularly in countries where dissonant voices are repressed and alternative perspectives discouraged. In that context, school textbooks merely tend to be "ideological, repetitive and mantra-like" (Talib and Tan 2003, p. xiii).[1] The narrative of origins in modern Lao-language history books and textbooks, instead of depicting a master version of a pacified history representing "idealized images of a harmonious, pre-colonial social order imbued of nostalgia" (Alonso 1994, p. 388), is, on the contrary, divided between three interpretations of the origins of the Lao, each situated in divergent geopolitical, political and ideological perspectives. The first and most popular reading is the "Ai-Lao" version that is dominated by the trope of migration and is an implicit response to the Thai nationalist historiography. The second historiography, with a Marxist-Leninist orientation, bears by contrast a resemblance to the Vietnamese communist narration. I suggest below that the (re)writing of the origins of the Lao nation epitomizes the fragmentary state of Lao historiography and, more precisely, its struggle to deal with competing ideologies. More significantly, as I suggest when dealing with the third type of historiography, as far as likely future trends are concerned the journey back to the "roots" in modern Lao-language history books, more than the search for "a screen on which desires for unity and continuity… could be projected" (Gillis 1994, p. 9), ultimately seems to reveal a quest for an autonomous history, i.e. a search for "a continuous Lao-centric history of Laos" (to paraphrase Smail's seminal words), which exposes the country's "underlying social structure and culture" (Smail 1993, p. 53).

The trope of migration: origins of the people

The myth of the "Ai-Lao"

The theme of migration is predominant in Lao school textbooks. First-year secondary school students learn in their social science manuals (which include history, geography and demography) the following version of the origins of the inhabitants of Laos:

> The group within the Thai-Lao family whose name was Ai-Lao, originally lived on a territory, on the upper area of the Mekong River in the valley in

the south of the Yang Zi Kiang River in China. They once constituted a developed and wealthy kingdom and were the masters of a country within the territory of China 3000–4000 years ago...

Not long after or before the Christian era, the group of the Thai-Lao family progressively went down to the south along the Mekong River, the Irrawaddy River, the Chao Praya River and the Black River, and mixed with other ethnic groups, who had been living for a long time in the Suvannaphum peninsula. Then, around the mid-thirteenth century, the Mongols expanded their domination to the south over various kingdoms in the south of China, which forced the group of the Thai-Lao family to emigrate further south... (Institute of Research in Educational Sciences 1996, p. 13).

The Lao nationalist historiography is not the only one to conflate legend and history. A historical discourse based on the tropes of migration and racial continuity is equally common in Thailand. Like the lowland Lao-based narration, the Thai racial historiography upholds the story of the emergence and development of a Thai race during a huge migration process from the Kingdom of Nan Chao (or Nanzhao)[2] in southern China during the pre-Sukhotai era (i.e. before the thirteenth century) to the present-day territory of Thailand. As Thongchai Winichakul comments: "Together, the Thai past was a linear movement of a great race from the time and place of Others to the time and place of self-realization as a sovereign race" (Thongchai 1995, p. 108). Despite denials from historians both outside and inside the country, the myth of a Thai identity of Nan Chao was disseminated by government publications up until the 1980s and still prevails in school textbooks (Terwiel 2001, p. 100). Yet, Thongchai has shown in his excellent overview of the new interpretations of the past in Thailand how a long tradition of contesting historical studies has developed over the last thirty years in Thai academia, thereby challenging the conventional historiography (Thongchai 1995) — in vain, as Patrick Jory seems to suggest in a recent contribution (Jory 2003), because of the Thai people's present lack of interest in professional history. Jory notes, thus:

What is today consumed as history by the Thai public consists of two forms: the royalist-nationalist history taught in the schools and popularized through bureaucratic channels; and products of the commercial media in the form of movies, TV dramas, and even advertisements, which are gradually becoming the dominant mode of reproduction of historical knowledge.

In consequence, the "dominance of the Damrong school of history (or Thongchai's royalist-nationalist historiography)", he suggests, may face its biggest challenge not from the new academic thinking, but from "new forms of dissemination and consumption of movies, TV dramas, and internet debate by new mass markets" (Jory 2003, pp. 9–10). It is too soon to tell which form of historical knowledge will prevail in Thailand. For the time being, the royalist-nationalist historiography remains unrevised in the textbooks.

To some extent, the politics of historiography in contemporary Laos may also be analysed from the perspective of the modern relationship between Thailand and Laos. Houmpanh Rattanavong, then Director of the Institute of Cultural Research in Vientiane, for instance, asserts that the term "Tai" or "Thai" did not yet exist (in reference to either the ethno-linguistic and cultural category or the ethnic group) before the sixth century; he claims, therefore, that "the so-called 'Tai' populations did not yet exist in North Vietnam nor in Laos. They were all called Lao" (Houmphanh 1990, p. 165). In other words, only the name "Lao" is original and authentic, hence implying the seniority of the "Lao" over the "Thai" (although there is no evidence that "Lao" then actually referred to the present-day ethnic Lao in Laos). Accordingly, the Lao post-colonial obsession with origins may also be read, at least in part, as a response to the local perception of an overwhelming Thai sense of superiority over Thailand's neighbours. Nevertheless, as Barend Terwiel points out, research on the prehistory of the Tai faces a major obstacle, which is that the Tai-speaking peoples are not mentioned in any text as such (Terwiel 1978, p. 240). Consequently, it seems highly speculative to attempt to identify a discrete and homogenous people as being "Lao" while different names were being used to refer to the populations living in what is now the Tai area.

In consequence, perhaps because of these shared roots and similarity of structure with the Thai nationalist historiography (i.e. "migration/racial continuity/racial domination"), Lao history textbooks have also been striving to distinguish "their" version of the past, and especially of the origins of the "Lao" people, by popularizing a "genealogy" different from the "Nanzhao" version,[3] that is, of the "Ai-Lao" people. Maha Sila Viravong, arguably the most renowned historian in Laos, was the leading figure of this lowland Lao-based historiography. His *Phongsavadan lao* ("History of Laos"), published in 1957, has been for nearly half a century the master reference for secondary school history textbooks, both in the "Old" and "New" regimes. Its impact, in fact, went well beyond the country's frontiers thanks to its English-translation that was available as early as 1958. With regard to historiography and ethnicity, Maha Sila Viravong's writings on the history of Laos have shaped a perennialist vision of the Lao nation by strongly relating Lao national identity to a myth of ethnic descent. The historian thus dated (in his *Phongsavadan lao*) the origins of the "Lao race" to some 2500 years ago "along the Hwang Ho river valley", and further claimed that their ancestors were an ancient people called the "Ai-Lao" who dwelt in the "valleys between the Hwang Ho and Yang Tse Kiang rivers in the heart of present day mainland China" (Maha Sila Viravong 1964, pp. 6–8).

The myth of a several thousand-year-old kingdom and civilization, or the "Ai-Lao ancestors", is still widely disseminated, both through school textbooks[4] and in the mass-circulation publications that are sold in the markets and bookshops in Vientiane and the major provincial towns at a fairly reasonable price.[5] For example, in a Lao history booklet, entitled *Anajak khunchiang* ["Kingdom of Khunchiang"], reprinted three times since 1996, Douangsai Luangpasi, a prolific Lao writer and keen amateur historian, explains the origins of the Lao people as follows, stressing the outstanding origins and traits of the Ai-Lao people:

According to what is said in history, the word 'Lao' means *Dao* ["star"], that is the people whose race has come down from above, having for instance for origins a region in the North, in high altitudes or heaven, skies. [...] The Ai-Lao, viewed as belonging to the *Dao* lineage, since adopted this word for their name. Then, the Chinese, who were going back and forth on the Huang-Ho ["Yellow River"], came to encounter the *Dao* or *'Dao* race', a civilized people, who possessed solid means of subsistence, a high culture and a benevolent and generous heart. They were willing to help the Chinese, some of whom were in transit and others who immigrated from elsewhere. Through their virtues, the *Dao* or *'Dao* race' is getting respect from the Chinese. In their pronunciation of 'Ai Dao', the 'D' is imperfectly pronounced by the Chinese and diverges to the 'L'; hence the name 'Ai-Lao' since then (Douangsay 2001, pp. 10–11).

Douangsay is not the only author to disseminate these views whose scientific value is nevertheless highly questionable (the author never quotes his sources nor mentions any references); they are also reproduced in school textbooks.[6] As a result, schoolchildren in Laos today are taught and made to believe that they are the descendants of an ancient people, the "Ai-Lao", who once ruled a prosperous kingdom in China thousands of years ago. The latter then migrated southwards, settled in the present-day territory of Laos, where they later founded the kingdom of Lan Xang. The students learn little, if anything, about the origins of the rest of the population. In other words, this historiography that promotes a monolithic, yet doubtful, ethnic Lao past neglects all other inhabitants of Laos. Yet, members of the Austroasiatic ethno-linguistic family (who comprise 23 per cent of the population according to the 1995 census, and are classified between the Mon-Khmer [22.7 per cent] and the Viet-Muong-speaking [0.3 per cent] ethnic groups), found throughout the country in both upland and lowland environments, are generally acknowledged (albeit mainly by Western academics) to be the original inhabitants of the country. The only non-ethnic Lao peoples that receive even scant attention are those who reigned over a significant portion of the former kingdom of Lan Xang but who either no longer exist or happen to live outside Laos and have been turned into "minorities" since the creation of national boundaries. The latter include the Khom,[7] the Môn and the Lawa. The history handbook for secondary school teachers, for instance, notes that

> ... the Lao racial community, presently called the Lao, is not the Lao from the Lawa or Lua lineage, because those Lawa, primitive inhabitants, no longer exist. What little remains of the Lawa is the Khmu community, which dwells nowadays in the forests and mountains, in northern Laos and Thailand (Institute of Research in Educational Sciences 1996, p. 17).

The linear logic of migration and racial continuity is therefore entirely focused on the ethnic Lao, as if the previous "multi-ethnic population" was wiped out by the huge wave of migration.

Recent studies in linguistics, history and comparative anthropology suggest that the original Tai homeland occupied an area extending from western Guangxi and southeastern Yunnan in southern China into northern Vietnam and northeastern Laos.[8] Likewise, a direct kinship relationship between these two populations, the "Ai-Lao" and the present-day ethnic Lao population in Laos, is hard to find. For instance, Terwiel again remarks:

> There is one early account regarding the Ai-Lao who are mentioned for the first time in Han times in the Hou-han-shu [...]. They were reported then to have lived in the Kwangsi-Yunnan area, the region of China bordering on Tongkin. At this stage we cannot be certain that these actually were T'ais (Terwiel 1978, p. 249).[9]

This assumption — that of the "Ai-Lao" being the direct ancestors of the present-day ethnic Lao people in modern Laos — has been rejected. Indeed, the founders of the kingdom of Nanzhao (or Nan Chao), established in the eighth century in Northern and Western present-day Yunnan, were not the descendants of the "Ai-Lao" but Lolo, a Tibeto-Burman speaking people (Terwiel 1978, p. 240). Martin Stuart-Fox concludes that it is "unlikely [...] that whoever the Chinese referred to as the Ai-Lao were directly ancestral to the Tai-Lao who founded the

Kingdom of Lan Xang well over a millennium later" (Stuart-Fox 1998, p. 23).

This trope of migration, underlining a logic of racial continuity and homogeneity and associated with mythical origins, epitomizes perennialist historiography whereby "the nation is a recurrent form of social organization and nationalism a perennial mode of cultural belonging" (Smith 1999, p. 11). It is the myth of an ancient, self-conscious, people that have existed from time immemorial to the present-day. In this sense, as Anthony D. Smith argues, the work of nationalist historians is comparable to those of archaeologists:

> the nation is multilayered, and the task of the nationalist historian and archaeologist is to recover each layer of the past and thereby trace the origins of the nation from its "rudimentary beginnings" through its early flowering in a golden age [ages] to its periodic decline and its modern birth and renewal. In this way the myth receives apparent historical self-confirmation over the longue durée, and a rediscovered and authenticated past is "scientifically" appropriated for present national ends (Smith 2000, p. 64).

It is far from certain, however, whether this perennialist historiography will succeed in imposing itself as the master narrative of Laos. Although it is mediated via school texts and some booklets for the general public, its audience is still limited because of the country's poor educational infrastructure, low literacy levels and scarcity of reading material. In addition, the Lao state lacks the mass media power (TV channels, programmes and movies) to popularize its nationalist history. Aside from these material restrictions, the elements that impede this historiography from achieving a position of hegemony are also historical, political and ideological. In this way, a comparative view with the Thai nationalist historiography can highlight the pitfalls of an ethno-nationalist history in contemporary Laos. I argue, that divergent adaptations of the concept of nation in Siam (now Thailand) and in Laos explain, to a significant extent, the contrasting degrees of hegemony of the nationalist historiographies in these two countries.

A curtailed policy of assimilation

One could argue that ethno-nationalist historiography is bound to fail in Laos because of the country's ethnic composition, which shows that over half of the population does not belong to the Lao ethnic group. Yet, according to Charles Keyes, the Thai ethnic group (i.e, speakers of Standard Thai, Central Thai, and southern Thai, but not including Sino-Thai, Thai Muslims or North and Northeastern Tai-speakers) in Thailand make up merely half of the total population (Keyes 2002, p. 1178). All the censuses since the 1920s, however, have shown very little ethnic diversity for the simple reason that Thai population surveys do not include ethnic self-identification in their criteria (Keyes 1997, p. 197). The supremacy of the Thai nationalist historiography has been achieved through modern technologies (a mass-education system, the technology of print, the mass media), but has also relied on a sophisticated and pervasive nationalist discourse that has from the late nineteenth century shaped Thai views of the outside world and of their own country — two nationalist resources which the Lao under colonial rule and successive modern Lao regimes (after the Second World War) were, for various reasons, unable to experience and develop.

Thai notions of nation, race, ethnicity and identity were shaped, to a great extent, by both the appeal of European "civilization" and the threats of colonialism.[10] In this regard, David Streckfuss offers a thought-provoking argument: French colonialism radically redefined Siam along *racial* lines. He argues that, in fact, French colonialism largely created the "racialist consciousness or 'Thai-ness' that has largely defined the Thai state and its ideology up to the present day" (Streckfuss 1993, p. 134). In the aftermath of the Pak Nam crisis of 1893, when the French seized the left bank of the Mekong River and established a protectorate over Laos, the Thai elite was forced to reassess itself in the light of the threat of French colonial expansion into the Mekong region. Hardly a coincidence, this era saw the birth of modern Thai historiography, much of it penned by or published on the authority of the "Father of Thai History", King

Chulalongkorn's younger brother Prince Damrong Rachanubhab. Streckfuss insists that more than the massive economic, administrative and political efforts of modernization that the kingdom made during that period, the most profound impact was ideological. The "logic of race" (i.e. a geographical and political entity can only claim to be a nation if it possesses a single language, culture and race) employed by the French colonialists so as to legitimize their claims over the Lao and Cambodian populations of Siam following their annexation of Laos forced Thai royalty to reappropriate and adapt the European concept of national identity. The Bangkok elite's response to the French threat was twofold: they reified the country's geographical space (by sending out armed surveying teams to demarcate the boundaries of Siam) and refashioned the population's (outer and inner) boundaries. Accordingly, the Siamese officials went on absorbing and homogenizing the disparate 'Other' peoples of Siam through the most simple, and yet ingenious, process: the merger of the concepts of nationality/ethnicity [*chon chaat*], race [*chaat, chu'a chaat*] and citizenship [*sanchaat*], within the single, all-inclusive and elastic term *chaat* (Streckfuss 1993, p. 141).

The modern Lao state has in the same way tried to define a politics of conflation between race (*son sat*), ethnicity (*son paw*) and citizenship (*san sat*) by implementing a bureaucratic use of the racial category. Amongst the data included on Lao identification cards, for instance, are the individual's race, citizenship and ethnicity. Except for citizens of Vietnamese and Chinese origins, the entire population, non-ethnic Lao as well as ethnic Lao, is classified as "Lao" under both the race and citizenship categories, but ethnicity remains a vector of distinction and classification. The same nomenclature is also applied to the compulsory household booklet. On this document, "citizenship", "race" and "ethnic group" are required, with "Lao" defining the first two qualities for Lao nationals, no matter what their "ethnic group". I argue, however, that the official policy of absorbing and homogenizing the population by subsuming racial and national identity has not (or perhaps not yet) captured people's imaginations in Laos, for three reasons: first, because of the weakness of the modern technologies of power in the hands of the state; second, as a result of a specific adaptation of the Western notion of the national identity from the early 1940s, which in contrast to Thailand's malleable and all-embracing concept of *chaat*, was intrinsically lowland-Lao orientated and had no assimilationist agenda; and third, due to the Marxist-Leninist influenced ethnography applied nationwide after 1975 that reinforced ethnic categorization.

Early Lao nationalism was built in reaction against other nationalist visions, real or potential, i.e. the political projects of pan-Thaiism and a Vietnamese-dominated Indochina. A series of social, economic, administrative and political reforms were initiated in the early 1940s, in tandem with the building of road infrastructure, in order to make the Lao elite feel that they had a future in French-Lao cooperation, and at the same time to counter the pan-Thai appeal of Bangkok. Greater financial resources from the general Indochinese budget were thus allocated to various spheres of Lao society. More significant for the constitution of a distinct Lao identity was the creation of a Lao movement — the "Lao Renovation Movement" — in 1941 under Decoux's auspices, the "first genuinely nationalist organization in Laos" (Christie 2001, p. 114). Charles Rochet, the Director of Public Education, played a key role in this reform movement, along with a small group of young, educated Lao patriots led by Nhouy Abhay and Katay Don Sasorith. Rochet believed that Lao culture and identity had to be restored and preserved by the Lao people themselves. His initiatives were based on a conviction that the main threat to Lao identity came, not from Thailand, but from the very Indochina entity envisioned by the French. A disquieted Rochet went on to warn in his book (*Pays Lao: Le Laos dans la Tourmente. 1939–1945*, published in 1946) that "[t]he Lao people were being steadily turned into aborigines in their own land [for which reason] he foresaw a real danger that a coherent Lao identity would eventually disappear altogether" (ibid., p. 116), mainly because of the French plans for massive Vietnamese immigration into Laos (and Cambodia) in order to build up their administration.[11] Rochet was not the first person to warn against the danger of unchecked Vietnamese emigration to Laos. As a matter of fact, as early as 1931, Prince Phetsarath clearly expressed in an interview his concerns over this immigration and the need to control it to avoid creating in Laos "a state within the state".[12] In other words, although the Lao Renovation Movement supported the development of a young Lao elite who would lead the cultural renovation, it did not create the emerging Lao nationalist identity. It was already there before the start of the WWII: Prince Phetsarath, in the same interview, asked for the unification of "Laos"; for him, "Laos existed", but not "Indochina".[13]

Early Lao nationalism was therefore primarily an elite lowland Lao nationalism, so as to ensure a viable nation–state at the international level. Moreover, the boundaries of Laos were not threatened by any colonialist expansion: except for the 1941–46 period,[14] the outer borders of Laos had remained unchanged since the Siamese-French treaties at the turn of the twentieth century. In consequence, the Lao nationalists had not been forced — in contrast to the Siamese elite in the late nineteenth century — to re-think the territorial and organic basis of the nation–state. As a matter of fact, equal citizenship was granted in the 1947 Constitution to all the races of Laos, including the upland minority groups and resident Vietnamese and Chinese, but the politics of national culture and identity during the war and in the immediate post-war period were not deliberately assimilationist. Lao nationalism was more outward than inward-looking — and, in any case, the state would have been unable to enforce integrationist policies given the weakness of the central administration. As Bruce Lockhart notes likewise:

> It can be argued that education under the RLG never succeeded in broadening its vision to build a Lao nation because it failed to incorporate the various ethnic groups whose position — though strategically important — was psychologically and culturally peripheral from the perspective of the ruling élite in Vientiane and Luang Phabang (Lockhart, n.p., p. 9).

Although in the aftermath of the Second World War Laos was no longer a French colony in a full sense, the country's educational system was still very much embedded in the colonial framework.[15] On the other hand, the insufficient degree of "laocization" under the RLG's schooling system seemed to be compensated for in the textbooks by an overwhelming focus on the lowland Lao lifestyle and religion (Theravada Buddhism), which automatically excluded a large portion of the population. In other words, the ethnic minorities were invisible in the school texts.

Laos and the lowland Lao elite, unlike the Siamese rulers from the late nineteenth century, were not forced to radically change the ways they thought about and ruled the country's space, or at least not until the national landscape became increasingly threatened by the growth of the Pathet Lao, as they expanded their control over the provinces and districts in the north and east of the country during the Indochinese Wars. However, the RLG's policy of integration proved to be too late and too little in both scope and means, whether through educational programmes or military operations.[16] The lowland Lao elite and leadership were less concerned about assimilating the upland and highland population than strengthening their culture, language and traditions in their own backyard, i.e. among the lowland Lao population themselves. Bruce Lockhart acutely remarks that the hierarchy between the ethnic Lao and the highlanders, pejoratively named *Kha* or *Meo*, was not solely defined along cultural lines or by civilizational degrees, but also in terms of ethnicity and socio-economic ranking (Kha is commonly translated as "slave"). "By contrast", he adds, "the Vietnamese terms — *Moi* and *Man* (the latter borrowed from Chinese) — have clear connotations of cultural primitiveness". In his view, accordingly, "[e]ducation, then, was perceived mainly in the context of socio-economic development (and thus of nation-building) rather than as part of a top-down *mission civilisatrice*" (Lockhart, n.p., p. 19). The RLG, in fact, perpetuated the political system and society based on the centre-periphery dichotomy. Put differently, it is reasonable to presume that the majority of the lowland Lao leaders in the mid-twentieth century were still guided by the traditional Buddhist concept and taxonomy that defined the relationships between rulers and ruled in terms of centre and periphery, on the one hand, and class and status (as well as race), at least as far as the ethnic groups encompassed under the "Kha" category were concerned, on the other.

Marxist-Leninist Ethnography and Collective Autochthony

Ordering and Fixing diversity

Another major contributing factor to the lesser impact of the lowland-Lao based historiography is arguably the radically different concept and discourse of identity propagated by the Communist leadership from before 1975. The latter promoted (at least during the first fifteen years of their rule) a policy of equality dominated by the class issue and the diktat of progress. The regime change opened a new era for the country: at the international level, Laos promptly joined the camp of socialist states. But perhaps it was internally that the changes were most dramatic, as the leadership began to redefine the very essence of the Lao nation in an attempt to "cleanse" the country of the "reactionary" legacy of the past. In speeches, policies and textbooks, the communists promoted a new image of the nation: from a (seemingly) monoethnic portrait, reproduced under the "Old Regime", to a multiethnic representation of the national community in which equality, diversity and unity were now the new key parameters and propaganda tools. Ethnic diversity was no longer overlooked and became, on the contrary, a national trademark. The new regime in Laos explicitly recognized "the Hill-Tribe Question" from the early years of the movement. Kaysone Phomvihane, the late President of the Lao PDR, called for greater attention to be paid to promoting education among ethnic groups, improving their living conditions and increasing production in remote minority areas. Furthermore, he insisted on respect being paid to the "psychology, aspirations, customs, and beliefs of each ethnic group" (Kaysone 1980, p. 233).

The principle was to give every member of the multiethnic state official recognition on an equal footing. The real objective was not to build a society based on national consciousness, though; rather, the concept of class was thought to be the new society's main axis of identification. During the first years of Communist rule, the Socialist Revolution planned to create a loyalty to the new state greater than the loyalties to particular ethnic identities. The ultimate goal for the Lao Communists, as it had been for their Soviet, Chinese and Vietnamese counterparts, guided by a historicist and evolutionist vision, was to eradicate the "old" identities and replace them with a new socialist one. National antagonisms and mistrust, however, were to be dissipated by a period of "national equality" first; this policy came to be known as "the flourishing of the nations". Although for Lenin nationalism was a secondary problem, it was essential to keep it under control. His strategy for neutralizing the national question was guided by his perception of nationalism as the result of past discrimination and oppression. The programme of promoting "national equality" was, nonetheless, only a prerequisite for a higher stage in the movement towards assimilation that Lenin perceived as progressive and inevitable.[17] It was predicated upon the belief that nations would naturally move closer together, a process described in the official Marxist vocabulary as the "*rapprochement*" or "coming together" of nations (Connor 1984, p. 201).

Lenin's apprehension about the risk of ethnic awareness in the Soviet Union led him to initially promote the policy of "national equality"; so too did the Lao PDR, as had previously the People's Republic of China (PRC) and the Democratic Republic of Vietnam (DRV). This vision of the achievement of historical progress thus became the landmark of the early communist projects in these three countries. Their governments all sent cadres to the highlands to enumerate the populations and collect data dealing with the material aspects of their lifestyles in order to promote the "culture" of the ethnic groups. Ethnographic studies and censuses reflected the belief that cultural recognition would narrow the gap between peoples.[18] The political objective was to classify the ethnic groups according to their degree of cultural development, since the ethnographic studies were strongly identified with a civilizing project vis-à-vis ethnic minorities. In effect, criteria for distinction or grouping were thought of as criteria of backwardness. The Communist state in Laos, as a vector of ethnicity, has tried to manipulate, create, suppress (or maintain) ethnic boundaries, the ultimate objective being the definition, categorization and classification of a national population out of real ethnic heterogeneity. As in China and in Vietnam, the census and classification of the post-1975 Lao population had ultimately "the effect of officially reducing [and] fixing diversity" (Keyes 2002, p. 1187).

After twenty-five years of Communist rule, the "ethnic problem" has not faded away, and Lao nationalist historiography still oscillates between the demands of Communist orthodoxy and a primordialist narration. As a result of this Marxist and Stalinist legacy, increasingly weakened by a culturalist form of nationalism, Lao Communist nationalism appears now to be defined, in Evans' words, by a "peculiar combination of both civic and ethnic nationalism" (Evans 2003, p. 215). On one hand, citizenship is granted to all, regardless of their ethnicity; on the other, the process of re-traditionalization since the early 1990s overwhelmingly focuses on ethnic Lao customs and religion. The theory of collective autochthony, which argues that all ethnic groups that inhabit the national territory have always lived together, exemplifies this irresolute nationalism, balancing the search for an inclusive identity against the revival of a dominant lowland-Lao ethnic identity.

Celebration of the mélange

It is in this context that another version of the origins of the Lao nation has recently emerged, in particular among institutionally-sponsored history books. Lao professional historians (some of them formerly affiliated with the now defunct Research Institute on Social Sciences, and now currently working under the History Department, Ministry of Information and Culture), much influenced by the national question in Marxist-Leninist theory and policy as well as by the Vietnamese communist historiography, depict a historiography that is much less focused on the origins of the ethnic Lao people — there is no mention in these texts of an ancient kingdom located in some remote area of China — and gives little attention to the trope of migration. The "nationalist genealogy", that is, the manipulation of cultural and historical elements to produce "blood" continuity between the past and the present (Keyes 1995, p. 143), is being replaced by its antithesis: the celebration of the mélange, intermingling, interactions between the different ethnic groups of Laos on the country's present-day territory. Thus, according to the authors of *Pavatsat lao* (1996):

> ... during the first millennium, continuous movements, intermingling and interbreeding between tribes took place on the Lao territory. The process of evolution can be summed up as follows: from the beginning of the Christian era in the seventh and eighth centuries, Laos' main area was constituted by the Mon-Khmer speaking ethnic population, of which the main group was the Lava. Some of the Thai [sic] people might also have lived with the Mon-Khmer population in some areas, notably in northern Laos. From the seventh century, the Lao-Thai grew with the addition of those originating from the North, progressively including all the Mon-Khmer tribes to become the main ethnic group in Laos. Afterwards, following historical evolution and development, the Tibeto-Burman, Hmong, Yao, Vietnamese and May (Meuang) [sic]-speaking communities who came to settle in the territory formed a community of Lao ethnic groups that has existed to the present day (Ministry of Information and Culture 1996, p. 11).

This thesis moves away from the linear and homogenizing migration-narration, and instead insists on the cohabitation between the peoples of Laos, and especially between the "Lao-Thai speaking community and Mon-Khmer speaking community" (Ministry of Information and Culture 1996, p. 12). This historiography actually suggests a collective autochthony in Laos, which allows, according to Yves Goudineau, the central lowland Lao authorities "to assert that all the ethnic or social groups have — in principle — the same rights on the national soil and that there are no first settlers on the territory that can be identified". In other words, he adds, "there are no truly indigenous minorities, no 'indigenous peoples'" (Goudineau 2000, p. 24), yet the interbred population are still led by the "Lao-Thai ethno-linguistic category". The authors of *Pavatsat lao* (1996) note in their book:

> The specificity of the living conditions and the relations between various ethnic groups engender favorable conditions for national harmony thanks to their [ancient] origins in Laos. Those large communities have unified

and the population is united. It is the population of Laos, with the Lao-
Thai speaking community [i.e. the ethnic Lao] as its core, in a multi-ethnic
structure (Ministry of Information and Culture 1996, p. 13).

The influence of Vietnamese historiography and ethnology is blatant
here. For example, a Vietnamese author wrote:

The Vietnamese have an important role, being the principal and largest
(almost 90%) group in the population of our country, with a long historical
evolution, and a major contribution to the task of building and maintaining
the country. In history, the Vietnamese are the nucleus, the core of solidarity
among the fraternal peoples who together have built and protected the
Vietnamese fatherland.[19]

The two late socialist regimes have been using the same metaphors to
discursively lessen the power relations and political hierarchy between
the ethnic Lao/Kinh (the ethnic Vietnamese, meaning "city" or "capital"
as opposed to Thuong, or "upland")[20] and the minority populations. Patricia
Pelley notes that the presence of ethnic minorities posed a problem in the
rewriting of national history in the Democratic Republic of Vietnam after
1945. The treatment of ethnic differences was erratic, oscillating between
two extremes: concealment and recognition of ethnic heterogeneity. When
the latter option was adopted, Pelley argues, it was done so in a way that
transformed the ethnic minorities. The metaphor of "flowers in a garden"
introduced a "new sense of topography and borders" by "converting
strange and hostile landscapes into familiar ones and [changing] barbarian
others into brothers" (Pelley 1998, p. 379). She writes thus:

When they talked about ethnic differences in Viêt-Nam, [Northern
Vietnamese] postcolonial scholars often borrowed from the idioms of
horticulture [...]. The sixty-four ethnic groups in Viêt-Nam, for example,
were reconfigured as flowers in a garden. The ideal garden is an exercise in
order: everything is in its place (Pelley 1995, p. 242).

"Diversity in order" has been expressed similarly through botanical
metaphors in Laos. Kaysone Phomvihane — President of the Lao PDR
(until his death in 1992) and celebrated at present in Laos as the inspirational

figure of the regime — poetically claimed that "[e]ach ethnic group has a nice and beautiful culture and belongs to the Lao national community, just as all kinds of flowers grow in a garden of various colours and scents" (Ministry of Information and Culture 1996, p. 13).

The ethnic Lao myth of the origins of the first inhabitants of Laos has likewise been diverted to reinforce this version of a collective autochthony. Lao communist historians presume that "this legend is perceived to throw a light on the realities of the history of the ethnic groups of Laos, that is, on their common origins..." (ibid., pp. 11–12).[21] Amongst other functions, the myth helps to legitimize the existing social order by conflating the latter with a putative natural order. It asserts the right of the ethnic Lao to rule over "indigenous peoples". It also justifies the politico-religious order by placing the Buddhist kings in the rank of deities, since they are the descendants of Khun Bôrom whose seven sons (the Lao kings, as the legend goes, descending from the oldest son) went on to establish different kingdoms in the northwestern region of mainland Southeast Asia. In lieu of legitimizing a social and political hierarchy, the communist reappropriation of the origin myth asserts the pacified and idealized metaphor of brotherhood, suggesting that the "multi-ethnic Lao people" are rooted in, and born of, the same soil. The authors explain thus:

> The pumpkin myth that has been told among the Lao illuminates historical realities with regard to the origins and national harmony in our country, Laos: the first group to be born are the *Lao Theung* (upland Lao). They are the eldest. Then, the *Lao Loum* (lowland Lao) followed, the younger of the two. And the last people are the *Lao Soung* (Lao of the highlands), the youngest of all three.[22]

This ill-defined legend connects blood ties (brotherhood, family) and territorial roots (country, soil). In this sense, Lao historians remain devoted to Stalin's definition of the nation, which, as is well-known, insists on the conflation of people, culture and territory.[23] This historiography, which celebrates the mélange while maintaining the hierarchy with the Lao-Thai speaking community at the top, not only serves the government's indigenist agenda, but also the idea of country. This "horizontal" historiography, by stressing and linking together the concept of territorial roots (geographical space) and kinship bonds (population), aims at transforming the geographical shape of Laos into a national space. In order to circumscribe a country, it is also necessary to fill and control that space, namely, to define the people in it. The communist ethnography has been pursuing this task over the last twenty years. In brief, the politics of classification, by defining a population, and the historiography of cohabitation and collective autochthony, by stressing the modern concept of a demarcated territory, define the very basis of a country through a top-down process of nation-shaping.

The theory of a (seemingly) ethnic Lao autochthony evoked lately in Lao official circles nevertheless shows the delicate balance between the demands of communist orthodoxy and the need for a primordial identity. Phongsavath Boupha, the Vice-Minister of Foreign Affairs, for instance, explains succinctly in the opening page of the English edition of his book, *The Evolution of the Lao State* (2002), that "there are two principal schools of thought among the historians who have attempted to discover the authentic identity and roots of the Lao people". The Nan Chao theory is one of them. "However", he swiftly adds, "modern Chinese, Lao and Thai historians have found sufficient evidence for seriously thinking that the Lao people were the original inhabitants of their land", although he admits shortly afterwards that: "While rigorous scholarly attempts are yet to prove this point of view with the help of archaeological and anthropological findings the final verdict is still awaited" (Phongsavath 2002, p. 1). This begs the question: by "Lao" does Phongsavath mean ethnic Lao or Lao nationals (i.e. those ethnic minority peoples, of Austroasiatic origins, who are considered the first occupants of the soil of Laos)? This thesis is still therefore at a preliminary stage, but it shares common ground with a more sophisticated and enduring historiography that has developed recently, and which focuses on the idea of an indigenous civilization in present-day Laos. This latest and third theory, however, does not entirely succeed in disentangling the vexed issue of the origins of the Lao people because it confounds once again the concepts of ethnicity and citizenship.

A third way? The indigenous civilization

Emergence of an "indigenized" historiography

A third thesis on the origins of the Lao people may be interpreted as a combination of the perennialist narrative and the Stalinist indigenist model — but the emergence of an "indigenized" historiography also expresses the desire among Lao historians and authorities to write a history autonomous from both the Thai nationalist version of the past and the Vietnamese ideological influence. One of the leading figures of this new Lao historiography is Souneth Photisane, a professional historian, who co-authored the massive volume (1,310 pages in total), *Pavatsatlao (deukdamban-pajuban)* ["History of Laos (Ancient Epoch-Contemporary Period)"], published in 2000 by the Ministry of Information and Culture. This book is, in fact, an expanded and edited version of two prior publications, *Pavatsat lao, Volume 3* [from 1893 up to present time], edited by Khamsing Sayvongkhamdi, published in 1989 (by the Institute of Research in Educational Sciences, Ministry of Education and Sports) and *Pavatsat lao, Volume 1*, printed in 1996 (Ministry of Information and Culture), which covered the preceding period, i.e. from prehistory until French colonial rule. The 2000 edition is becoming a major reference within official circles, including university lecturers.[24] Souneth is one of the few Lao historians to have completed his PhD thesis in a non-socialist country (following five years of study in Mongolia). He undertook his doctoral studies in Australia under the supervision of Martin Stuart-Fox, the most well-known foreign historian of Laos. From the outset, Souneth's historical perspective appears "unconventional": he shows no interest in the trope of migration southwards (whether the migrants set out from Central Asia, Sichuan province or Central China between the rivers Hoang-Ho and Yang Tse-Kiang). He also refutes the version of the Ai-Lao ancestors and the Tai kingdom (the Nan Chao theory) located in northeastern Sichuan province, China. Neither is he convinced that the ethnic Lao were the indigenous people of the present-day territory of Laos. He acknowledges, instead, that the ethno-linguistic theory whereby the Tai-speaking people were originally from an area that encompassed present-day southern China and the northern regions of Vietnam and Laos is the most plausible and accepted hypothesis (Souneth 2003, p. 66).

As a matter of fact, this Lao historian, in a paper during a conference on the history and literature of the Tai ethnic groups in Chiang Mai (Thailand) in March 2001, clearly expressed his desire to move away from the partial and traditional versions of the history of Laos that are, in his view, the "Buddhist", "traditionalist", "royalist", "tai-ist", but also "nationalist" and "Marxist" historiographies. He supported, instead, what he calls "the modernist history", which he succinctly defines as follows: "[The modernist history] emphasizes historiography according to principles of historical research, with the appropriate use of data, evidence, documents, under the scrutiny of research and analysis" (Souneth 2003, p. 66). As such, Souneth shows his attachment to the historian's scientific credentials based on logic and evidence. Helped by this methodology, he has been pursuing for a number of years, along with fellow archaeologists, the reconstruction of the prehistory of Laos. Indeed, from the volume *Pavatsat lao (Volume 1)*, printed in 1996 to the *Pavatsatlao (deukdamban-pajuban)*, published four years later, a sophisticated theory has come into being that argues for the existence of a pre-Indian and pre-Chinese culture and society on the present-day territory of Laos (and beyond). In this same article presented in 2001, Souneth outlined the *Pavatsatlao (deukdamban-pajuban)* edition, or in his words, "the tendencies of Lao contemporary history, from the stone age to the period prior to Fa Ngum". He claimed, thus:

> One may therefore correctly declare that Luang Prabang, in northern Laos, has been for a long time a cradle of civilization. In any case, with the knowledge that the Lao are originally from the lower Mekong, what we

will take into account afterwards is the expansion of the Indian and Chinese civilizations on the borders of the Mekong and the mixing with the population's indigenous culture of this area, which have laid down the cultural foundations of the lower Mekong as well as the creation and the development of the city-states in the region (Souneth 2003, p. 66).

Souneth's conference paper is important because it facilitates our understanding of this apparently positivist historiography, the objective of which is nothing less than the rewriting of the history of Laos as an autochthonous and autonomous history. In this regard, Souneth's conviction is evident as he comments: "the society of clans and ethnic groups embraced a mixing of cultures that were their own and were very advanced in many areas, before receiving the cultures from India and China" (Souneth 2003, p. 74). This reassessment of the prehistory of Laos prior to Indian and Chinese influences is constructed around two main arguments: on the one hand, the predominance of a cultural substratum (even of an indigenous civilization), and the capacity to adapt to external influences, on the other. In other words, a socio-cultural matrix appears to have developed and consolidated in the period prior to the first Indian and Chinese contacts in the lower Mekong in general, and in Laos in particular. The description and reconstruction of technological progress and of the formation of socio-economic, political and administrative centres — of an earlier type of urbanism — between prehistorical and proto-historical periods (i.e. between Neolithic and post-Neolithic) is a major element that reinforces the theory of an advanced autochthonous society:

> The increase in population is such that it allows the construction of dykes, and from dykes of irrigation systems… When there are natural resources, such as iron, salt, etc., this configuration leads to exchanges, hence the creation of social, economic, political and administrative and cultural centers. This process starts off in small *muang*, and then expands to become a village farming society. It is also the era of agricultural production… (Souneth 2003, p. 68).

Similarly, a capacity for artistic production is revealed and seemingly identified with a nascent religious orientation:

During this period [6000–1200 BC], several cultural activities worth examining appeared: ceramic and pottery that, in Laos and in the lower Mekong, are similar to those in other regions of the world. They are in use among populations that permanently settle in villages and carry out subsistence activities, such as agriculture (rice, corn) and farming.... Decorative pottery possesses esthetical qualities, or denotes applied arts. The highly esthetical features of this period result from a certain ideal, a philosophy and belief... (Souneth 2003, p. 68)

Archaeology as a political tool

The second major characteristic of this historiography is its perennialist aspiration, that is, a search for cultural continuity between ancient epochs and the present. Archaeology is therefore expected to follow a linear narrative and, as such, to overcome the problematic periodization between prehistory and history, that "sharp discontinuity between the Neolithic "tribes" of Southeast Asian prehistory and the "Indianized" and "Sinicized" states" (Bentley 1986, p. 276). That continuity is made possible through the process of *localization*. The eminent historian, Oliver W. Wolters, once defined the process and its consequence as follows: "The term "localization" has the merit of calling our attention to something else outside the foreign materials. One way of conceptualizing "something else" is as a local statement, of cultural interest but not necessarily in written form, into which foreign elements have retreated" (Wolters 1999, p. 57). Put differently, this approach allows us to look at something foreign from a local point of view rather than to interpret something local from an external source. Craig Reynolds argues that this process of reappropriation, of writing back, "against the foreignness — of "influences" and of evidence — [...] must constantly be negotiated because of the nature of the sources for early history"; so that, he adds: "The thing that has an Indic name or is written in Chinese characters is... made demonstrably Southeast Asian" (Reynolds 1995, p. 433). Souneth suggests that some contemporary Indianized cultural items in Laos (in this case, stone boundaries in Buddhist pagodas) developed originally from indigenous materials. He explains:

... the standing stones [in Sam Neua] represent the belief in spirits back to 3000 years ago under prehistory. During the following period, under the Indian influence, the standing stones were transformed into the cities' pillars, then into stone boundaries of Buddhist pagodas, which were used to delineate the temples, often decorated with beautiful carvings, such as lotus, spears, pagodas, the Jataka and the life of Buddha, devoted to Buddhism... These stone boundaries are therefore an improved form of the standing stones and constitute items of an ancient Lao culture, for such practices do not exist either in Sri Lanka or in India. These stone borders are located in Laos and in northeastern Thailand, which demonstrate that these populations who were interested in standing stones or stone boundaries belonged to the same group since very old times (Souneth 2003, p. 71).

More strikingly, Souneth argues strongly, again in his 2001 conference paper, that the "stone chairs (*kao y tcheuang*) [in northern Laos]...

... are thought to be older than the bronze drums due to their simple aspects that prove their antiquity. New findings have been made in the province of Luang Prabang. It is said that there are more, albeit only few, in polished metal, in the regions of Phu Sam Sum and Phu Khao Lêp in Luang Prabang province... Some have drawings of frogs or toads on them, others of birds, which are found bountifully on bronze drums. These stone chairs probably preceded the bronze drums, which actually originated from the former... And scholars, who had been unable to do so previously, find out now that the origins of the bronze drums are located in Laos, and that the latter are a result of the evolution pattern from the stone chairs (ibid., p. 72).

The "cult of antiquity", in Pelley's perspicacious expression, is thriving in neighbouring Vietnam as well. The bronze-age culture (500 B.C.), and in particular the Dông Son bronze drums that epitomize it, has in fact become one of the country's most powerful national symbols, endlessly replicated in plaster factories as a whole or in distinctive pieces, for "pedagogical" reasons (Pelley 2002, p. 156) that somehow recall the mass techniques that give birth to imagined communities. The fact that this recent Lao-language historiography claims that *these* bronze drums are actually originally from the present-day territory of Laos (and, moreover, that they derive from older archaeological artifacts also found in this area) suggests that official narratives of the Vietnamese and Lao pasts may be engaging in a nascent battle for antiquity, reminiscent of the heated debates that have opposed Vietnamese and Chinese scholars on the origins of the bronze drums. Yet, the centre of diffusion these drums still remains undetermined.[25] Nobody has, however, proposed Laos as a possible option (except for the Lao historians and archaeologists). Although a few bronze drums from the Dông Son period have been found in central (Khammouane province) and northeastern (Hua Phan, Xieng Khouang plateau) Laos, these pieces have been acknowledged to most likely be "imports" (Giteau 2001, p. 56).

There is a fine line here between the capability for agency and the modern nationalist agenda.[26] Trigger suggests that archaeologists establishing their regional or national prehistoric sequences could provide a justifiable collective pride in the past and help resist colonial and imperial domination (Trigger 1995, p. 277). Kohl and Fawcett, on the other hand, warn against an archaeology in the service of the state, which, in their view, runs the greater risk of distorting evidence in order to promote a chauvinistic nationalism by promoting the interests and domination of one particular ethnic group (Kohl and Fawcett 1995, p. 6). I argue, however, that modern Lao historiography, focused as it is on the early periods, is less about supporting policies of domination and control over the rest of the population within the country than a desire to write an autonomous history against foreign influences. The will of "writing back" in Lao historiography is perhaps even more acute than elsewhere because of the successive and various kinds of political domination to which the different Lao kingdoms, and then the state of Laos, were subjected — from the Siamese and Vietnamese subjugations in the eighteenth and nineteenth centuries, followed by French colonial rule, then the Civil War triggered by foreign powers, to finally the integration into a Vietnamese-dominated socialist alliance from 1975. The interpretations of the prehistoric excavations in the Khorat plateau in present-day northeastern Thailand (commonly called "Isan", which means "Northeast" in Pali) must be read, to some extent, in this geopolitical context. In this regard, what Lao archaeologists and historians have formulated in *Pavatsatlao (deukdamban-pajuban)* from excavations at the Non Nok Tha and Ban Na Di archaeological sites is particularly revealing.

These two sites belong to a larger area, the Khorat plateau, which has a long history of archaeological research, stretching back to the French colonial period and the pioneering works of the cohort of scientists it brought with it, including archaeologists and amateur anthropologists. Closer to our time, the search for prehistoric material began again in this region in the mid-1960s (Higham 1989, p. 95). The authors of *Pavatsatlao (deukdamban-pajuban)* have included Charles Higham's authoritative book, *The Archaeology of Mainland Southeast Asia* (1989), in their references, yet have derived significantly different archaeological reconstructions from the findings. They write:

> ... with respect to the culture (*vattanatam*) of Non Nok Tha, the studies of the terracotta objects and of the grave-digging techniques have shown that the population that lived on this site have had one unique and same culture throughout all the epochs, that is, the one that belongs to the ancient Lao (*lao buhan*) ... (Ministry of Information and Culture 2000, p. 17).

It is not certain to whom they refer when they use the term "the ancient Lao", whether this refers to ethnic Lao only or the whole population of present-day Laos (again, the absence of distinctive Lao-language terms that could differentiate between the two notions of ethnicity and citizenship regarding the ethnic Lao group is a handicap, while favouring the ethno-nationalist project). Archaeological evidence has indeed suggested that human settlements in the Isan region stretch back to at least 2000 years ago (Grabowsky 1995, p. 110). Nonetheless, ethnicity can never be securely traced. Even with a position that accepts that a partially apprehensible objective reality cannot be totally reduced to invention or social construction, it is difficult to agree with the argument of continuity and homogeneity of one particular group of people "throughout all the epochs" because of the inevitable changes that the group will experience over time (that is, its ethnomorphosis [Kohl 1998, p. 232]). The authors may not be referring to contemporary ethnic Lao when they use the term "ancient Lao", since they mention, a few pages further on, a wave of migration from the present-day province of Vientiane of "actual Lao" (*lao pajuban*) to the site of Non Nok Tha between zero and 800 AD, a period during which they suggest that the civilization of the "actual Lao" emerged and developed in this area (Ministry of Information and Culture 2000, p. 19). The concluding statement, however, adds to the uncertainty by stating that "[i]n brief, Non Nok Tha has found remains of the Lao from different epochs and additional evidence that bear that the Lao people have emigrated from territories outside Indochina".

Archaeology arguably plays an important role in reinforcing the conception in Lao contemporary historiography of a collective, (ambiguously) perennial and primordial identity. Equally important, it moves the roots of the "Lao people" away from "Indochina" and further West, closer to the Thai-Lao speaking world, as if the end of the Cold War in Southeast Asia and the resultant reduced imperative for showing international socialist solidarity has had an impact on the prehistory of Laos. Contemporary Lao historiographers reconstruct the early period by expanding "Lao" autochthony to include the right bank of the Mekong (present-day northeastern Thailand), hence seemingly recreating the former Lan Xang kingdom's territory. They stress the antiquity of the area and their people, for example by arguing that knowledge of brass-production and -working was gained by local people (the "ancient Lao") in Non Nok Tha 4,700 years ago, well before the first Indian and Chinese contact (Ministry of Information and Culture 2000, p. 20). And, although Higham dated the excavations in Non Nok Tha and Ban Na Di roughly from 3600–3000 B.C. until about 500–300 B.C. (Higham 1989, p. 99), the Lao historians in *Pavatsatlao* (*deukdamban-pajuban*) estimate that the sites may be as old as 7,000 years (Ministry of Information and Culture 2000, p. 16).

Modern Lao-language historiography pushes back the date of a distinctively and autonomous "Lao" culture and society in the interests of establishing an authentic, pre-Chinese and pre-Indian civilization, as Vietnamese post-colonial (after 1945) historiographers have done through an intensive work of desinicization.[27] "The stress on localizing agency", as Reynolds comments, "shifts the focus on Southeast Asia and their future, away from their suspect origins as mere borrowers and culture brokers" (Reynolds 1995, p. 431). Pelley has similarly remarked that the rewriting of Vietnamese history in this westward perspective (a "self-generating instead of derivative mode") "establishes Vietnam as a focal point of Southeast Asia rather than an insignificant periphery of East Asia" (Pelley 2002, p. 156). It remains, nonetheless, equally important to bear in mind the political orientation of archaeology, which is almost inevitable as long as nation–states remain the dominant type of polity, especially where post-colonial states are concerned. But national*ist* archaeology is the misuse of evidence to pursue the creation and the consolidation of national identities, often by undermining the identities of others within and/or outside the state (Kohl 1998, p. 226). Contemporary Lao historiographers likewise localize, indigenize and, because the process occurs within the boundaries and by means of civil servants of the state, nationalize, "Lao" culture by stressing pre-Chinese and pre-Indian local genius and creativity. They tend to do so, however, by emphasizing the Tai ethnic roots of a segment of the population at the expense of the non-Tai population of present-day Laos.

Conclusion: Geographies of the national body

The key distinction between the former regime and Communist rule lies in their concept of national identity, its practice and discursive content. While the RLG focused on the definition of the inner "essence" and qualities of a people, i.e. the ethnic Lao/Majority's identity, the Marxist-Leninist-inspired regime turned the perspective upside down and looked at a more systematic definition and classification of the ethnic minorities. In other words, they incorporated into the national space — or in Thongchai Winichakul's seminal expression, into the *geo-body* of Laos — the peripheries, i.e. the upland and highland minorities, which were traditionally located outside the national lens under lowland Lao politics and nationalist historiography. The newly independent state of Laos in the aftermath of the Second World War lacked the administrative grip to integrate the "savages" on the frontiers of the kingdom and was less concerned about a "civilizing project" than consolidating its centre of power, i.e. the lowland Lao areas (at least in the first years of communist leadership). Unlike Thailand from the late nineteenth century, the central authorities in Vientiane were never able to establish territorial and population management throughout the country.

The Communist ethnography, guided by the so-called "policy of national equality" embedded in an evolutionist vision, went on defining, categorizing and classifying the whole population of Laos (except the ethnic Lao themselves, who are categorized as an "ethnic group" in the census but are not scrutinized and itemized). The Communist rulers, ethnographers and historiographers together have engaged in the redefinition of the "nation" by emphasizing territory and Marxist-Leninist rhetoric and politics. The trope of migration associated with the Ai-Lao version is incompatible with this diversity-cum-equality ideology. The huge wave of migration of the Lao race descending from the Far North and marginalizing all the "weaker" and "backward" people on their way by absorbing them is undoubtedly not the right discourse to promote in this context. History, and especially prehistory, have to be modified accordingly. The recent new trend in officially endorsed Lao historiography that stresses collective autochthony rather oddly aims at reconciling the demands for Communist orthodoxy — based on the principle of equality among all the ethnic groups and the Stalinist conflation of people, culture and territory — and the call for a perennial and primordial identity, i.e. the domination of the ethnic Lao. Yet, the trope of migration, and especially the Ai-Lao narrative, much influenced by the former regime's textbooks, remains unrevised in school textbooks and prevails in mass-circulation publications. This form of nationalism, attempting to balance Communist convention and ethnic nationalism, inevitably leaves the writing of the origins of Laos unsettled in modern Lao-language history books.

The writing of an autonomous history requires a quest for local and authentic origins; it demands a beginning that is not derivative. The objectives of the recent and growing "indigenous civilization" narrative, promoted by Lao historians and archaeologists, are threefold: to establish an autonomous history of Laos prior to external influences, i.e. pre-Indian and pre-Chinese, capable of adaptability and creativity; to engage in a race for antiquity for nationalistic purposes, and to move the origins of the "Lao" (either referring to the ethnic Lao or to the whole population — the use of the term will always remain ambiguous) closer to the former Lan Xang Kingdom's territories. In that latter sense, the prehistorical period in Lao-language modern historiography is also a bid to win very contemporary debates: Lao scholars reinterpret the early period in accordance with a geopolitical rationale that erodes the country's links to Indochina, and especially to Vietnam. Lastly, displacing Lao origins to the West in the reconstruction of the country's prehistorical past, outside the actual national boundaries but embedded in a perennialist perspective, suggests that some historians and archaeologists in Laos have yet to come to terms with the nation's modern spatial identity: to reverse Chris Baker's plain expression (inspired, in turn, by Thongchai's argument),[28] this nationalist history does not take (only) the present-day national territory as its space.

In recent years, other interpretations of the country's past have emerged, however, that strike a very different chord to the ethnic Lao-dominated narration. Coincidentally or not, the authors of these divergent historiographies happen to be well-educated officials of ethnic minority origins. A few years ago, one of them, Sisouk,[29] a high-ranking official in the LFNC Research Department on Ethnic Groups, wrote a paper with the convoluted title, "Opinions and our Party's General Policy towards Ethnic Groups during Each Period of the Revolution". The essay narrated the history of Laos from a multiethnic perspective. The overall canvas — the chronology and the themes — was not original. The central thematic of resistance by the "multiethnic national community" to foreign aggression constituted the leitmotiv that sustained the regime's construction of the past. Contrary to the contemporary tendency to weaken the non-ethnic Lao component of the "struggle", the author stressed the central role of Lao people of ethnic minority origins during the French and American Wars, i.e. the "struggle for national liberation". He wrote, thus:

> Our Party rallied the highland peoples, such as those who lived along the Lao-Vietnamese, Lao-Chinese and Lao-Cambodian borders, and turned them into the bastion of the revolution. Our Party trained the children and grandchildren of these ethnic groups, who joined our troops to become political militants on the ground, guerrilla fighters and skirmishers. They then rose to become regular soldiers equipped with modern weapons of the Revolution. Thanks to the support, the supplies, the care and the collaboration of the ethnic population, the revolutionary forces took form and spread from the highland and remote areas to the plains, and surrounded the towns that were the enemy's bases.

His historical account is not anti-patriotic. He does not allow any historical autonomy for the "highland peoples". The Communist Party guided and formed them (the author mentions in a later paragraph the long-term education policy for the young people who were sent to study in Vietnam, China and the Soviet Union during the war). In his version, it is precisely under the Party's leadership that the periphery moved to the centre. The epicentre of the revolution was located in the Eastern mountainous zones, "strong bedrock of the revolution" and "safe bastions of the economic, social and cultural revolution" (Sisouk n.d., p. 5): the socialist nation was first built up in the East.

A strikingly similar narrative is found in the writings of another high-ranking official of ethnic minority origins, Khamphone. In an unpublished paper (1999), he recollects, blending personal and collective memories:

The National Democratic Revolution, under the Party's leadership and led by the Neo Lao Issala — which later on became the Neo Lao Hak Sat — ... mobilized and created bases for revolutionary operations in the upland and ethnic minority areas. Children and great-children of the ethnic minority peoples have supported the Revolution's just and legitimate political policy. They made sacrifices by leaving their families, their towns and villages to join the revolutionary movement in order to liberate the country, to win again the independence, to create equality and generate prosperity (1999, p. 28).

Sisouk and Khamphone's writings and opinions cannot be dissociated from their personal backgrounds and early lives. Both men were born in the aftermath of the Second World War near the Lao-Vietnamese borders. The Vietnam War transformed their lives. It embarked them on a journey that took them from the upland regions of Laos to the outskirts of Hanoi and as far as to the former Soviet Union. Khamphone was born in the northeastern province of Huaphan. His parents were farmers. In 1959, at the age of 12, he left for Northern Vietnam. Lao communist soldiers had come earlier to his village and offered free schooling for the children of the village, at the end of which they would come back and "become teachers themselves".

Our parents were of course very excited!, Khamphone recalled. Can you imagine? Three months at school, nothing to pay, and we'd become teachers! I wanted to go. My father was also happy to let me go. But my mother was more reluctant. She asked me twice if I really wanted to go, and I replied each time "yes". That really showed that she didn't want me to leave... Three months at school and then becoming a teacher... it was a lie. But it was a lie with an honourable purpose since it was meant to give us an education.

Khamphone is not certain how the children were selected. The size of the family was one criterion — not all the children could have gone and left their parents on their own. Children were needed for rice planting and harvesting, as well as for looking after the cattle. "We were four children in the family, and I was the only one to go. Besides, my father was the chief of the village and he wanted me to receive an education."

Khamphone left with a few belongings wrapped up in a bundle with a small amount of money and a knife that his mother gave him. His joined a group of about thirty children:

> We started early in the morning after eating a bit of rice that we took with us. We walked all day. At every village we stopped the Lao Issara soldiers recruited new children. Then, after three or four days of walking, we reached the Vietnamese border. We saw many soldiers. But we weren't sure if they were Lao Issara soldiers or those of the enemy, you know. Luckily, they were our soldiers! The following day, the children were put onto trucks. There were enough of them to load three vehicles, which were completely covered in order to keep their passengers out of sight of the local population. It was a secret operation to prevent the Vietnamese villagers from suspecting that there were Lao soldiers and children in their country.

They arrived in the military camp and were divided into two groups: the older children joined the army ranks and the younger ones were sent to school. Khamphone himself moved around several times during his stay in Vietnam as he was sent to different schools. In the first one, he estimated that there were nearly 2,000 pupils from all over Laos. He remembered:

> We were all together! We learnt the Lao alphabet at the primary school, and then the teaching was conducted in Vietnamese at the secondary and high-school levels. The teachers were Vietnamese soldiers who had fought in Laos. We were well looked after. They washed our clothes. They fed us. They even gave us candies once a week. We played sports all together. But we were not allowed to leave the school area, which was surrounded by fences, neither to have contacts with the local population.[32]

After finishing high school, the students were dispatched to stay among Vietnamese families. It was not a happy time for Khamphone, though:

> I was on my own. I cried at night. I missed my friends. I wanted to go back home. But I hanged in there, telling myself that it wouldn't last long, that it was nearly the end... My parents died before I returned. I still remember

the day when I was told that my mother passed away. I kept crying in the classroom. I was all alone, the rest of the students were all Vietnamese. The teacher asked me if I were having problems, if I had enough to eat. I said nothing. I hanged in there, telling myself that it would be over soon.

I asked him if he ever thought of staying in Vietnam.

No, never, he replied adamantly. I wanted to go back to my homeland, Laos. The Vietnamese and the Lao are too different. For example, the Vietnamese eat bread by dunking it in the soup, and we, Lao, eat rice. But we are grateful that they gave us an education. The teachers themselves used to tell us: "After receiving your education, you will go back to your country and you will develop it." They did not want us to stay either.

Sisouk left his minority village in Savannakhet Province at the age of 13 to join the Lao Issara army in the late 1950s. Like Khamphone, he was considered to be too young to fight and instead was assigned to serve as a cook for the soldiers. The circumstances of his involvement in the communist ranks are interesting to note. They are fairly characteristic of the atmosphere of confusion that defines that period. His father was the chief of the village, which like many others was located in a disputed zone; the village therefore had no choice but to show allegiance to both camps, "the Vientiane side" (i.e. the Royal Lao Government) and "the Lao Issara", for which his father also worked clandestinely. Sisouk was his only child, and to protect him from "those dangerous activities", his father planned for his son to go and study in a Buddhist monastery. Sisouk was not very keen on this idea, however. He was in fact already taking part in clandestine activities that consisted of supplying food to the Vietnamese "workers" operating inside Lao territory. One day on his way to their camp, he met Vietnamese soldiers who offered him to go and study in Vietnam so that he could "come back and help to develop his country". Following this encounter, instead of entering a monastery, Sisouk became an apprentice communist. He joined the "hundreds of children" from his area who were taken secretly to northern Vietnam by truck, hidden away from the local population (they were told not to speak in Lao to them). His anti-colonial sentiments were not clear at that time, though. Only when his Vietnamese instructor asked him why he joined the Revolution was he forced to think of an "acceptable" reply: his father was the chief of the village and the French treated him badly. Added to that, his uncle was brutalized by a Lao soldier under the orders of a French commander for failing to feed the troops properly. Sisouk candidly explained forty years later: "I was full of hatred, so I joined the Revolution to take my revenge! But I didn't know anything about the Liberation War or the Revolution. Only after studying in Vietnam and in Russia did I find out what I had fought for". Sisouk remained and studied in Vietnam for the next thirteen years. We will meet him again in the next chapters.

Khamphone and Sisouk's early lives share many parallels: the two men are of ethnic minority origin and come from a rural background. Although they were neither rich nor powerful, their fathers held positions of authority. Both of them were village chiefs and Sisouk's father was also working (clandestinely) for the communists. Although probably not the sole factor, their fathers' position and status may have helped them to be selected to go and study in Vietnam. Education is also particularly stressed in the two narratives; both fathers had encouraged their sons to get a "good" education. More importantly, their socialization began in Vietnam: it was in the neighbouring country that their social and political identity awakened and developed. The two boys gradually became "Lao" in a most unusual experience of socialization, that is, away from their home village and outside their own country. In other words, their journey across the borders deeply shaped their perception of national membership. As Khamphone pointed out, the Vietnamese themselves had no intention of letting their Lao charges remain on their soil. On the contrary, their educational programme was aimed at forming a generation of qualified and patriotic Lao young people so that the latter could return and help to defend and rebuild their own country after the end of the war.

In my opinion, however, Khamphone and Sisouk embody each in their own style the claims and paradoxes of Lao officials of ethnic minority origins in post-socialist Laos. Their identity politics reveal hesitations, if not contestations, over the very core of the Lao nation as narrated and represented by the present regime.

Not only is Khamphone's essay about remembering what it is fading away within the national(ist) historiography, it is also, and perhaps above all, a criticism of the structure and trends of present-day writings of the past in Laos. In a rather unusual style, the Lao scholar denounces in the same paper the "confusion between legend and history". He demands instead to read a history book of Laos that would apply a clear distinction between "history of the nation" [*Pavatsat khong sat*], "history of the origins" [*Pavatsat kwam pen ma*] and "history of the ethnic groups in Laos" [*Pavatsat khong son phaw*]. By way of his condemnation of a current type of historiography focusing on the idea of indigeneity and obsessed by origins, Khamphone appears to call for the dismissal of history, or to be more exact, for the rejection of history as narrated by the Majority; in another words, for the historicization of the Majority (national) identity. He asserts, thus:

> To be sure, these communities [i.e. the five ethno-linguistic categories in Laos: Mon-Khmer, Thai-Lao, Hmong-Yao, Tibeto-Burmese and Sino-Ho] have not gone through the same historical process: some are indigenous peoples, others have immigrated from elsewhere and have settled down with the rest; others, still, have immigrated at a later period. Such are those historical realities that nobody can deny nor distort. More importantly still, these communities have united within one Lao national community. Each group graciously contributed in the past through their duties and responsibilities to the preservation and the development of the country. We may therefore argue that all the communities are the masters of the soil of Laos. All can claim to belong to the country, to contribute to its defence, its development and its prosperity. And they all must have the right to political, administrative, economic and religious advantages, as well as to the promotion of their arts and culture in a spirit of equality and according to each group's specificities (1999, p. 27).

What this Lao scholar seeks is not merely an effective application of the principle of "unity and equality" repeatedly emphasized in the Constitution of the Lao PDR. He also tries to contest the dominance of the Majority by positioning the other ethno-linguistic "communities" on the equal basis with the Tai-Lao, culturally, socially and politically. They are clearly placed on the same level, all "masters of the soil of Laos". In consequence, the mainstream/periphery mentality no longer defines the national culture and identity: all become visible and "unassimilated". "Lao-ness" and "nation-ness" no longer lie on the majority/minority divide, or within the dual process of incorporation and exclusion. In the next chapter, more voices will be explored and will add to the multiple interpretations of the Lao past.

Notes

1   Quoted, in turn, from Charnvit Kasetsiri, "History: 'In and Out' of Textbooks in Thailand", Paper presented at the Conference on Southeast Asian Historiography since 1945, 30 July to 1 August 1999, Penang, Malaysia.

2   Nan Chao existed as a political entity in the present-day Chinese province of Yunnan from the first half of the eighth century AD until its invasion and occupation by the Mongol armies of Kublai Khan in 1253.

3   Interestingly, Lao school texts, despite some strong hints, e.g., pointing out the same geographical location, never use the name of Nan Chao to refer to that ancient kingdom in China.

4   The secondary school manuals (whose latest edition dates back to 1996) are on sale at 8,000 kip each (less than a dollar), while students in high school must copy their lessons from the teacher's dictation. University students are given a brochure, which is a condensed version of the lessons prepared by their lecturers.

5   Between 15,000 and 20,000 kip; that is approximately between US$1.5 and US$2.

6   Ministry of Education, Centre for Teachers' Training, *Pavatsatlao samaybouhan lè samaykang* [*History of Laos in Ancient and Middle Ages*] (Vientiane, 1998), p. 8.

7   The origins of the term are not clear but it seems that *Khom* was an old word used by the Tai peoples in ancient times — perhaps before the foundation of

the Lan Xang kingdom — to designate the Mon-Khmer-speaking population of Laos. Later on, the ethnic Lao texts, such as the *Nithan Khun Bôrom* ("the Legend of Khun Bôrom"), would refer to them as *Kha kau* ("old slaves"). See Martin Stuart-Fox, *The Lao Kingdom of Lan Xang: Rise and Decline* (Bangkok: White Lotus, 1998), pp. 17 and 164.

[8] See James R. Chamberlain, "The Origin of the Southwestern Tai", *Bulletin des amis du royaume Lao*, No. 7–8, (1972): 233; Terwiel, "The Origin of the T'ai Peoples Reconsidered", pp. 252–53; and David K. Wyatt, *A Short History of Thailand*, (New Haven: Yale University Press, 1984), pp. 5–6. For further details on the fallacious Nan Chao (or Nan Zao) thesis, see, for example, He Shengda, "The Theory of the Nanzhao Thai Kingdom: its Origins and Bankruptcy", *Social Sciences in China* 3 (1995), pp. 74–89. I would like to thank Sun Laichen for the latter reference.

[9] The choice of this spelling, as Terwiel explains in a note, is to indicate the aspiration by means of the apostrophe.

[10] See Thongchai Winichakul, *Siam Mapped: A History of the Geo-Body of a Nation* (1994), and "The Others Within: Travel and Ethno-Spatial Differentiation of Siamese Subjects 1885–1910" (2000a); David Streckfuss, "The Mixed Colonial Legacy in Siam: Origins of Thai Racialist Thought, 1890–1910", in *Autonomous Histories. Particular Truths. Essays in Honour of John Smail*, ed. Lauries Sears, pp. 123–53.

[11] For more details on the French migration policy for Laos, see Martin Stuart-Fox, "The French in Laos, 1887–1945", *Modern Asian Studies* 29, no. 1 (February 1995): 123–34.

[12] *France-Indochine*, "La question laotienne : opinions du Prince Phetsarath", No. 3,416, 21 March 1931, p. 1; quoted, in turn, from Christopher E. Goscha, *Vietnam or Indochina? Contesting Concepts of Space in Vietnamese Nationalism, 1887–1954*, NIAS Reports, No. 28, Copenhagen, p. 58.

[13] Ibid.

[14] In 1941, the Phibunsongkram regime of Thailand forced French Indochina to cede to it the southern territory of Champassak and, in the north, the Sayaboury region of the Luang Prabang kingdom. These territories were returned to Laos after the end of the war in November 1946.

[15] French remained the main language of instruction above the primary level

(thus creating a de facto barrier for those wishing to pursue secondary studies, since children in rural and poorer areas would be most unlikely to have had the opportunity of acquiring a good command of French), while the curriculum still reproduced to some extent the colonialist history tainted with racist representations of the indigenous population (Lockhart, "Education in Laos in Historical Perspective", p. 8).

[16] In contrast, as Thongchai has brilliantly shown, the threat and influence of colonialism, along with the introduction of Siam to the world market and commodity economy, led the Siamese authorities to implement a new style of territorial management as early as the late nineteenth century. In Thongchai's words, thus, "[t]he space of *chao bannok* [a derogative term for 'peasants', equivalent of 'bumpkin'] was becoming administratively domesticated, economically exploitable as natural and human resources. The trope of the narratives of the 'Docile People' is that of state-territorial exploitation, for production, for civilisation.", Thongchai, "The Others Within...", p. 50.

[17] While the work of Marx and Engels centres on a critique of capitalism and includes analyses of societies characterized by slavery and feudalism (the stages thought to be the immediate predecessors of capitalism on the evolutionary scale), they drew heavily on the work of Lewis Henry Morgan when they turned to analyse "primitive" societies. Morgan's theory of social evolution outlined three main stages: savagery, barbarism and civilization (Lewis H. Morgan, *Ancient Society* [New York: Holt, 1877]).

[18] However, the Soviet authorities were careful to avoid using the term "assimilation", for they argued it conveyed a negative meaning, as it was connected with capitalist societies and their coercive process of acculturation conducted by the state's dominant group towards the minorities. On the contrary, the Marxist-Leninist approach was claimed to be different: the process of merging together was doctrinally based upon absolute national equality and on the basis of voluntary cooperation.

[19] Quoted from Bruce Lockhart, "Looking Down from a Tightrope: Ethnology in Vietnam", unpublished paper, p. 23.

[20] Ibid.

[21] See "Myth and Cosmology" in chapter 2.

[22] Tibeto-Burman speakers arrived recently from southwest China, while the

Hmong-Mien (Miao-Yao) peoples, likewise recent arrivals, came from southern and southeast China. These latter two families are confined primarily to highland areas in the northern provinces.

[23] Stalin defined a " nationality" by five criteria: a stable community of people, a language, a territory, an economic life and a psychological make-up or "national character".

[24] Interview with a Lao professor in history at the National University of Laos, April 2002.

[25] For more details on the disputes between Vietnamese and Chinese scholars on the origins of the bronze drums, and their political ramifications, see the article by Han Xiaorong, "The Present Echoes of the Ancient Bronze Drum: Nationalism and Archeology in Modern Vietnam and China", *Explorations* 2, no. 2 (1998): 27–46. I would like to thank Haydon Cherry for this reference.

[26] Grant Evans has made a similar point by arguing that the search for a deeper "indigenous" cultural layer, that is, for the "real" cultural essence, underneath (and outside the influence of) foreign imports, is methodologically flawed partly due its nationalist modern agenda (Grant Evans, "Between the Global and the Local there are Regions, Culture Areas, and National States: A Review Article", *Journal of Southeast Asian Studies* 33, no. 1 (2002), p. 158).

[27] Tran Quoc Vuong, "Traditions, Acculturation, Renovation: The Evolutional Pattern of Vietnamese Culture", in *Southeast Asia in the 9th to 14th Centuries*, edited by David G. Marr and A.C. Milner (Singapore: Institute of Southeast Asian Studies; Canberra: Research School of Pacific Studies, 1986), p. 272; Pelley, *Postcolonial Vietnam*, pp. 148–56.

[28] Chris Baker's exact sentence is: "National history takes the national territory as its space, and tells the story of the rise and fall of the state inside that container, usually overlooking that the definition of the territory and the idea of the state are very recent" (Chris Baker, "Afterwords: Autonomy's Meanings", in *Recalling Local Pasts. Autonomous History in Southeast Asia*, edited by Sunait Chutintarinond and Chris Baker [Chiang Mai: Silkworm Books, 2002], p. 170). Through this remark, Baker succinctly recalls Thongchai's argument whereby "a national history is the biography of a spatial identity", that is, imagined, conceptualized, materialized and reified where it did not exist before Western colonialist expansion in Southeast Asia (Thongchai Winichakul, "Writing at

the Interstices. Southeast Asian Historians and Postnational Histories in Southeast Asia", in *New terrains in Southeast Asian History*, edited by Abu Talib Ahmad and Tan Liok Ee (2003), p. 9.

[29]   I use a pseudonym here.

[30]   As a Lao woman in her mid-forties told me, fondly recalling her years in a school for Lao children near Hanoi during the late 1960s: "We were all together, studying together, playing together. We were all united and helping each other regardless of our ethnicity." This woman was born in Luang Prabang province. Her father was a Lao Issara agent. She was first educated in Vietnam and then pursued her studies in agronomy in the former Soviet Union. Upon her return to Laos, she entered the Ministry of Agriculture and Forestry.

5

An "Heroic Village"

If it is commonly acknowledged that representations of the past are central to the symbolic constitution of national consciousness, the relationship between collective history on the one hand, and memories based on personal experience on the other, is a vexed one, even when a coercive state is responsible for the production of history. Perhaps it is wise to adopt Rubie S. Watson's cautious statement when she writes: "it is important that we do not credit the socialist state and its agents with too much power or its citizens with too much boldness" (Watson 1994, p. 2). People are not mere passive receivers; nor are they constantly resisting. Homi Bhabha sees the relationships between individuals and the nation's narrative through a dual lens, or in his words, in "double-time". The people are the "historical 'objects' of a nationalist pedagogy", but they are also

> the 'subjects' of a process of signification that must erase any prior or originary presence of the nation-people to demonstrate the prodigious, living principle of the people as that continual process by which the national life is redeemed and signified as a repeating and reproductive process (Bhabha 1995, p. 297).

It is precisely this duality that allows individuals a space for contesting the official representation of the past, which claims to configure the imagining of the national community. Elizabeth Tonkin argues that people are both subjects[1] and agents in the account of memory and the constitution of history. Social conditions and political rhetoric mould identities; yet, individual subjectivity is not entirely dominated by the social, or by the actions of the nation–state. Personal and social identities are clearly intertwined; however, people have a margin for criticism and self-reflection. She states: "[…] oral accounts no less than written ones can be means of comment and reflection, in which different pasts are conceptualised, and, often, contradiction and failure admitted" (Tonkin 1992, pp. 130–31). In other words, totalizing narrations of national history are not themselves homogenous. They serve as a framework, the content and bounds of which may be re-presented by people. The working of power is neither total nor unilateral. Alonso, in her dense article about the struggles between the official and popular historical discourses in Mexico, points out the effects of power on public memory whereby the state imposes its "truth" of past events in order to establish its hegemony. However, as she stresses, the "past is neither transparent nor given; 'what really happened' is a focus of conflicting representation" (Alonso 1988, p. 50). She provides the example of the resistance of Mexican rural communities to the dominant representation of the past. They display a counter-history, which repudiates the role of "The Revolution", as presented by the Mexican state. On a more general scale, for Gillis this ongoing process of the state's "memory work" contesting with that of the people has become more democratized, to the level of a personal matter:

> [t]oday everyone is her or his own historian… Most people have long since turned to more heterogeneous representations of the past… the reality is that the nation is no longer the site or frame of memory for most people and therefore national history is no longer a proper measure of what people really know about their pasts (Gillis 1994, p. 17).

While acknowledging the existence of space for dissent, we should also, on the other hand, be careful not to reify the other posited field of memory, i.e. collective. What happens on the personal level when the narrative of the nation shifts? In this chapter, my intention will be to transcribe the narratives of some people of ethnic minority origin that have remained concealed in the authoritative national history, and to show that, in the manner of Bhabha, "no political ideologies [can] claim transcendent or metaphysical authority for themselves" (Bhabha 1995, p. 299). I will point out the divergent interpretations performed by the state and the villagers of Ban Paktai in Sekong Province (in Southeastern Laos) concerning Ong Keo (an ethnic leader who fought against French colonial rule in the early twentieth century and was turned into a patriotic figure for the sake of the nationalist history), through investigating the memory of some of these villagers. More significantly, in a second section, I argue that these villagers' narratives about Ong Keo ultimately aim at contesting the state's historical discourse of the "30-year struggle". There are similarities as well as potential differences between the narratives of the rulers and the stories embedded in the lived experience of the ruled. In the context of contemporary Laos, where orthodox communist ideology is slowly giving way to "more purely nationalist sources of legitimation" (Evans 2004, p. 99), the official historiography of the "French and American Wars" is now better defined by the authorities' growing amnesia than it is shaped by collective remembrance; my final reflection in this chapter will focus on the missing link between the war dead and veterans and the Revolution in today's commemorations of the past in Laos.

A "Heroic Village"

I will focus my analysis on the case of Ban Paktai in Meuang Thateng,[2] Sekong Province, also called *Ban Ong Keo* or *Ban Vìlàsòn* ("heroic village") as this village was the birthplace of the minority leader, Ong Keo. As I have explained in my methodology, my request to do research on ethnic minority revolts with the support of the LFNC was a pretext to be introduced to villages perceived as having a significant revolutionary history. I was realistic enough to acknowledge the tremendous ideological burden behind the stories of these rebellions' ethnic leaders who were resistant to any kind of encroaching domination.

A revolutionary story

I was introduced to Ban Paktai during my research trip with Sisouk, the high-ranking official introduced in the previous chapter. The village is located on the main road that links Pakse to Sekong town, the municipality of Sekong Province. It is composed of three units, totalling 58 households with 271 people (Integrated Rural Accessibility Planning [IRAP] 1997). The numerically and politically dominant ethnic group is the Ngae, accounting for 90 per cent of the villagers. Thirteen ethnic Lao families from Ban Maknao moved into the village in 1997 as part of the government's resettlement scheme to give people access to the road, and there are also a few Alak people. Ban Paktai is an old village: it moved closer to the road in 1973, but has always been located on the Sekong plateau. The main agricultural practice is that of shifting cultivation, mixed (for a very few families) with sedentary rice farming.

The village was without doubt an obligatory stop on our so-called historical investigation. As soon as I arrived in the municipality of Sekong Province, the local LFNC recommended to Sisouk and myself a route to follow for our research. For the entire duration of our trip, I felt as though I was on a guided tour, organized by the LFNC officials. They told us that, among the few witnesses still living, there was an "old hero" called Uncle Tin (who lived in the town a few metres away from the administration building) and a number of people in Ban Paktai in Meuang Thateng, the district that is bordered by Champassak Province to the west. Obviously, these witnesses clearly were the officially approved informants, and the fact that they were located in places accessible by road was no coincidence. I certainly would not have been allowed to go to remote places in search of less well-known witnesses by myself — the memory of "national" history is kept under firm control. I will begin by describing my first encounter with the village of Ban Paktai in late August 1999, so as to show the false assumptions, but also the accurate observations, that I then made; both the assumptions and the observations proved to be equally fruitful for the more rigorous analysis I developed when I had the opportunity to return to the village and stay for longer periods.

We arrived in Ban Paktai in the afternoon. Sisouk and I were accompanied by a local LFNC member and the son of the head of the LFNC as driver. Our group certainly looked fairly official at first glance: Sisouk and Saveng — the local LFNC member — were both dressed in white shirts and grey trousers, and my physical presence, though mute most of the time, was sufficient to arouse curiosity among the women and children. We quickly realized that all the men in good physical shape had gone to cut some trees for the construction of a new school. Sisouk then asked to meet the head of the village LFNC branch while waiting for the return of the younger men, but it transpired that this individual had also gone into the forest. The village men, however, soon returned from their labours — they had probably been told about our visit by a runner shortly after our arrival — and some of them joined us at the village head's house. The first surprise, ironically, was that nobody in the village was able to give us information on Ong Keo. In fact, the sole authoritative informant, Thongkham, had moved to a neighbouring village, Ban Songkham, to marry. His father had been one of Ong Keo's fighting companions. Upon the villagers' insistence, it was decided to bring him to the village, instead of us going to meet him.

Thongkham was a 75-year-old man. He introduced himself as a member of the Ngae ethnic group. He looked fit at that time and the tone of his voice was still assertive; his face was heavily scarred, and he had lost an eye. Soon after Sisouk finished asking him questions about Ong Keo, he spontaneously started telling us about his own life as a war veteran and, especially, his experience of torture by the "enemy". I have reconstituted below the circumstances of his capture, drawing upon elements of the story I heard unexpectedly during that first visit and upon complementary information I recorded when I interviewed Thongkham again during my second visit to the village.

He started his "revolutionary activities" in 1951 as the leader of a group of skirmishers. Three years later he "sacrificed" (*sàlà* "to sacrifice", *khat* "to be torn"[3]) his family and joined the resistance. In 1957, the "enemy" captured him. Thongkham gave two slightly different reasons for his arrest: he told Sisouk that the "enemy" had arrested several men distributing political pamphlets who then denounced him as their leader, whereas he told me that he was caught by the "enemy" while carrying secret documents. In any case, he was accused of plotting against the government, despite his protestations: "All I said was that I wanted the two sides to stop fighting. I wanted an united government between Souphanouvong and Souvanna Phouma so that the Lao and the Vietnamese would stop killing each other!".

These claims did not prevent the "enemy" from beating him up so as to extract information from him. Here, I let Thongkham recount the story in his own words (derived both from the account he gave in Sisouk's presence and his later interview with me):

> They arrested me and threatened to kill me. They took me to an isolated place by car, but I refused to get out. I told them that if they wanted to kill me, they might as well do it in the car! Instead, they took me back and locked me up in a small hut with just one hole for seven days and seven nights. They used electric shocks, they hanged me upside down. I was so badly beaten up that I fainted and lost one of my eyes. Thongkham added in the interview: But I was determined to keep the secret and to die for the country (*tay pheua sat*). If I had given information, I would have lost the country (*sia pàthetsat ban meuang*). If I had to die, I would die alone and save the country (*pàthet sat nyàng*). But, I was determined.

He was finally freed and carried on the "struggle". He would be arrested three times during the war, but he said that his first arrest was by far the worst.

Thongkham's narration bears a remarkable similarity to the model stories of "revolutionary heroes" published in the communist propaganda documents. For example, Kaysone Phomvihane told the following "heroic" story of Sithong, a "revolutionary model", in his speech during the Youth Lao Hak Xat Congress in 1968:

> Comrade Sithong joined the revolutionary path at an early age. While he was doing his work, the enemy arrested him. At the beginning, the latter tried to corrupt him, to offer him money [...]. But Sithong rejected these offers. Having failed in using soft methods, the enemy employed violence. They tortured him with electricity, burnt him [...]. But Sithong remained calm and didn't lose his courage. During his transfer, with other comrades, he escaped, joined the Revolution and pursued his revolutionary struggle (Kaysone 1975).[4]

These stories stressed equally such values as integrity, courage, sense of self-sacrifice and patriotism, but also invariably involved elements of physical and emotional violence. Here is another dramatic extract:

> Comrade Chantha was caught by the enemy in the act of achieving his mission. The latter tortured him, beat him savagely, branded him, used electroshock, made him drink whitewash liquid, etc. But Comrade Chantha refused to reveal the secret. On the contrary, he insulted the man who carried out the torture with all his energy and resisted until the last minute. Before he died, he cried to his enemies: "Kill the imperialists and the henchmen! Glory to our victory! I keep the revolution in my heart, how can you possibly know?" (Norindr 1980, p. 483).[5]

In his book (1998), Evans mentions that the third grade Lao primary school textbook (issued in 1996) has reintroduced the story of "The Hero Si Thong", his capture and torture by the "foreign imperialists" and his escape, for which he received a medal on Army Day in 1956 (Evans 1998, p. 164). To some extent, Boulom to use Bhabha's words, is the "historical 'object' of a nationalist pedagogy, giving the discourse an authority that is based on the pre-given or constituted historical origin or event" (Bhabha 1995, p. 297). Thongkham certainly selected the most vivid recollections of his "revolutionary activities", relying on his memory of the narrative authority (i.e. the communist leadership's narrative). He thus may have exaggerated, or *a posteriori* omitted, some events — yet the scars I saw on his face were very real. The issue, again, is not so much the facts as the meaning produced by the narrative. Memory is not modelled on an immutable essence; it evolves and it mutates. The violence and the suffering of their past, which also define their days of glory, have remained entrenched in their memory and have contributed to the shaping of their identity. As Ricoeur poetically observes, identities are sustained through "a creative fidelity grounded in founding events which place them within timeness" (Ricoeur 1992).[6] The composition of their stories configures and synthesizes, moreover, a multiplicity of events into a meaningful whole, which can be understood from the end to the beginning and from the beginning to the end, allowing one to "read time backwards" repeatedly (Ricoeur 1980, p. 183). Thus narrative allows, in Ricoeur's words, through repetition and memory, "the retrieval of our most basic potentialities inherited from the past in the form of personal fate and collective destiny" (Ricoeur 1980, p. 183).

I therefore argue that the narrative of this man embodies "heroic revolutionary" narrative themes by delivering an interpretation of his experience, as reality perceived by his consciousness. It is not a "mere experience". For Victor Turner, a "mere experience" is "simply the passive endurance and acceptance of events" whereas "an experience" is "formative and transformative" because of its emotional power and (negative or positive) effects. Thus: "[w]hat happens next is an anxious need to find meaning in what has disconcerted us, whether by pain or pleasure, and converted mere experience into *an* experience. All this when we try to put past and present together" (Turner 1986, p. 36, original stress). By re-enacting his past, Thongkham attempts to maintain his role within the present-day world. To put it differently, his narrative is constitutive of his identity. As Bruner asserts,

> [i]t is in the performance of an expression [in this case, a narrative] that we re-experience, re-live, re-create, re-tell, re-construct, and re-fashion our culture. The performance does not release a pre-existing meaning that lies dormant in the text. Rather, the performance itself is constitutive. Meaning is always in the present, in the here-and-now, not in such past manifestations as historical origins or the author's intentions (Bruner 1986, p. 11).

Thus, the experience-cum-past is never monolithic. Experience structures narratives, which in turn structure experience, while all interpretations and expressions are historically, politically and institutionally situated. As Bruner comments:

> There are no raw encounters or naive experiences since persons, including ethnographers, always enter society in the middle. At any given time there are prior texts and expressive conventions, and they are always in flux. We can only begin with the last picture show, the last performance. Once the performance is completed, however, the most recent expression sinks into the past and becomes prior to the performance that follows. [...] Life consists of retellings (1986, p. 12).

In the next section, I will show that narratives also change under new historical and political conditions. I will focus on the divergent interpretations of the history of Ong Keo, the minority leader turned into a "national hero" in Ban Paktai, and show how his "legacy" is reflected in the present divergent interpretations of the past.

From a *Kha* leader to a "patriotic hero"

I have already mentioned the name of Ong Keo, the leader of a minority revolt on the Bolovens Plateau in southern Laos under French colonial rule in the early twentieth century. I will first present his actions from the perspectives of scholars and of Lao official historiography. Then, I will comment on the "legacy" of Ong Keo's actions in Ban Paktai, based on the villagers' accounts. My brief account of Ong Keo's history is principally drawn from the works of Moppert (1978, 1981), Gunn (1985) and Murdoch (1974).

Ong Keo's real name was "My"; hence, he was condescendingly re-nicknamed by the French as "Bac My" (which may be roughly translated as "that bloke My"). He was an Alak,[7] born in Ban Paktai from a relatively modest background — his father was a village chief. However, he rapidly distinguished himself by his charisma and intelligence: his command of Lao, and also of Pali,[8] no doubt helped him to build up a certain prestige among his fellow men. He began his actions around 1900 amidst the highland peoples' resentment and anger, caused by the French authorities' harsh and insensitive rule. He performed religious *phi* ("spirit") ceremonies on Phu (Mount) Tayun, located a few kilometres east of his native village, during which he urged his followers to "throw out the invaders". The rituals attracted an increasing number of people. He was soon proclaimed Phu Mi Boun, "the Holy Man", by his followers, and rapidly became known as Pha Ong Keo or Ong Keo (*Pha* means "saint", *Ong* "king, prince or a divine person of high rank" and *Keo* "diamond or precious stone"; Moppert suggested the following translation: "the Saint who possesses the miraculous stone" [Moppert 1978, p. 78]). In April 1901, Ong Keo launched his first spectacular attack on the French local authority in Thateng, in Eastern Province (now Sekong Province). It was clearly in retaliation for the French authorities' destruction of the temple of Ban Nong Mek, Ong Keo's stronghold, on the Bolovens Plateau a month earlier. The ambush opened a 6-year period of armed actions and repression between Ong Keo and his partisans and the French in the mountainous eastern region of the Bolovens Plateau.

Finally, in October 1907, the Phu Mi Boun surrendered, following the dispersal of his troops who had been seriously undermined by various factors, including military defeats, epidemics and famine. However, he never really submitted to the French conditions — for instance, he did not relinquish the title of *Chao Sadet* ("Great King") that he had bestowed upon himself, and he continued to perform very popular *bouns*, religious ceremonies mixing both Buddhist and Alak rituals (Moppert 1978, p. 171). He even implicitly encouraged his disciples, notably Kommandam, to carry on the struggle. Eventually, incensed by his "arrogant" attitude, the Commissioner of Saravane, Dauplay (who had played a crucial role in the rebellion's repression), decided to get rid of him. He set up a meeting in November 1910 with the clear intention of killing Ong Keo. Debates still surround the circumstances of his murder. Some sources claim that he was killed by Dauplay himself, who hid a gun under his hat (Moppert 1978; Murdoch 1974);[9] others argue that it was Dauplay's men who bayoneted Ong Keo to death (Gunn 1985, p. 51).[10]

History writing by the state and its agents in Laos and Vietnam necessarily implies the taming of minority/non-national elements and their incorporation into the national body, where they are assigned a fixed place and a muted part. In other words, their destiny is to be led by the ethno-cultural Majority, whether they be Kinh (in Vietnam) or the ethnic/ lowland Lao (in Laos). The task seems simple enough for the state's historiographers. But this historical discourse contravenes the rhetoric of ethnic equality and solidarity, still an essential component in the Marxist-Leninist history writing that cannot suffer accusations of Majority chauvinism. The narratives of war that have shaped to a great extent the Vietnamese and Lao twentieth-century historiographies, have allowed official history writers to reverse the representation of ethnic minorities: from a liability ("barbarians", "primitives") they became an asset when transformed into pro-independence fighters.

Rebellions in the highlands of French Laos have thus been consistently reinterpreted by Lao nationalist historiographers as the country's pioneering independence movements. However, the objectives of these armed revolts varied: some of the rebellions were millennarian movements; others, more prosaically, were attempts to resist the imposition of French — and to a lesser extent, lowland Lao — administrative and political authority. For Geoffrey C. Gunn, the "shared Montagnard ethnic identity or sense of separateness from outsiders" may explain the insurrections, although he prefers to stress the material causes, such as colonial tax, *corvée* requirements and the abuses of the *lam kha* [middlemen] (Gunn 1985, p. 59). According to François Moppert, though, the main factor behind the revolts is to be found in the form of the traditional dichotomy between "valley peoples" and "hill peoples": the latter had been able to preserve their political autonomy to a certain extent, thanks to the topography of the region; hence, there remained amongst them a strong sentiment of independence, which was ferociously defended on the ground, through armed resistance if necessary. The French administration neglected this fundamental attribute of the highland peoples, and consequently had to face the consequences of their policy (Moppert 1978, p. 227).

The material causes of these revolts led by highland peoples against the colonial administration have not been revised in state-sponsored history manuals and school textbooks since these movements serve well the need of the state to fill in the blanks with factual heroic events. Their "patriotic resistance" against "foreign domination" is accentuated while their true motivations, as well as the ethnic origins of their leadership, are played down. In other words, local conflicts have been recast as proto-nationalist movements, such as in this article published by the state-monitored English-language newspaper, *Vientiane Times*, which emphatically claims: "['the armed struggles of the people of various ethnic groups'] showed the spirit of steadfast and unyielding struggle of the valiant Laotian people who refused foreign domination. They ignited the revolutionary flames of patriotism of the multiethnic Lao people which have continued to burn inextinguishable" (*Vientiane Times*, 8–11 January 1999).

Rhetoric of struggle and local traditions

However, the villagers of Ban Paktai showed a divergent interpretation of the "hero" Ong Keo, which does not follow exactly the national narrative. In fact, they interweave the theme of struggle with local traditions. During his interview, Thongkham thus portrayed Ong Keo as having supernatural powers, as a true "Holy Man"; below is his narration (my transcription follows his words as closely as possible):

> One evening, Pha Ong heard the Phi Bang Bot,[11] who came down on his horse. But he couldn't see him. He could only hear him. Ong Keo was in the spirit house. He learnt the chants and the prayers from the Phi Bang Bot during three days and three nights. After the third night, Ong Keo saw the candles in the spirit house. He still couldn't see the Phi Bang Bot but his horse only. From then on, Ong Keo had the power. If he ordered the buffaloes to crush, they would; if he told people to fight against each other, they would. So everybody, without exception, in Meuang Thateng believed that he was a *Pha Ong*, the most powerful; that he could defeat the French. And Ong Keo said that he wanted to defeat the French because they were oppressing the people.

The attribution of special powers to a charismatic leader is common, especially in non-Buddhist traditions; as Murdoch explained in his essay on the "Holy Man's" revolt:

The panels found in the Saravane area portraying Ong Keo as a *Thevada* suggest the invocation of the proto-Bodhisattva Maitreya[12] tradition. In addition there were repeated references to "Phu Mi Bun" (he who has merit) and "Thammikarat" (Ruler of Law or Ruler of Justice). On the Lao side of the river [Mekong], and specifically among the non-Buddhist Kha, the more common reference was to invulnerability — as though invulnerability to bullets or personal harm was a kind of "proof" of the "legitimacy" of the Phu Mi Bun and his cause. The tradition of sorcery, spirit-mediums, and invulnerability is particularly strong in the Kha tradition, as has long been acknowledged by the Lao. [...] The background religious elements of the traditions of the Maitreya, the *Phu Mi Bun*, and the invulnerable sorcerer were to be incorporated by the leaders of the rebellion. By drawing on these elements, the rebellion's leaders became focal points for the dissatisfaction of the populace. Without this religiously sanctioned leadership, it would have been far more difficult to have organized the rebellion's followers (Murdoch 1974, pp. 64–65).

In effect, the tradition of sorcery and invulnerability has remained carved in oral history, as demonstrated in Thongkham's account of Ong Keo's execution.

The *Phu Mi Bun* was summoned to a meeting by the Commissaire of Saravane, Dauplay,[13] in Vat Tai in Thateng. But as soon as he and his soldiers (there were six of them) entered the room, Dauplay locked the door. The French officer then issued Ong Keo with a deadly challenge to his special powers: if by dawn he were unable to escape, he would be killed. The next morning, Ong Keo was still entrapped and Dauplay therefore ordered his men to fire at him. But the bullets did not reach him. Dauplay then ordered his men to stab him to death, but their blades could not penetrate his flesh. Eventually, a *sin* (the Lao woman's sarong) was wrapped around a rifle's bayonet. The blade this time pierced his body and Ong Keo died — but there was no blood.

Invulnerability was Ong Keo's proof of his legitimacy (Murdoch 1974, p. 64). Only an "impure" element, the *pha sin*, could disrupt his power. The official historiography has completely left out the religious aspects of Ong Keo's rebellion, but the villagers of Ban Paktai, on the contrary, incorporate them as the central element of their narration while also acknowledging

Ong Keo's fight against the French colonialists. They are not challenging the national narration; rather, they are adding to it a mystical dimension, which belongs to the local traditions.

"War genealogy"

Ban Paktai's reactions to the national narrative of Ong Keo, however, have been ambivalent. While they are grateful for the attention he is receiving, they express bitterness at what they feel to be a dispossession. During my first visit to Ban Paktai, the villagers sitting on the balcony of the village head's house listened silently to Thongkham. They sometimes nodded, but never interfered in the conversation. Thongkham seemed to be a well-respected figure in the village. After he finished his story, he soon left and went back to his village. The atmosphere between the villagers and we outsiders was now relaxed. There were six villagers: the head of the village, Pim; the Front man, Nieung; the secretary of the Party, Phumi; and three other men of indeterminate position, Khamsing, Bounmak and Sim. The look of suspicion[14] on their faces had disappeared. As the atmosphere became more and more relaxed, with the aid of rice alcohol and Sisouk's jokes, some dissonant voices began to emerge. I cannot recall who was the first to speak, but all the villagers who were present approved the criticism. They complained that we were the third group to come and ask them to tell the story of Ong Keo. Thongkham had already told it to some Lao provincial officials and to some foreign scholars. Yet, they had never heard of these researchers again, nor had they been informed of the results of these investigations. The villagers then expressed the wish to have a museum of Ong Keo in the village, and insisted that it should be "nowhere else".

When night began to fall, I started to think that it would be nice to get some rest. As soon as we finished eating, however, we were led to another house at the edge of the village. By then, a few other men had joined us, and the bottles of rice alcohol were drained at an even faster pace. As inhibitions weakened further, Phumi, clearly drunk, suddenly told Sisouk in a surprisingly distinct and firm tone that Thongkham deserved to be raised to the rank of "national hero" (*vìlàsòn heng sat*), like Sithon Kommandam (the son of Ong Kommandam) and Ong Keo: "I agree with your research", he said to Sisouk, "but I think that other valorous soldiers, who are still alive, should also be decorated. Thongkham should receive the first-class medal that he never got; all his medals are second-class ones.[15] Thongkham deserves it; he was tortured and he fought for the nation".

The other villagers at first remained quiet, then reproached Phumi for his tempestuous behaviour. They defended Sisouk who, after all, had come to study their ancestor. Phumi, in turn, retorted that he had never criticized this research but that, to his mind, Thongkham should be awarded the title; also, we were not the first people to show interest in Ong Keo. The villagers did not say anything but nodded. In his interview, a few weeks later, Phumi again stressed the leading role of Uncle Thongkham in the shadow of Ong Keo:

Pholsena: Were there many revolutionaries in Ban Paktai?

Phumi: Yes, there were. To tell you the truth, from the start, it was Uncle Thongkham who formed [(*sang*) literally, "built up"] two comrades. Then, it developed from 1954 to 1956. Then, from 1956 to 1960, there were 12 comrades. It was Uncle Thongkham who made them up. He's a true hero. The enemy's barbarity, it's not nice. The tortures he suffered from, it wasn't nice. He didn't tell you the other day. He was modest. But, we, his children, know his actions. He's an authentic hero of the province of Sekong. He's the number 1. The number 2 is... [hesitation] Khamsong. The number 3 is... [hesitation] Khamdieum... [hesitation] Khamlieun. These three comrades were tortured, beaten up, until they bled and were wrecked.

Pholsena: All these three comrades are from the same ethnic group?

Phumi: Yes, all three were Ngae, from Ong Keo's lineage. They are his children.

Pholsena: They were from Ban Paktai?

Phumi: Yes, all of them.

Phumi had been back in the village for 14 years now. He left the village in 1969 to "join the revolution" at the early age of 13. He was a soldier at the district level in Meuang Vienthong in the former Eastern Province until 1973, when he joined a battalion. Soon afterwards, he was sent to Vietnam for seven years to study and obtained a degree in "military studies". Then, back in Sam Neua, he carried on studying mechanics for one year and a half. He "started [his] service" in 1981. He went to Udomsai, Phongsaly, Luang Namtha, Luang Prabang, Xieng Khuang, and then to Vientiane in 1982. Finally, he was sent to Sekong, then a newly created province, in 1984. He retired the following year. His father also participated in the "revolutionary struggle" in the early 1950s. He was a "recruiting agent on the ground"(*phànàkngan khònkway damlòngpheunthan*), involved in secret activities in the district of Lamam in the Eastern Province (now, Sekong Province). He supplied the Issala soldiers and recruited new fighters in collaboration with the northern Vietnamese troops. In 1954, following the fall of Dien Bien Phu, most of the "civil soldiers" (*thàhan fayphònlàheuan*) of Ban Paktai rallied to the troops in the newly "united two provinces" of Sam Neua and Phongsaly to join the battles.[16] His father came back to the village a few years later, in 1957, to carry on the struggle in their native area. Phumi did not start his "revolutionary activities" when he left the village. He was still a child when he supplied the Issara soldiers who hid in the rice-fields and the forests. Phumi was 10 when he started some "minor activities" because his "parents and relatives were also involved in the revolution". The long journey to Sam Neua was thus the logical pursuit of a wartime education that had begun several years earlier.

Ong Keo is being included by the villagers of Ban Paktai in what I term a "war genealogy". The figure of the ethnic leader is being reinterpreted to endorse a story that follows neither the "national" history nor the story of ethnic rebellions. He is no longer the static and monolithic figure of the national past. Instead, Ong Keo appears to be being recast as the ancestral figure of the "revolutionary" struggle of Ban Paktai. His patriotic figure is reappropriated to legitimate his putative descendants' claim for recognition of their role during the Vietnam War. His story is being retold to support their claims. Indeed, Phumi's protest to Sisouk that night well expressed claims to the right for homology between the "great" and the "small" fates,[17] i.e. Thongkham, like Ong Keo and Sithon Kommandam, is a local hero as much as a national hero. In other words, Phumi disputed and claimed back the genealogy of the village by linking the "great" history to the "small" fates. Also, in a certain manner, Thongkham's narration is also that of Phumi; that is, a story of suffering, deprivation and violence caused by the war, of wounds that are not yet healed. However, Phumi expressed a new narrative, which does not follow the "revolutionary" story exactly. His narrative asks for another ending: the recognition of himself and his fellows within the "national" history. It reconstructs a past that looks towards the future. As Bruner observes, "[s]tories give meaning to the present and enable us to see that present as part of a set of relationships involving a constituted past and a future. But narratives change, all stories are partial, all meanings incomplete" (Bruner 1986, p. 153).

The content of the official historical account tends to imply that the Communist-led nationalist movement in Laos was based on a genuine popular awakening to anti-colonialist consciousness of the whole population, of which the ethnic minorities formed only one component. This claim leads implicitly to the weakening of the non-ethnic Lao role in the revolution. An article published in the *Vientiane Times* (8–11 January 1999)[18] on the 50th anniversary of the creation of the Lao People's Army (LPA) claimed that the Pathet Lao soldiers gained the ethnic minorities' confidence, as they did with other sections of the population: "we won the people's support after lengthily explaining them [sic] our goals and showing them the justness of our cause". Ethnic Minorities were among "the people" who happened to be "there" to support the movement. Ethnic minorities, like the rest of the "patriotic people", gave their "sons and daughters" to the revolution. They are no longer presented as key actors in the "revolutionary struggle" as they once were in the early historical representations. For example, thirty years before, a Neo Lao Hak Sat publication stressed the active participation of ethnic peoples during the war. It was thus asserted:

> The multinational character of Laos also reflects itself in the composition of the revolutionary army. In all units, from the biggest down to the smallest, there are men of various nationalities enjoying complete equality of political and other rights. Each nationality has one or several famous names in the army: Si Thoong is of the Lao Lum nationality, That Tou of the Lao Sung, and Thao Kong of the Lao Theung (Neo Lao Hak Sat 1966, p. 25).

As Grant Evans notes:

> There is a tendency to de-emphasise the minority aspect of these revolts and to stress the idea that they were part of some more general 'Lao resistance' to colonialism. Similarly, narratives about the 'war against the Americans' (i.e. the civil war with the Royal Lao Government) stress the solidarity between the different ethnic groups in the struggle, but no key minority figures stand out in the struggle (Evans 1998, p. 149).

This is the reason why the concept of narrative is liberating — it allows individuals to tell their own signifying stories. Thongkham and Phumi's narratives are split between the "pedagogical" and "performative" signifiers. Their stories have a similar pattern — patriotism, loyalty and sacrifice — but they also claim difference. Ong Keo's memory has been invested with an ideological content taken from the nationalist movement, but the reaction of some residents of Ban Paktai has been to reappropriate the figure to assert their role as ethnic fighters in the "national" history. In brief, they reject their marginalization to a peripheral role and ask, instead, for the recognition of their full participation in the construction of the Lao nation.[19]

It is a commonplace in the study of nationalism that the construction of national identity necessarily relies on the creation and use of narratives — part history, part myth — that imbue nations and nationalist projects with coherence and rationale. But the connection between the collective discourse and the personal narrative is often missing. Works on nations and nationalism tend to neglect to address individual interpretation. For instance, Fox's comment on Anderson's imagined community is rather valid when he notes: "for Anderson, the imagined community of the nation is a mass fiction; it is never clear who, if anyone, imagines particular communities, or if there is any difference in the resulting fictional community depending on who imagines it and how they do so" (Fox 1990, p. 7). In one sentence, "why and how do people invest themselves in nations and nationalism?" (Hearn 2002, p. 745). The answer may lie in the ontological desire that guides one's life story, Jonathan Hearn suggests. The person uses his/her narrative to make sense of his/her own life by attaching it to larger stories, "public narratives", by connecting his/her individual identity to the destiny of a collectivity. Hearn writes,

> [w]hen a person identifies with a collective narrative, of the nation for instance, they do not simply locate themselves within that orienting story; they invest themselves in and identify with the central protagonist, the collectivity, the nation… It is through an *isomorphism* between the individual and the collective as protagonist that people become attached to narratives" (Hearn 2002, pp. 749–50, my emphasis).

The villagers of Ban Paktai seek to legitimize a link between themselves and the nation. Through the logic of an invented descent line — being Ong Keo's "revolutionary children" — they try to attach their "small" fates to the "great" history. Following the socialist rhetoric that stresses the deeds of extraordinary individuals as models for others, the villagers of Ban Paktai feel that some of their fellow men and women also have the right to bear the title of "national hero" for their actions during the Vietnam/American War. Their claims to being "revolutionary heroes" reflect their identification with a collective identity. More precisely, their narratives reveal the imagining of a nation, born of specific historical, political and ideological contexts: during wartime when the "enemy", i.e. the rightist Royal Lao Government and the United States, served as the contrasting and defining figure of the Other, and when "being an ethnic person" (*pen khòn sòn phaw*) had the positive connotation of being attached to the ideals of revolutionary fraternity. In other words, these members of minority groups show loyalty to a country where once ethnicity and socialist ideals blended.

In the present-day historiographical agenda of the Lao PDR, "national" history gives little weight to history "on the ground", especially when it is recounted by ethnic minority voices. The latter's narratives are now going "against the flow":[20] their stories are being alienated from the encompassing narrative, they run contrary to the state's historical discourse. Sadly for these villagers, their stories do not fit the history of their village, a *Ban Vìlàsòn*, as told by the authorities. The title was given on the grounds of their ancestor Ong Keo's so-called anti-colonial struggle against the French administration, and not because of their involvement in the Vietnam/ American War. Despite an autobiographical narrative embedded in socialist historical discourse and their assertion of an unbroken revolutionary tradition between Ong Keo and their own fighting, the district and provincial officials disregard these villagers' vision of the past and their claims upon the present official historiography. It may be for a trivial reason, simply due to a lack of interest in these "peasants" and "minority people". It is not implausible. I argue, however, that the indifference is less a matter of prejudice than a consequence of the state practice of the "technology of amnesia" (Watson 1994, p. 19, speaking of Eastern Europe and the Soviet Union) regarding its war dead and veterans.

Amnesia as commemoration of the past

Heroes and Revolution: the missing link

Revolutionary regimes that come to power, in the attempt to transform and to appropriate the people, systematically deploy the techniques of awards and celebrations of exemplary members. The French historian, Benoît de Tréglodé (2002), argues that the production of "New Heroes" in the Democratic Republic of Vietnam (DRV) in the 1950s and the 1960s contributed to the forging of a link between the centre and the periphery.

In other words, the celebration of exemplary members played a role in the political unification of the "national" territory by filling the figure of the local hero with a "national" aura. Similarly, Shaun Kingsley Malarney shows that the Vietnamese Communists, in their effort to legitimize American/Vietnam War (1963–75), developed a new set of definitions for noble and virtuous actions. The critical element in the construction of the new virtue was the "transcendence of self-interest and the selfless devotion to the collectivity" (Malarney 2001, p. 49). Among those tribute policies for those who fought and died, and for their families, the most important ceremonial innovation by the government was the creation of an official and secular memorial service for the war dead.

One hundred and forty-eight revolutionary fighters were rewarded with the title of "New Heroes" between 1950 and 1964 by the DRV (Tréglodé 1999, p. 21). The hero under the DRV was an elusive figure, though. The aura of mystery surrounding the figure of the hero enhances his reputation and prestige. He was, in a way, a superhuman and his exceptionality was to remain beyond the reach of the masses as an example to aspire to but probably never to attain. In consequence, it was very rare for villagers to have met or seen a hero during their lifetime; heroes' appearances were carefully orchestrated by the authorities (Tréglodé 2002, p. 230).

To my knowledge, there was no such degree of production of heroic biographies, "heroes" or "revolutionary martyrs" by the Pathet Lao or the communist regime during the war or after 1975. This bureaucratic production of "national heroes" does not appear to have occurred in Laos during or after wartime. Unlike in the DRV, the Lao Communists did not attempt, at least not in such a systematic way, to replace class by heroism through ritual, carefully crafted responses. Although patriotic emulation and revolutionary heroism were very much inscribed in the Lao communist propagandist agenda, there were no similar institutionalized practices at the local level to glorify people's sacrifices and for the Lao communist leadership to ceremonially display their gratitude and appreciation for those who died for the "just cause". When I asked former "revolutionaries" (*khon pativat*) (soldiers, nurses or "agents on the ground") what the word *vilason* ("hero" in Lao) meant and who deserved to receive such title, I invariably received the same vague and standard answer: "A *vilason* is the fighter who is more courageous than the others, who would volunteer for dangerous actions when no one else would". I would then ask: "Do you know many *vilason* who are still alive?". "Most of them are dead" was the common reply. To be *vilason* does not therefore necessarily mean to sacrifice one's life; nonetheless to die for the Revolution may be seen as logical since the *vilason* would always take greater risks than anybody else.

It is quite revealing that a "National Federation of War Veterans" (*Sahaphan naklop tosou heng sat*) was created in Vientiane only in September 2003 under the auspices of the Ministry of Labour and Social Welfare. I was told that the late implementation was due to the lack of funding in the past, but also in order to comply with ASEAN standards (Laos joined the regional organization in 1997). The Federation's representative recently came back from an ASEAN meeting in Vietnam that gathered all the member countries' associations of war veterans. Since the creation of the Federation in Laos was so recent, it was granted observer status along with Brunei's and Cambodia's veterans associations. This association seems to have more welfare-oriented objectives (to provide material support to war veterans from the Army and the Police, widows and orphans) than a commemorative mission, though. One of the Federation's senior members admitted that the organization was still underfunded: "this federation exists only in name given its means", he said, "the title has been chosen, nonetheless, to give it an equal status with the other federations, the Lao Women's Union, the Youth Union and the Workers' Union".

The Federation unsurprisingly includes, under the category of "war veterans", those who fought for the "right side", i.e. against the French and the "Former Regime" (the Americans and the Royal Lao Government), as well as those who help at the present time to "preserve peace and security" in the country. Yet, a former Pathet Lao colonel (of Khmu ethnic origins) recently observed in his interview that the "Vientiane side" (i.e.

the Royal Lao Government and the American) soldiers should also be included in the welfare programmes; as he added in a stunning counter-discourse: "They were also unwilling victims of the war".[21] However, this view is still fairly isolated in present-day Laos. Although the Federation welcomed people such as myself who took an interest in their mission and activities, when I asked to come back and interview some *vilason*, they backed down and refused my request. A few days later, while discussing my meeting with the Federation with a Lao colleague, he strongly advised me not to use the term "revolutionary activities" (*khieunvay pativat*) in my interviews because "people may think that you want to spy on their past and to find flaws".

Practice of the "technology of amnesia"

This piece of advice was, after all, hardly surprising for a regime that still imposes state autobiographical guidelines on individuals' life stories, but it is not the only reason for the remaining mentality of secrecy and paranoia. While the colonial period offers grounds for emphasizing such values as unity and solidarity, the multiethnic narrative undermines, if not omits, certain historical periods that may not appear politically acceptable as they reveal conflicts and divisions among those very people who were supposedly all united against a common enemy. Grant Evans (1998, p. 164) notes that in the 1996 school textbooks the episode of the so-called "American war" (1954–75) has disappeared to be replaced by the narrative of a one long patriotric struggle under the leadership of the Communist Party (when compared to the former 1979 edition) (Evans 1998, p. 164). As he observes,

> Laos today is still in search of a convincing national narrative, because 'fratricide' there was not only in the distant past but very recent — and it is still not 'reassuring'. The civil war, which lasted from the late 1950s until 1975, must be borne in mind because it is the process by which the new regime came to power, but it also has to be forgotten as a period of disunity (ibid., p. 188, emphasis in original).

The national narration involves, in Ernest Renan's famous formula, the dual selective process of remembering and forgetting. The past appears seamless because it is constructed as such. The representation of the nation loathes disruptions and discontinuities. One may easily argue that history as written by authoritarian states constitutes the most extreme example of a highly selective, if not distorted, representation of the past. History must be "correct", that is, legitimizing the leadership's rule, and in the case of communist states, history must also follow the single party-state's vision. This genre of historiography is still commonly available in Vientiane, the capital of Laos. The state printing press continues to churn out memoirs of Party leaders and histories of Laos as well as of "heroic" provinces (i.e. those that fought the toughest battles against the "enemy" and subsequently suffered the most, e.g. Huaphan and Xieng Khouang in the north, or Saravane/Sekong in the south), all of which follow the same underlying pattern, i.e. the celebration of the party-state's righteous and flawless guidance that led to the liberation of the "Lao people" from "colonial tyranny" (the French) and "imperialist forces" (the Americans) 30 years ago.

A hard-cover book entitled *Pavatsatkwaengsalavan* (History of Saravane Province) was published in Laos in 2000. The monograph belongs to the series of historical studies written by local authorities (the authors of the *History of Saravane Province* were the Saravane Provincial Publication Committee). The decentralization of the production of knowledge has not resulted in independent works and divergent narratives of the country's colonial and post-colonial history, however. Only the geographical scale has been narrowed down to the provincial level, with no variation from the state historical discourse being apparent. It is therefore hardly a surprise that so far only those provinces known for their "heroic" battles against the "enemy" have published a version of their recent past. These publications serve mainly to enhance the province's profile nationwide.

The *History of Saravane* offers a particularly interesting case: A truer title would have been the *History of Saravane* and Sekong, since events related in the book straddled the border of the two neighbouring provinces. But Sekong was only created in 1981, as a result of which four districts (Thateng, Lamam, Kalum and Dakchung) were removed from Saravane's administration. The territory of present-day Sekong (former Saravane province under the old regime) was a strategic site during the American War as the "Ho Chi Minh trail" ran through the area. The trail was thus dubbed the "road of the three nations" as it was possible to reach both North and South Vietnam from "Sekong". However, the battles differed greatly from one district to another due to the great topographical variations between them. As the road (National Road 16) in the plains going from Saravane to Attapeu (the southernmost province of Laos) and passing through the former Lamam District (now located in present-day Sekong Province) was under the close control of the rightist Royal Lao Army (RLA) posted on the Bolovens Plateau, the Viet Minh and the Pathet Lao used the trails located in the Eastern districts of Dakchung and Kalum (Sekong Province), bordering South Vietnam. In consequence, these two mountainous and remote areas were heavily bombed from as early as the 1950s. How then does the monograph deal with the civil war in those southeastern mountainous regions where the fighting was particularly confusing, with the "enemy" and the "patriots" sometimes controlling the same villages and people shifting sides between the "imperialists" and the "communists"? How does it incorporate the ethnic factor in areas where the majority of the population who suffered from the bombings and the battles were of ethnic minority origins? In a nutshell, how much of the civil war's fragmented past is remembered and forgotten in the *History of Saravane*?

The title of the chapter on the Vietnam/American War leaves no room for ambiguity; it opens as follows: "The struggle against the American imperialists and neo-colonialists from 1954 to 1975 in Saravane Province". The United States is clearly identified as the "most cruel enemy" (Saravane Provincial Administration Office 2000, p. 70). They replaced the French as evildoers. The Royal Lao Government, "the

Vientiane side", on the other hand, merely followed the American orders: they were their "lackeys". The book seems to argue that the causes of the civil war were external: the United States masterminded and fuelled the country's political and ideological divisiveness because it "fundamentally aimed at transforming Laos into a new form of colony and a military base" (Saravane Provincial Administration Office 2000, p. 75). The Lao communists, conversely, were those who fought for the "reunification of the Lao people" (Saravane Provincial Administration Office 2000, p. 70). They drew together "tens of thousands" of men, women and children, who formed the forces of the "patriotic Lao multi-ethnic people" in the two northernmost provinces of Laos, Huaphan and Phongsaly, while supporting and training those left behind in the "zones under the enemy's control" to fight for the "new revolutionary era". In short, the interpretation of this highly complex period is overly simplified and encapsulated in a most basic Manichean frame.

There is no mention, on the other hand, of the ethnic origins and identity of the communist recruits in the chapter. Likewise, the crucial support of the Viet Minh, the Vietnamese communist movement, is very much minimized. In the name of Vietnamese-Lao long-term friendship it would not have been politically correct to completely erase the Vietnamese from the narrative, in the way the *History of Saravane* does with ethnicity in its narration of the Vietnam/American War. On the other hand, the Vietnamese and, particularly, the Lao leadership are equally wary of potential accusations of Vietnamese domination over their Lao "apprentices".[22] Historiographies in Laos, in consequence, usually apply sombre terms when they describe Vietnamese aid during the war. The Vietnamese communist armed forces and advisers are thus modestly referred to as "volunteers". Yet it has been proven that the Lao communist leadership and army depended to a great extent on their Vietnamese counterparts for both their military and political training and organization, as well as for manpower and material supply and logistics.[23]

For these reasons — the civil war, ethnicity and an imported revolution — the state's commemoration of the war dead and support for their survivors has been inconsistent, if not superficial, in Laos. The commemorations of the past in this country could perhaps be better defined as "willed amnesia" than "hyper-mnemosis"; in other words, more by a process of forgetting than a willingness to remember (Ho Tai 2001, p. 8), the consequence of which is inevitably to widen the gap between the official narrative and the history "from the ground", to negate the linkages between the political leadership and the people.

Conclusion

For Ricoeur, narrative originates in lived experience: the composition of a plot is grounded in a "pre-understanding of the world of action" (Ricoeur 1984 [1983], p. 54). However, one may comment critically that it is wrong to assume that people's "lived experience" is nothing but their own consciousness, that there exists an essence of things "out there", ready to be picked up. Miller thus vigorously asserts that "there is no such thing as an 'experience of being in the world and in time' prior to language. All our 'experience' is permeated through and through by language" (Miller 1987, p. 1104).

The vocabulary and "heroic" style of the narratives of Thongkham, Phumi et al. shows how socially constructed they are. They are produced in a particular social context, a regime of power conveyed by a State that emphasizes values such as patriotism, sacrifice and heroism. Phumi and Thongkham have internalized these principles to the extent that their behaviours and thoughts may deceptively appear to them as being natural and rational; in Foucault's words, they are "an effect of power" (Foucault 1980, p. 98). However, does this mean then that Phumi, Thongkham et al. are not worth hearing, let alone worth listening to, because their voices may in fact be disempowered? Or, worse, because they may be the "claim of another's *will of power*" (Ricoeur 1978, p. 45, original stress)?

Ricoeur's argument is that there is no lived reality, no human or social reality, which is not already *represented* in some sense, or *mediated* by ideology. In other words, there is no non-ideological place (or, in Foucault's vocabulary, there is no social space that is not within a regime of power): all individuals belong to a group, hence there is no knowledge totally open to critical reflection. "All *objectifying* knowledge concerning our position in society, in a social class or in a cultural tradition is preceded by a relation of *belonging to* [...] which can never become completely transparent to reflective thought" (Ricoeur 1978, p. 58, original emphasis). Having stressed the constraints, external as well as internal, upon individuals' actions, Ricoeur nonetheless argues that a critique of ideology — or individual agency — is possible, although it will never be "total": "it is condemned to remain partial, fragmentary, insular" (Ricoeur 1978, p. 59). As Alonso writes, "we are simultaneously the subjects, in both a political and a phenomenological sense, and the objects of our own understanding" (Alonso 1988, p. 51).

Ricoeur's argument is that "the 'language-game' of narration, the "inventive power of language" or how narration, the act of telling a story, can create meaning, ultimately reveals that the meaning of human existence is itself narrative (Ricoeur 1986, p. 17). The power of narrative subsequently opens up the multitudinous possibilities of re-telling history; in Ricoeur's words:

> ... the history of the vanquished dead crying out for justice demands to be told. As Hannah Arendt points out, the meaning of human existence is not just the power to change or to master the world, but also the ability to be remembered and recollected in narrative discourse, to be *memorable*. These existential and historical implications of narrativity are very far-reaching, for they determine what is to be 'preserved' and rendered 'permanent' in a culture's sense of its own past, of its own 'identity' (ibid., original stress).

The narratives of Phumi and Thongkham may be partial and fragmentary; but their words of suffering are not dictated by techniques of government and technologies of self (although they may be *a posteriori* ordered in a narration that is influenced by social forces); these words spring initially from these individuals' own feelings and reasoning. As Ricoeur reminds us: "We tell stories because in the last analysis human lives need and merit being narrated". In the context of post-war Laos, my informants' narratives seek to legitimize their belonging to a political community whose national narration has changed, however. While people on the ground, and especially war veterans, have kept a vivid and personal memory of the past, the state and its agents are determined to reduce the events of the last fifty years to a simplistic and fuzzy rhetoric of "us" against "them". The next chapter will reveal a similar reductionist strategy through the analysis of the Lao state's attempt to control people's ethnicity so as to transform a fragmented and fluid cultural reality into an orderly and fixed ethnic landscape.

Notes

1   "Subject" is used here to refer to an individual who is subjected to the actions of an authority.
2   Meuang Thateng was created in 1993. It was previously under the administration of Meuang Lao Ngam, Saravane Province. Meuang Thateng is bordered by Meuang Saravane and Meuang Lao Ngam (Saravane Province), Meuang Lamam (Sekong Province) and Meuang Paksong (Champassak Province), to the North, the West, the East and the South, respectively.
3   Although the expression *sàlàkhat* does not exist in Lao, Somseun may have combined the words "to sacrifice" and "to be torn" in order to stress the magnitude of his sacrifice.
4   "Le camarade Sithong s'était engagé dès son jeune âge dans la voie révolutionnaire. Pendant qu'il accomplissait son travail, il fut arrêté par l'ennemi. Au début, celui-ci essayait de le soudoyer, de lui promettre de l'argent et (?) [sic - original translation]. Mais Sithong rejeta ces offres. Ayant échoué avec la politique de la carotte, l'ennemi recourut à la violence. Il le tortura à l'électricité, le brûla avec le fer rouge. Mais Sithong garda son calme et son courage. Pendant son transfert, en compagnie d'autres camarades, il s'évada, rejoignit la Révolution, et poursuivit son combat révolutionnaire." Kaysone Phomvihane (1975), "Discours au Congrès de la jeunesse LHX", 25/08/1968, Editions du NLHX, (page non-specified); quoted from Norindr (1980, p. 484).

5   "Le camarade Chantha, dans l'accomplissement de sa mission fut arrêté par
     l'ennemi. Celui-ci le torturait, le battait sauvagement, le brûlait avec le fer
     rouge, le soumettait au magnéto, le faisait boire de l'eau de chaux, etc. Mais le
     camarade Chantha refusa de révéler le secret. Au contraire, il injuria son
     tortionnaire de toutes ses forces et résista jusqu'à la dernière minute. Avant de
     rendre le dernier soupir, il cria en face de ses ennemis: "A bas les impérialistes
     et les valets! Vive notre victoire! La révolution, je la porte dans mon cœur,
     comment peux-tu savoir?" *Les gars du 97*, Ed. Neo Lao Hak Xat, date and page
     non specified; quoted from Norindr (1980, p. 483).

6   Quoted, in turn, from Poutignat and Streiff-Fenart (1995, p. 180).

7   According to all three authors (Moppert [1978, p. 50], Gunn [1985, p. 43],
     Murdoch [1974, p. 55]).

8   The sacred language of Theravada Buddhism.

9   Murdoch, in turn, quotes from Burchett's book (1957, p. 242). The latter
     interviewed the son of Ong Kommandam, Sithon, who gave him this version
     of Ong Keo's death. Moppert did not indicate his sources, although they are
     most likely to be the same as Murdoch's.

10   Gunn, in turn, quotes this second version from a report by Dauplay: AOM Aix
     F6, "Mort de Bac My et capture de ses lieutenants" (Dauplay to the Resident
     Superior of Saravane, 19 December 1910). However, considering the fact that
     Dauplay was the main investigator into Ong Keo's death, one may wonder
     whether his testimony is entirely trustworthy.

11   A malevolent spirit.

12   In Buddhism, Maitreya (Sri Ariya Maitreya) is the future Buddha (who, it is
     believed by many of the faithful, will come 5000 years after the death of
     Gotama Buddha) (Keyes 1995, p. 90).

13   In the interview, Somseun pronounced the name "Complay". I surmise that it
     is a deformation of Dauplay.

14   One of the men even asked us if we had an official permit from Vientiane to
     come and do research in the village. Sisouk just laughed, and the man did not
     insist. I later asked Sisouk about that incident but he said that I must have
     misunderstood, for it never happened.

15   A villager whom I could not identify at that time mentioned a badly conducted
     investigation into Thongkham's deeds at the time the medals were awarded.

[16] Occupied and administered by the Lao communists and the Viet Minh since 1953.

[17] I have borrowed the expression from Tréglodé (1999).

[18] Another paper relating the "struggle for independence" from 1939 to 1946, published in the LFNC magazine, introduces the "Lao people" as "the *great popular mass* [who] understood that in order to re-gain independence and freedom, they had to rely on their own strength and joined the appeal made by the Indochinese Communist Party" (Sinsay 1998, p. 23, my stress).

[19] In his interview, Lieusai, a retired *vìlàsòn avuso* of Sekong — a title that rewarded him for the years he spent fighting with the Pathet Lao — was categorical in insisting that it was the "Lao Theung", and "not the Lao", who fought during the American War in what was then the Eastern Province. Moreover, did not Thongkham himself confide to Sisouk that his father once told him to join the battle only if the struggle were in the "East"? The common story I often heard, though I do not have it confirmed officially, is that the creation of Sekong (the vast majority of whose population is non-ethnic Lao) in 1984 was to reward its people for their participation in the "revolutionary struggle". There are thus clear historical and ideological boundaries between Sekong and Saravane, the neighbouring province. The latter was known as the "enemy" province, and the stigma of the wrong side appears to remain. In effect, Saravane "chose the wrong nation", a military officer told me, "whereas the Eastern zone was truly a heroic zone (*khet vìlàsòn*)".

[20] I have borrowed the expression as used in the context discussed in Hearn's article (2002).

[21] Interview in December 2003, Vientiane.

[22] We borrow the term from the title of a book by McAlister Brown and Joseph J. Zasloff, *Apprentice Revolutionaries: The Communist Movement in Laos, 1930–1985* (Stanford University, Stanford, California: Hoover Institution Press, 1986).

[23] See, for instance, the pioneering studies of Paul F. Langer and Joseph J. Zasloff, *North Vietnam and the Pathet Lao: Partners in the Struggle for Laos,* Harvard University Press, Cambridge, MA, 1970, and MacAlister Brown and Joseph J. Zasloff, *Apprentice Revolutionaries: The Communist Movement in Laos, 1930–1985,* Hoover Institution Press; Stanford, CA, 1986. More recently, Christopher Goscha (2004) shows that in the aftermath of the Second World War the Vietnamese

communists began to form and consolidate revolutionary bases, structures and cadres in Laos and Cambodia, whereas before 1945 their efforts to build up and run revolutionary networks in Western Indochina relied almost entirely on Vietnamese locals in French Laos and Cambodia. Motivated by strategic imperatives and driven by deeply-rooted convictions, they tried, and sometimes succeeded, to win the local population's support despite the hardship and relentless efforts this entailed (Goscha 2004, pp. 154–56).

6

Ethnic Classification and Mapping Nationhood

The modern State, in the Foucaldian sense, is that hegemonic apparatus whose raison d'être is to control and administer the body of the population through a series of discourses that together form the "regime of truth", which Foucault defined as follows:

> Each society has its regime of truth, its 'general politics' of truth: that is, the types of discourse which it accepts and makes function as true; the mechanisms and instances which enable one to distinguish true and false statements, the means by which each is sanctioned; the techniques and procedures accorded value in the acquisition of truth; the status of those who are charged with saying what counts as true (Foucault 1977, p. 131).

Truth is not transcendental, "out there": it is produced here and now. Indeed, modern states, among other agents, participate in a continuous and uninterrupted process of generating "truth" through the use of "technologies of power" in order to legitimate and naturalize their authority. They transform innovations into everyday practice "by constant reiteration of [their] power through what have become accepted as natural (rational and normal) state functions, of certifying, counting, reporting, registering, classifying, and identifying" (Cohn and Dirks 1988, p. 225). My intention in this chapter is thus to show the determinant role that administration in general, and population censuses in particular, play in the modelling of Lao society in the image of a national community. In other words, the State in modern Laos has operated the census as a vector of ethnicity (through the manipulation of ethnic boundaries) in order to fashion an imaginary nationhood out of real heterogeneity.

Description and interpretation of the early censuses

Insightful works have shown the long-lasting impact of the knowledge produced by colonial administrations on the independent states they once governed.[1] For instance, Cohn, in an article that analyses the conduct of the censuses in India under British rule, argues that the censuses that classified the Indian population into castes significantly influenced "scholars' and scientists' views on the nature, structure and functioning of the Indian caste system" (Cohn 1987, p. 242). Indeed, the colonial State contributed to shaping the ruled population according to a new conceptual framework by operating instruments of domination, or technologies of power, which included the census, the map and the museum (Anderson 1991, p. 167).

The French administration

The French censuses of the population of colonial Laos were basic. The data reported in the 1911, 1921, 1931, 1936 and 1942 censuses (see Appendix 1: *Ethnic Composition of the Population of Laos, 1911–1955*) were mainly based on general administrative reports, such as the *Annuaire Statistique du Laos* and the *Annuaire Statistique de l'Indochine*.[2] Only major groups were listed. There were nine of them, namely, the "Lao", "Tai", "Kha", "Meo-Yao", "Vietnamese", "Chinese", "European", "Cambodian", "Indian and Pakistani" (though, for the two last groups, the data is patchy and is completely missing from the 1942 survey). The table gives the

"Ethnic Composition of the Population of Laos" as a general title, and the neutral term of "group" is used to head the ethnic classifications column. As a consequence, presumably, the nine statistical categories were considered as "ethnic groups".[3] Yet, more detailed statistics were available from other sources, such as military reports, ethnographic studies (conducted by both French and foreign researchers), and provincial statistical records. However, the subcategories were simply not listed in the ethnic composition of the whole territory. There seem to be several related reasons for the basic classification, as follows.

The French administration classified the population into categories that followed racial lines; hence, inevitably, the use of rough methods of categorization. That could also explain why the "Lao" and "Tai" groups were invariably placed at the top of the list, despite the fact that the "Kha" outnumbered the "Tai" population in general (see Appendix 1). The classification was indeed based on the assumption that the "Kha" were not situated at the same level of civilization as the "Lao" and "Tai" (Hirschman 1987, p. 568). One could equally well ask why the "Europeans" were usually put at the bottom of the list. Economically as well as strategically, French authorities saw Laos as a mere extension of Vietnam — especially after the failure of the *mise en valeur* policy (see Chapter 2). Consequently, marking the domination of the ruling Whites over the subordinated Asians was probably not such an issue, in a possession that has been called a "colonial backwater" (Gunn 1990). The inadequate data collection system, aggravated by poor communications, especially in the upland areas, were certainly other factors that contributed to the dearth and inaccuracy of the statistics (Pietrantoni 1953). However, the lack of usefulness of detailed statistics on ethnicity was probably the primary reason for using such simplified categories. The taxation administration needed only simple distinctions to do their work: the Lao and the non-Lao (the Europeans — French and others — and the Asian foreigners — including Chinese — were subject to a different tax system [Pietrantoni 1953, p. 28]). Later on, the system became slightly more complex, but the French administration's classification still followed the same pattern as that of the census[4] — or, on the contrary, was the latter following the administration's interests? In any case, rough, i.e. racial, categories were apparently sufficient for the functioning of the colonial tax system that was emphatically the backbone of French Laos.

The Royal Lao Government's administration

The first post-colonial census under the RLG appears to have been conducted in 1955, while the last colonial countrywide census seems to be dated as far back as 1943 (Pietrantoni 1953, 1957). The official departure of the French from Indochina in 1954 did not remove the colonial imprint, however, and their classification inscribed their image of the Lao population on the post-colonial censuses. Indeed, the latter kept the same pattern, i.e. the naming and the categories (see Appendix 1, the year 1955), which meant that the racial lines were insidiously perpetuated. However, the Lao authorities brought about one significant change that reflected the imperative of forming a self-conscious Lao national community. They gathered the "Lao" and "Tai" groups together under a single category (see Appendix 2: *Ethnic Composition of Laos, 1954–1955, by percentage of ethnic groups in each province*), resulting in an increase in the figures in favour of the ethnic Lao, at the expense of the "Kha" population. In addition, there were suspicions on the part of some individuals involved in the census that the "Kha" figures were underestimated in the censuses (See Appendix 1).[5] On the other hand, there is no evidence that the underestimation was systematic and politically orientated, and it could simply have been due to the difficulty of listing populations living in remote areas.

In the 1950s, the use of the seminal terms "Lao Lum" or valley Lao, "Lao Theung" or Lao of the mountain slopes and "Lao Sung" or Lao of the mountaintops, was initiated under the RLG. It was a stroke of genius. That classification is still being used in present-day Laos and is widely applied, even among academic works and in spite of the authorities officially forbidding its use (of which later). And yet from the beginning it was clearly a political attempt to emphasize the unity of the country by suppressing the pejorative nature and the racial connotations attached to the previous naming system, and by denying the reality of cultural differences (Halpern 1964, p. 5). The mapping of Lao society was first shaped by a racial theory in the form of scientific discourse engendered and developed by the colonial authorities, with the support of a certain type of ethnography and in response to a demand from the administration. The racial discourse was then naturalized through a "repertoire of routines of rule" (Cohn and Dirks 1988, p. 225). In the aftermath of colonial rule, the discourse was perpetuated and reproduced under a new terminology by the newly independent state. The "Lao Lum", "Lao Theung" and "Lao Sung" categories referred exactly to the same major ethnic groups ("Lao and Tai", "Kha" and "Meo-Yao", respectively) as defined by the colonial administration. The categorization was as arbitrary as the previous one, but it endured because it coincided with the "truth" that had been produced and already legitimized during the French period.

That classification was furthermore encouraged by the RLG because it served its project of building Laos as a nation, and, as such, was widely used. As a matter of fact, some in the RLG saw the use of these gross ethnic categories as an indicator of the integration of the non-ethnic Lao peoples into the ethnic Lao cultural mainstream. Katay Don Sasorith thus wrote in 1953:

> Indeed, the ethnic issue in Laos won't be as complex as it is in Siam, because in Laos, the Lao element clearly and undeniably predominates, in terms of numerical importance as well as by its degree of social and cultural development. [...] Some educated and developed Boloven or Mèo [sic] tend to get closer to us, as much in their way of dressing and their lifestyle as in their patriotic ideal, to such an extent that they now want to be called under the name "Lao Theung" [...] (Katay 1953, p. 21).[6]

That "truth" was also legitimized by other agents, such as foreign scholars. Indeed, those who criticized the Lao Lum, Lao Theung, and Lao Sung stratification also recognized the logic of it. For example, the American anthropologist, Joel Halpern, wrote in the 1960s:

Leaving the Mekong plain the land abruptly changes to rugged mountains cut by narrow valleys. The observer looking closely at the settlement pattern below can discern almost a textbook illustration of ethnic stratification and economic-geographic adaptation to the land based on varying degrees of altitude (Halpern 1964, p. 5).

A "truth" had been produced and legitimized, naturalized through a series of discourses, which were operated, integrated and transmitted by diverse and multiple agents, i.e. the colonial administration, the post-colonial state, scholars and the population. They all underlie a fundamental action: a "truth" had been produced and developed, maintained and naturalized through a political economy (Foucault 1977, p. 131). The "truth" was sometimes criticized and even denied, but it was the starting point from which the debates over ethnic classification were departing. It was this "regime of truth" that the Pathet Lao, and later on the socialist regime, attempted to break and to replace with their own discourse of the nation.

Socialist regime: Break with the past

The "Policy of National Equality" and the Civilizing Project

On 2 December 1975, the monarchy was abolished and replaced by the Lao PDR. The propaganda for socialist construction became an appeal for a united patriotic front. Ethnic minority people were called upon to join the struggle for the triumph of socialism against the "imperialists and the reactionaries". Indeed, as Martin Stuart-Fox rightly observed, "[n]ational solidarity and defence had to proceed hand in hand. So long as ethnic and social divisions remained, these could be exploited by the 'enemies' of the new regime" (Stuart-Fox 1981, p. 63). The new regime explicitly recognised the "Hill-Tribe Question". Kaysone Phomvihane, the then leader of the Party, thus declared in a 1982 speech:

> No tribe can be regarded as the majority as nearly 70 tribes [sic] with different levels of economic, cultural and social development live in Laos. The tribal question is one of the major problems of the Lao revolution and socialist construction in Laos. Our Party is trying to resolve this issue while

carrying out its overall cause of socialist transformation. The Party is striving to tighten unity among the nationalities and tribes, taking into consideration the special aspects of each tribe and our harmonious interests in the struggle for a bright future (Kaysone 1982).[7]

He called therefore for greater attention to be paid to promoting education among ethnic groups, improving their living conditions and increasing production in remote minority areas. Furthermore, he insisted on respect being paid to the "psychology, aspirations, customs, beliefs of each ethnic group" (Kaysone 1980, p. 233). On the tenth anniversary of the Lao PDR in December 1985, Kaysone announced that minority traditional culture had been preserved through schools of dancing, music and handicrafts. Lenin's apprehension about the risk of ethnic awareness in the Soviet Union led him to initially promote the policy of "national equality"; so too did the Lao PDR, as had previously the People's Republic of China and the Democratic Republic of Vietnam.

When the PRC was proclaimed in 1949, the traditional Han goal of forced assimilation was rejected. The objective of the Chinese Communist Party (CCP) was to end the inequality between the ethnic groups through a programme of gradual cultural, economic and political equality. Stevan Harrell offers a concise definition of the work as

creating autonomous regions, implementing educational and developmental plans, bringing leaders of the peripheral peoples into the fulfilling of the promise that all *minzu*,[8] equal legally and morally, would march together on the road to historical progress, that is, to socialism (1995, p. 24).

The slogan was then "Unity in Diversity" or "Unity and Equality". All the minorities were allowed to keep their cultural distinctiveness. For the Chinese Communists, the two great evils that had to be overcome now were the attitude of Han cultural superiority ("Han chauvinism") and the fear the minority groups had of Han domination ("local nationalism"). In the 1950s, party cadres were sent to the minorities' areas to collect data on their customs and lifestyle, the objective also being to make their minority propaganda and the training of a socialist proletariat among the minorities more effective (Dreyer 1975, p. 52).

The Viet Minh's policy towards the minorities was very similar to the Chinese model. Article 3 of the amended 1959 Constitution of the Democratic Republic of Vietnam reiterated the policy of autonomous zones[9] while asserting that such autonomy was to be within "the territory of Vietnam [which] is a single, indivisible whole from North to the South" (Article 1) (*The Constitutions of Vietnam*, p 39). In reality, the right of self-determination was subordinated to socialist ideals. As within China's autonomous zones, the minorities were expected to follow the path to "progress" by going through all the evolutionist stages — from primitive communism to feudalism, then to capitalism and finally to socialism. As Jean Michaud observes:

> In a new country where the collective project has to be popular, national and scientific, there was little room left for the ways of the past. Following this frame of mind, and despite an openly egalitarian state rhetoric, montagnards were considered culturally and economically backward unless they accepted the cultural supremacy of the lowland majority (Michaud 2000, p. 357).

Lao ethnography

Following the Chinese and Vietnamese communists, the Lao authorities launched data collecting campaigns in areas inhabited by minority populations, first in the "Liberated Zones" during the war, and then, after their victory, throughout the country from the late 1970s. As mentioned above, the ethnographic works were guided by similar Marxist-Leninist theories, i.e. "policy of national equality" and "evolutionist theory". In 1981, Kaysone made clear that the incumbent terminology, i.e. the three large "national categories", "Lao Lum", "Lao Theung" and "Lao Sung", was to be replaced by a new ethnic classification. He wrote thus:

> [Each ethnic group] has [...] its own characteristics. As the revolution developed, the various ethnic groups became integral parts of the nation of their own free will, under the *then* political denominations: Lao Lum (of the plains), Lao Theung (of the slopes) and Lao Sung (of high altitudes). The Central Committee of Ethnic Groups must co-operate with the various

branches and with our brothers, the workers from the various ethnic groups, to conduct together research and discussions with regard to the names and the lists of ethnic groups, *in order to establish official rules* (Kaysone 1981, p. 47, my stress).

As a consequence, the new regime started using a new system of classification for the population census. The threefold categorization with the "Lao" prefix was deemed to be anti-revolutionary and its use was abandoned in political documents, although this terminology is still widely used in Laos.

The ethnographic research methodology in the Lao PDR is probably best exposed in a working manual, entitled "References and criteria for conducting research on ethnic groups across the country for statistic purposes", and written by Sisouk,[10] a high-ranking official working in the LFNC Research Department on Ethnic Groups.[11] The document is also worth mentioning as it was used as the official guide during the data collection campaign for the 2000 census.

The methodology applied is directly based on Kaysone's definition of the nation that he gave during a "Conference on Ethnicity" in 1981, in which he declared: "The national question has four criteria or characteristics, which are: common language, common territory, common socio-economic organisation, and common psychology" (Sisouk 1999, p. 1). This definition is itself clearly inspired by Stalin, who defined a "nationality" by five similar criteria: a stable community of people, a language, a territory, an economic life and a psychological make-up or "national character" (Stalin 1913).[12] But only two of the four criteria are to be applied for ethnographic research in the Lao PDR, i.e. language and "material and spiritual ways of life" (*sivìt dan vàttù làe chìtchai*)); a third criterion is also added, namely, the origins and migrations of the group. Laos being a predominantly rural country, Sisouk argues that there is not enough variation in socioeconomic organization for this to be a factor of differentiation. As for territory, there is simply no autonomy granted to ethnic groups in Laos.

It rapidly appears, however, upon closer scrutiny, that the ethnographic element is accompanied, if not dominated, by the objective of controlling ethnicity and producing fixed and "correct" identities. Sisouk even admits that "spiritual" as well as "material ways of life" are not such reliable criteria, especially the former because "some ethnic groups mingle with others' culture. Sometimes, some ethnic groups adopt others' culture as theirs. As a consequence, we must be careful to collect an adequate amount of clear data for comparison" (Sisouk 1999, p. 8). The data collection seems in effect to be guided by two political aims: (1) to contribute to the national culture and (2) to censor "bad" while promoting "good" culture. Indeed, as Sisouk bluntly explains:

> [...] in general, all the ethnic groups' psychological and cultural features mentioned above do not conflict with the overall psychology, with the national community's culture. On the contrary, they enhance the psychology and the culture of our Lao nation. They also provide us with information to conduct research for clarification as well as for supporting the Party-Government in its policies and socio-economic development plans that lead all the ethnic groups into the path of development and prosperity. [A few pages below, he specifies the aim:] Once the data is collected, we will write an assessment report and submit it to the appropriate organisation in order to set up short and long-term plans to view the backward practices and to promote the correct ones (Sisouk 1999, pp. 3 and 18).

Ethnographic works produced by Marxist-Leninist regimes have always been strongly identified with a civilizing project vis-à-vis ethnic minorities.[13] Thus, the scientific study of ethnic groups in these regimes thrives on an ideology strongly influenced by evolutionist theories, the objective of which is to "classify the ethnic groups according to their degree of cultural development"; in effect, criteria for distinction or grouping are thought of as "criteria of backwardness" (Goudineau 2000, p. 23). An "ethnic group" in this sense is probably better defined as a "tribe", i.e. a group of individuals, seen as being clear-cut and isolated, around which are traced artificial boundaries for administrative and political reasons. To be exact, the idea of "tribe" came from an illusion: at the ideological level, "tribes" are a colonial concept that reflected the conception held by Western culture of the rest of the world at that time, key themes of which were imperialist expansionism and the dichotomization of humankind into the "civilized" and the "uncivilized" (Cohen 1978, p. 384). There is clearly a double agenda attached to ethnographic studies in the Lao PDR (on the one hand, promotion of cultural diversity and on the other, political control of ethnicity). An "ethnic group" appears as a fixed entity on which is imposed a set of characteristics that have been accepted as "correct" and distinctive enough. That seems to be in effect the basis for an "ethnic group" to appear on the census list. I suggest that the pattern of the Lao PDR population census not only reflects Marxist-Leninist ideology, but also parallels the shaping of the nation. As such, an analysis of the construction process and the structure of the latest population census is most helpful.

Case study of the 2000 population census

The messy job of classification

Data collection for the 2000 census was once more driven by the constant imperative to list and to identify the exact number of ethnic groups, an obsession that Lao officials commonly share with their Chinese and Vietnamese counterparts. In Laos, as in Vietnam, the figure has been subjected to several revisions.[14] An official document mentions the successive figures of 200, 177, 150, 131, and even up to 820 and 850 ethnic groups (Sisouk 2000, p. 1)! Unfortunately, it does not specify any dates, but according to Grant Evans, the number of 820 self-named ethnic groups was the result of the 1983–85 census (Evans 1999, p. 178). It was not until 1985 that the Party approved an official estimate of 47 ethnic groups; and yet, even after the publication of the 1985 population census, the deliberations continued (Goudineau 2000, p. 22).

The 1999 data collection campaign, once again, aimed at clarifying this forest of anarchy, uncertainties and confusion. And, after five years of apparent stability, new figures emerged: 49, instead of 47, ethnic groups, which were distributed between four, instead of the previous six, ethno-linguistic categories (see Appendix 3: "Assessment of the ethnic groups' names in the Lao PDR accepted during the LFNC meeting on 13–14th August 2000"). The issue is not, of course, to debate the figures' accuracy, since the census is anyhow arbitrarily constructed. Rather, I attempt here to analyse how and why the changes occurred or did *not* occur. By addressing these questions, the answers may, in turn, help to interpret the broader picture, i.e. the nationalist discourse.

Teams, composed of officials from the LFNC Research Department on Ethnic Groups, were sent across the country in groups in Spring 1999 to collect data on the ethnic populations. The campaign lasted nearly four months until September of that year. Each team stayed for about one month in the provinces, which had been divided into five major geographical areas.[15] Except for two members, the teams had little, if any, knowledge or academic background relating to ethnographic methodology. Before they left for the field, they received only a few days' training at a seminar taught by Sisouk, who supervised the census. To be fair, their task was not to conduct an exhaustive investigation as had been done in the past; in fact, it merely consisted of collecting the population censuses from the provincial LFNC organizations. Some ethnographic studies were nevertheless carried out to fulfil the imperative of clarification, but these works were performed by an exclusive few, including Sisouk himself.

In reality, the changes in the census went far beyond the addition of two new ethnic groups. In fact, the first assessment of the provincial censuses gave a list of 55 ethnic groups (see Appendix 4: "Assessment of the provincial LFNC censuses 1999–2000: list of 55 ethnic groups"), which was whittled down to 49. Ironically, the main objective of the census coordinators was not to check information in the field but rather the data provided by the provincial LFNC organizations. Indeed, the authorities, alarmed by the confusion that was reigning throughout the country and among the officials themselves, placed a high priority on keeping the proliferation under control. Sisouk, thus, recounted in his report:

> According to the data of the Committee on Population Census, the population amounts to 4,574,848 inhabitants, among whom 24,084 have not specified their ethnic affiliation and 10,201 do not appear on the list of 47 ethnic groups. Many problems, however, occurred after the population

census [of 1995] documents were sent to the Party-State's provincial organizations. The Statistical Department has received letters and phone calls from the Central Committee's offices and ethnic group representatives in the provinces, pointing out the absence of ethnic groups' names as well as names that did not satisfy the ethnic groups (Sisouk 2000, pp. 4 and 5).

Finally, thirteen new ethnic groups, which were not listed on the national census, appeared in the provincial data.[16] In total, five new ethnic groups were officially recognized for inclusion in the national census at the LFNC meeting held on 13–14th August 2000, though only two of these had been listed in the provincial data (these were the "Thaen" (out of the "Kmmu" group) and the "Thai Neua" (out of the "Phuthai" group), the latter being listed in no less than three provinces[17]) (see Appendix 3). Two of the other groups recognized for inclusion, the "Tai" and the "Idu", seem to have been proposed at the central level, as neither of them appeared on the provincial data at all. The fifth ethnic group, the "Lahu", was a new name in the official list.[18] It encompassed the "Kuy" and "Musser" peoples, which disappeared from the census by becoming sub-categories.[19] The construction of the 2000 census was also probably inspired in some ways by the Vietnamese census. Indeed, in total eleven names (some of them attributed (supposedly) to the French colonisers and/or being perceived as derogatory in the authorities' eyes) were replaced by "correct" ones, among which four were already listed in the Vietnamese census.[20] That similarity could also possibly explain the apparition of a "Tai" group (extracted from the "Phuthai"), which is found among the 54 Vietnamese official ethnic groups.

This cultural objectification is most unlikely, however, to have any short-term impact on the population, all the more so as the names still remain subject to possible revisions, depending on whether they will fit the evolving standard of "correctness" (Sisouk 2000, p. 8). During a trip to a village in 1999 in the province of Sekong, I was intrigued when an official kept repeating to the villagers that they should no longer call themselves "Lao Theung" or "Ngae", but "Krieng". However, a month later, when I came back to the village, the answers were still "politically incorrect". I then asked the village's Party Representative the ways in which he usually described himself:

Pholsena: What is your national group (*sònsat*)?

Mani: Lao Theung! [the man replied at once. He then started enumerating the different national groups:] There are the Lao Theung, the Lao Lum, the Lao Khong,...

He stopped, looking hesitant, and then mumbled a few more words I was unable to understand. I asked his nationality (*sànsat*). He replied without hesitation:

Mani: Lao.

Pholsena: Your ethnic group (*sònphaw*)?

Mani: Ngae. [He then specified:] We belong to the 68 ethnic groups like the Lao Sung, the Mèo,... [He stopped and inaudibly mumbled again.]

During our whole stay in the village, I never heard someone spontaneously introducing himself or herself as "Krieng".

"You must be Bru!"

Accompanying Sisouk on another short trip to a Ngae village in Sekong Province the same year, I witnessed an intriguing scene involving the LFNC official and the villagers. Sisouk declared that their ethnic group actually belonged to a larger category, the "Bru" (an ethnic group officially classified under the Austro-Asiatic category in the Vietnamese census, but invisible in the Lao version, which apparently refers in Makong language to "the people from the mountains"[21]). He argued that both ethnic groups indeed shared some traditions, such as offering to special guests the boiled feet, head and giblets of a chicken. The villagers looked puzzled, but silently submitted before the central authority.

Sisouk is often depicted as a pro-Makong (the official ethnic group to which he belongs, and which is referred to as the "Bru Makong" in the census' sub-categories) chauvinist. I would suggest, rather, that this high-ranking official is lobbying for the cause of the "Bru" as an official category. In effect, as Cohn similarly observed in India:

> The implied argument is that the census was one of the situations in which Indians were confronted with the questions of who they were and what their social and cultural systems were. I don't think that the act of a census enumerator asking a question of a peasant contributed too much to the process. [...] If there was a direct effect of the census [on the mass of the Indian population], it was on the enumerators (Cohn 1987, p. 248).

In addition to the list of 55 ethnic groups resulting from the Lao Front provincial censuses, Sisouk proposed a much-condensed list of only 34 groups (see Appendix 5: "Assessment of the names of 34 ethnic groups"). Among the causes of that dramatic reduction was the grouping of eight ethnic groups listed separately in the 1995 census within a single one, the "Bru".[22] The desirability of being recorded as "Bru" might come from the benefits, however symbolic, such a denomination would bring. As he explained to some villagers in Sekong during the trip:

> We must no longer name the Makong, Pàkò, Tri, Kàtang, Ngae, Katu, Tà-Oy, Suay, one by one. Each of them, singled out, makes too low a number, whereas the "Bru" would amount to more than 300,000 persons. That makes a bigger population, more influential!

His cause was echoed in a project financed by the International Labour Organisation (ILO). The latter became involved in Laos in 1996 through its Project for the Promotion of ILO Policy on Indigenous and Tribal Peoples. In 1999, it started a study on the "Government's policies regarding the ethnic groups in rural development" (ILO 2000). In the following year, upon completion of that study, a two-year pilot project (with a budget estimated at US$140,000) was initiated in the province of Khammuan. According to the Project Document, the five target villages were mainly populated by the "Bru", with the Phuthai occupying second position (these two ethnic groups accounted for 78 per cent and 22 per cent of the population, respectively). This ethnic distribution apparently justified the inclusion of "Bru" and Phuthai as the project's languages, along with English and "Laotian". Similarly, the candidate for the post of Project Manager was required to possess knowledge of the "Bru" language (ILO 2000).

I have no evidence that conclusively proves Sisouk's direct influence on the choice of area or on the outline of the project; however, there are some disconcerting elements that make coincidence appear to be a less convincing alternative explanation. First, the LFNC, along with the Central Leading Committee for Rural Development, was the Government's agency for the project. Consequently, Sisouk was directly involved since he was responsible for all the foreign projects asking for the LFNC's cooperation. Although he had limited executive power, no project could be pursued without him as supervisor or coordinator. In addition, the project's target area was his very own native district, with which he still keeps in regular contact, notably via relatives and business partners. Yet, Sisouk is not the only scholar to argue for the existence of a "Bru" group in Laos. James Chamberlain, a linguist, also lists in his census of the ethnic groups of the Lao PDR the "Bru" as an Austro-Asiatic group, which corresponds, according to his classification, to the Makong and So peoples within the Lao nomenclature (Chamberlain 1995). It should also be noted that Chamberlain was the main author of the 2000 ILO consultants' report. One may conclude that Sisouk and Chamberlain's concordant positions, in addition to Sisouk's unique position within the project, have played a significant, if not decisive, role in the selection of the "Bru" as the main target ethnic group. The "Bru" became a living, distinct entity as far as the ILO project was concerned.

Could Sisouk's own ethnicity be defined as strategic? His involvement in the ILO project seems to support that analysis. Ethnic solidarity is reinforced as the reaction of a culturally distinct periphery against the centre. Under these circumstances, ethnic differences do not disappear and indeed may form the basis for collective action by members of the peripheral communities against the central community because ethnic identity cannot be detached from one's economic and political interests within the system. Sisouk is, through his project of creating a "Bru" ethnic identity, his own cultural agent. As a Lao anthropologist, he has been, and still is being, strongly influenced by the Soviet and Vietnamese ethnographic traditions. His study of minorities, like his conception of the "Bru" cultural identity, is therefore very much guided by taxonomic principles, whereby cultures are conceived of as bound, static and objective. For instance, he explained to me in a vague fashion that the eight ethnic groups[23] shared the same language — or, at least, they could understand each other — as well as a few traditions, though he did not specify which ones.

However, during a discussion with him on criteria for ethnic classification, he himself admitted that even the villagers from his native area were not conscious of their "Bru" identity. He also acknowledged that language could be a tricky criterion for drawing distinctions, as two ethnic groups could share the same language. He gave the example of his own father's village, Namtok, in Savannakhet, where no one spoke "Bru" any longer. In addition, they were all Buddhist. I then asked him how they introduced themselves. "Lao" he replied, a hint of disappointment in his voice. "But it doesn't matter!" he added. "They know in their heart that they're ethnic people (*pen khòn sònphaw*)!" Yet, there was no evidence of a higher degree of ethnic incorporation. Thus, the anthropologist, Stephen Sparkes, who carried out a study for the Nam Theun 2 dam project in Khammuan Province in 1997, reported that the people living in the area were embarrassed about his (Sparkes') use of the term "Bru" as it had derogatory connotations. Worse, another anthropologist who visited a few "Makong" villages in a district in Savannakhet in March 2001, revealed that the people dismissed the name "Bru" as a colonial term![24] In essence, the process of identification seemed to remain limited to a restricted number of persons, namely, Sisouk and his followers. Some of them were themselves LFNC officials in Khammuan and Savannakhet Provinces, Sisouk's territorial strongholds (his mother and father's native provinces, respectively). These two provinces, with Bolikhamsai in central Laos, were the only ones to list the "Bru" as an ethnic group in Sisouk's version of the 2000 census, the most extreme case being Savannakhet where there were only three groups listed — Lao, Phuthai and "Bru" — despite this being the most populous province of the country.

The reason for his ethnic chauvinism cannot be reduced to a mere competition for resources either. Sisouk cleverly understands the politics of culture and the desire of the international community to protect so-called "indigenous people". However, at the present time the benefits from such a strategy of ethnic incorporation remain largely uncertain. The newly released 2001 Lao census by the LFNC still does not recognize the "Bru" as an official ethnic group. Moreover, Sisouk lacks the support of those he seeks to categorize as "Bru". To sum up, his ethnicity is socially irrelevant outside his group of followers. In such uncertain conditions, Sisouk's actions are for the present unlikely to influence the government's official ethnic labelling and classification. He may count on the long-term effect of the labelling process, through which the name becomes the identity. As long as these people regard the name "Bru" as a colonial legacy and ignore it, however, it is difficult to see a process of self-identification occurring again as a result of the input of an external categorization. In 2002, Sisouk took early retirement from the LFNC. His views on ethnicity and ethnic classification apparently no longer corresponded with those of the mass organization. He was replaced by a Phunoy official who, coincidentally or not, succeeded in having the ethnonym of "Phunoy" (literally meaning in Lao "small people") replaced by that of "Singsili" (another name used for the province of Phongsaly) in the official ethnic classification, without consulting any other members of the ethnic group at the local level (many of whom still disagree with the name change[25]).

People — foreigners and Lao — who know Sisouk usually describe his ethnic chauvinism as if it were another aspect of his eccentric character, a sort of joke or piece of wishful thinking. Nevertheless, as a high-ranking official, how could he entertain such unorthodox ideas as regards the egalitarian rhetoric, thereby challenging the political and cultural (national) homogeneity? My suggestion is that what Balibar has called the "community of race" (Balibar 1997, p. 136), which along with the community of language forms the "fictive ethnicity", is flawed in present-day Laos. By "community of race", Balibar refers to the sentiments of common roots and shared history felt by one people within a bounded territory. However, the newly reformulated narrative of the nation in post-socialist Laos, which is increasingly centred on an essentialist ethnic Lao core, appears to be less effective in subsuming cultural differences.

I would predict that statistical stability will remain the authorities' imperative. In Richard Handler's acute observation, nationalist discourses are "attempts to construct bounded cultural objects" (Handler 1988, p. 27). Consequently, too dramatic a change (in one way or another) of the census would indubitably disrupt the whole picture of the nation. As Eriksen notes: "[N]ationalism reifies culture in the sense that it enables people to talk about their culture as though it were constant" (Eriksen 1993, p. 103). The Lao PDR's authorities are still in search of the symbol of national identity in the form of an almost sacred number, i.e. that of the total of ethnic groups. In order to keep the number of 47 ethnic groups they could have turned their back on the claims discussed above. I suspect, however, that pressures for clarity and order were too strong to be ignored. In the final section below, I furthermore argue that the census' pattern has been influenced by Kaysone Phomvihane's 1981 guidelines on ethnicity and nationalism in Laos.

Kaysone Phomvihane's theory of nationhood

Kaysone's guidelines on nation and ethnicity

Kaysone Phomvihane's guidelines still strongly influence Lao nationalist discourse. In particular, his booklet entitled, "Expanding Roots of Solidarity between Various Ethnic Groups within the Lao National Community", written in 1981, is still referred to as the ideological bedrock for works on ethnic groups, including the censuses and the ethnographic studies. In one section, Kaysone explained the different processes that led to the emergence of nations. He develops his views in a lengthy argument, of which large extracts are well worth citing in order to understand the idea of nationhood that still permeates the nationalist ideology in the Lao PDR:

Clans: [...] (kòk)] and tribes [(law)] [...] are communities of individuals living only in a primitive subsistence society that lacks stability and relational consistency. In the present day, in some underdeveloped countries, there are still remains of this type of society of clans and tribes: based on kinship, ancient stratification, psychology, lineage, 'animist' practices and wedding rituals, etc.

Then, along with the development of production, the society divides into classes (sònsàn). The clans and tribes, in general, disintegrate due to the broadening of relationships between peoples from different clans and tribes, and to the apparition of new economic bases. A new human community has been created. That is the ethnic group [(phaw)].

Ethnic group: Each ethnic group has its own language. But there is as yet no language unity in each area. There are even real differences, due to the fact that individuals from the same ethnic group went to seek refuge and mixed with those from another ethnic group. The ethnic groups' economy is based on self-sufficiency, which does not promote the development of economic and cultural exchanges, and which also explains the non-homogenous character of ethnic groups' languages.

The ethnic group formed with the slavery system and subsisted until the feudal period in the history of human society. It can be the basis for the formation of a nation, as in the case of Austria, Hungary, Russia, Georgia, etc.

An ethnic group can be the constituent basis for a certain number of nations, as is the case of the Russian ethnic group, which is the common origin for Russian, Ukrainian, Byelorussian ethnic groups, which later on became Russia, Ukraine and Byelorussia.

A certain number of ethnic groups in a country can blend into a nation, as is the case with France, Germany, Italy, England, etc.

Some ethnic groups in certain countries can progressively get along with one another in the fields of language, psychology, as well as in economic and territorial areas so as to become nations. This is the case with ethnic groups that united throughout historical periods to struggle against external aggression and to protect the nation subjected to the feudal system, such as Vietnam, for example.

As a matter of fact, this is the case with the ethnic groups of all colonies, which unite to resist imperialism, to achieve independence, freedom and to become a nation [...] as well as a united country [...], such as some Asian and African countries in the history of the contemporary world.

Thus, the word "<u>nationality</u>" [(*sat*)] (*nation*)[27] [...] is not the outcome of man's will, neither of the administrative power's imaginative efforts. It is the consequence of the impact of economic and social laws. Consequently, a nationality is a community of individuals that normally emerges in history, on the basis of common language, territory, economic lifestyle and psychology that reflects a cultural community. This is what appears in Western European countries, such as England, France, Italy, while feudalism collapses and capitalism develops. As far as eastern countries are concerned, such as Laos, Vietnam and Cambodia, etc., they emerged during different historical periods. Despite their different ways of forming, the national communities, once created, are characterised internally by four characteristics, i.e. language, territory, economy and culture. An ethnic group also possesses these four features, but they are not consistent. Dealing with the improvement of national unity simply means dealing with the improvement of these four features. [...]

<u>A nation (*pàthet sat*)[...]</u>: is clearly distinguished from "race" (*seuasat*) [...] and "nationality" (*sat*)[...]. A nation is the whole community or a group of several communities, each of them having different features, but united within the same historical destiny, with the will of living on the same territory, under the same administration, constitution and laws. A nation can consist of only one nationality (*sat*) [...] (for example, Korea, Eastern Germany, Japan, etc.), or of several nationalities (*sat*) or several ethnic groups (*phaw*) (for example, several Asian and African countries) (Kaysone 1981, pp. 19–25).

In their book on *Asian Forms of the Nation*, Tønnesson and Antlöv classified the nationalist "route" that the Lao PDR, like China, Vietnam, and to a lesser extent, Cambodia, followed, as *class struggle* or *social revolution*, during which the population seized power from the colonial state to form a "state based on an ideology of class struggle" (Tønnesson and Antlöv 1998, p. 22, original emphasis). During the first years of communist rule, the Socialist Revolution indeed planned to create a loyalty to the new state greater than the loyalties to particular ethnic identities. In other words, the priority was to overwhelm the ethnic identities with "the principle of the primacy of politics" (Gunn 1991, p. 530), which claimed to be able to outline an ideal social and political order on the basis of universal ideas and then to act politically to realize it. The regime's real objective was not to build a society based on national consciousness; rather, the concept of class was thought to be the new society's main axis of identification. The ultimate goal for the Lao communists, as it had been for their Soviet, Chinese and Vietnamese counterparts, was to eradicate the "old" identities and replace them by a "socialist" one. Kaysone asserted in 1976: "The building of socialism does not only consist of creating new relations of production and new productive forces, but also in contributing a new superstructure. If one wants to create new relations of production and new productive forces, there must be new, socialist men" (Kaysone 1977, p. 78).[155]

However, by the time Kaysone wrote his booklet, the second phase of the regime had been underway for two years. The Seventh Resolution of the Supreme People's Assembly was endorsed in December 1979. This document proposed a number of important changes in economic policy in order to improve the disastrous economic performance that characterized the first four years of the new administration. It admitted that, while Laos might be in the process of "bypassing capitalism", it was going to take time to construct a socialist economy. Restrictions on private production and internal trade were liberalized; price controls were abolished for goods sold on the free market. Economic management of state enterprises was reformed by adopting profit as the criterion of efficiency (Stuart-Fox 1986, p. 61).

In 1981, Kaysone certainly believed in the construction of a socialist society, but ethnicity persisted as a vertical phenomenon that cut across class and socioeconomic strata, despite the land reform and collectivization campaigns. Ethnicity did not fade away as expected. Kaysone's classification of social entities suggests an ethnic character to his theory of nationhood: "one ethnic group can form the basis of a nation". However, he clearly rejected that "route" in explaining the creation of Laos as a nation. Meanwhile, Kaysone cleverly proposed the idea of nationhood based on sentiments. Ethnic groups, thus, may share nothing but the will to pursue a life in common and thereby form a nation. They are joined together, in Kaysone's terms, "within the same historical destiny, with the will of living on the same territory, under the same administration, constitution and laws". They united to fight and defeat the "imperialists" together. The sense of solidarity that allowed them to gain victory has endured since then. The emotions that emerged under hardship have become the cement of the new nation. Kaysone's theory of the creation of the Lao nation is arguably subjectivist, civic-orientated and modernist. Paraphrasing Gellner's famous words (1964), the drive for "independence and freedom" led to the emergence of the Lao nation where it did not exist before. It also transcends linguistic and cultural differences, as the constitution of a nation is defined by the concomitance of territory, national community and the modern state. In other words, in Kaysone's theory, the peoples who live within the national boundaries belong to the Lao nation–state, but this population needs controlling and subordinating under the State's project of constructing a nation.

Control of ethnicity

In his glossary of human organizations (1999), directly inspired by Kaysone's 1981 writing, Noychansamon Denchaleunsouk (pen name of an LFNC member) highlights the distinction between "ethnic group", "nationality" and "nation". He points out the fundamental distinction between the juridical/political and ethno-cultural concept of nationality. Likewise, he reapplies Kaysone's subjectivist and civic definition of "nation". His definitions are as follows:

Ethnic group [sòn phaw]: [...] community of individuals forged by history, on the basis of common language, roots and naming, sharing thoughts and psyche that reflect a cultural community. [...]

Nationality [sànsat]: community of individuals that belong to the same country, on a legal basis, no matter what their physical and cultural differences;

Nation [*pàthet sat*]: all the communities having different characteristics which join in the same historical destiny, and which are willing to live on the same territory, under the same administration, constitution and laws.

Nationality [*sat*] or National category or large ethnic group [*sònsat* or *sòn phaw nyai*]: it is not formed by human aspirations, or by the will of the executive authority. It is the result of the impacts of the whole socio-economic system. Therefore, a nationality truly means all the human communities that emerged in history, on the basis of common language, territory, livelihood, thoughts and diverse cultural features (Noychansamon 1999, pp. 1 and 2).

According to the above definition, a "nationality" (in the ethno-cultural sense) — or "national category" or "large ethnic group" — has similar characteristics to those of an "ethnic group", but the difference is that a "nationality" would arise from socio-economic inequalities: some "ethnic groups" would dominate, and eventually absorb the others. The Lao State, applying the Stalinist model of ethnicity, defines an ethnic group as a cultural totality. An ethnic group is identified by a set of taxonomic features, and according to the evolutionist theory used by Kaysone, it succeeds the "clan" and the "tribe" but is the predecessor of the "national community" or "nationality". Kaysone's distinction between "nationality" and "ethnic group" is not always clear; these terms sometimes appear to be interchangeable in his text. Nonetheless, "nationality", in the sense of cultural community, seems to suggest a more advanced stage, whereas "ethnic groups" are still described as "inconsistent" and "non-homogenous" entities. In Laos, the "ethnic groups" have not reached the status of a "national category" or "large ethnic group", and probably will not under the present ideology for the authorities are careful not to allow the formation of "nationalities" (or "national category" or "large ethnic group") among the existing, officially recognized, ethnic groups that could numerically rival the size of the ethnic Lao majority. This is the reason why claims such as Sisouk's (for the admission of the "Bru" as an ethnic category) have little chance of success. Anyhow, this LFNC official and member of the Communist Party is certainly conscious of the risk of politicizing his ethnicity, for which he would likely be accused of threatening the equilibrium of the nation.[28] For the purpose of controlling ethnicity, the state in Laos defines what is "correct" in terms of language, locality, and culture — regardless of a group's subjective belief in its existence as a people or in the legitimacy of these state-defined cultural traditions. The deviant peoples will not become full members of the ideologically defined nation unless they stop claiming their right to a self-defined identity.

This rule, however, does not seem to apply to the ethnic Lao group. In the Lao language, there is only one term ("Lao") to designate both the ideas of ethnicity and nationality. The ambiguity is therefore as much linguistic as conceptual. Used in the legalistic sense, the term "Lao" should be viewed as an a-ethnic and a-racial status, attributed to members of all ethnic groups. The term "Lao", in other words, is used as a synecdoche for the whole population. Thus, ambiguity thrives on the equivocal use of the term. Yet, textually, "Lao" refers to an ethnic group since it derives from a group to whom are attached specific characteristics. But this rule never strictly applies to the ethnic Lao, because the "Lao culture is shared by all the ethnic groups. It is composed of the best of each ethnic group's culture. The ethnic Lao language is the vernacular language, and the script is the national script for all the ethnic groups" (Kaysone 1981, p. 49). Again, Kaysone wrote:

> Our country is among those that have several ethnic groups, of which the ethnic Lao group has a greater population than the others, located in almost all the provinces and holding a superior degree of economic and cultural development. Each ethnic group shares common characteristics with the Lao national community (ibid., p. 47).

The census, accordingly, perfectly depicts this form of the nation. Indeed, the ethnic Lao are always put at the top of the list followed by the scattered "ethnic groups".

Conclusion

The egalitarian policy that held all ethnic groups to be equal (economically, socially and politically) was initiated under wartime conditions as part of the Communists' survival strategy. The goal was to gain highlanders' loyalty and their support for the Pathet Lao troops. After 1975, the strategic plan was turned into an ideological programme of preservation and promotion of every ethnic group's "culture". The principle, copied from the Stalinist model, was to give every member of the "multiethnic" state official recognition on an equal footing. In consequence, the new regime created "ethnic groups" as equals in their membership of the nation. In reality, the egalitarian ideology serves another purpose: the State, as a vector of ethnicity, actively manipulates, creates, suppresses (or maintains) ethnic boundaries, the ultimate objective being the formation of a homogenous national culture out of real heterogeneity.

Meanwhile, the concepts of ethnicity and nationality seem to be conflated with regard to ethnicity of the ethnic Lao. As Banks comments, "the nation's defining group, the one that claims the national label as its own [...], is not then simply another 'ethnic group', it is very deliberately and self-consciously everything and nothing" (Banks 1997, p. 160). Two interdependent processes are involved in the construction of a nation, once state control is achieved: on the one hand *reifying diversity* — through which ethnicity is enhanced and controlled *outside* the cultural mainstream but *within* the national paradigm, and *homogenizing* — the blending-in process where ethnicity both as a process and as a category is suppressed.

However, in the case of Laos, these two processes of mapping nationhood are hampered by inconsistency, which reduces their effectiveness. As has been discussed, the 2000 population census, behind its ordered facade, is in reality the product of multiple negotiations and arbitrary decisions that leave members of some ethnic groups confused and sometimes resentful. It is the lack of consistency that prevents this technology of power from becoming "natural" and from becoming integrated in individuals' minds. The continued popular and official use of the threefold category, Lao Lum, Lao Theung and Lao Sung, in contemporary Laos, despite Kaysone's 1981 call for its replacement, thus epitomizes the Lao state's deficit of power. Sisouk's lobbying for the visibility of the "Bru" in the census may be another example of the regime's deficiencies in controlling ethnicity. Nonetheless (and this will be the focus of my next chapter) the state's strategies of control over people's ethnicities are facing an unexpected backlash from those very persons whose self-identification these policies aim to mould.

Notes

[1]   See, for instance, Charles Hirschman (1986 and 1987).

[2]   For the 1911 census figures, the data came from the *Bulletin de l'Office colonial* (No. 62, February 1913).

[3]   However, in 1953 the term "nationalities" was used for the heading of a census referring to "European, Vietnamese, Chinese and Cambodian" populations. These appeared to be Lao citizens, since there is another table referring to the same populations based on the same source but which gives the list of the "proportion of each nationality in the foreign populations" (Halpern 1961, p. 45. quoted, in turn, from *Annuaire des Etats Associes*, 1953). But, the distinction between "ethnic groups" and "nationalities" appeared rather fuzzy and did not seem to follow a coherent pattern (for example, in the 1955 census, the Vietnamese, Chinese and European populations were still included in the ethnic composition of the population as "group") (Halpern 1961, p. 19. quoted, in turn, from *Annuaire Statistique du Laos*, Lao Ministry of Interior).

[4]   See the 1940 system of taxation in "The Colonial System of Taxation", Chapter 2.

[5]   Curiously enough, a handwritten note was added below the original table of the Appendix 2 suggesting that the non-Lao groups were indeed underestimated.

[6]   Certes, le problème ethnique au Laos ne sera pas aussi complexe qu'au Siam, car au Laos, l'élément lao prédomine nettement et indiscutablement, tant par son importance numérique que par son degré de développement social et culturel. [...] des Bolovens ou des Mèos [sic] instruits et évolués tendent à se rapprocher de plus en plus de nous, tant dans leur façon de s'habiller et dans leur manière de vivre que dans leur idéal patriotique, au point de vouloir se faire appeler maintenant sous le nom de "Lao Theung" (Katay 1953, p. 21).

[7]   Quoted, in turn, from Luther (1983, p. 44).

[8]   Chinese term, of Japanese origin, that can be translated as "nation", "people", "nationality" or "ethnic group" (Gladney 1998, p. 117).

[9]   After their victory over the French, the Vietminh rewarded its minority supporters by creating in 1955 and 1956 two Autonomous Regions — respectively, the Tai-Meo zone in the northwest and the Viet Bac zone in the northeast. However, the reunification of the country in 1975 heralded a return to the minority policy of the 1946 Constitution that had made no mention of self-determination. Thus, ignoring the provisions of the 1960 Constitution, the government announced on 29 December 1975, its decision to dissolve the Autonomous Regions.

[10] I use a pseudonym here. See also Chapter 4, pp. 107–8, 110, 111.

[11] I have the version updated in 1999, but apparently Sisouk has been using these guidelines since the late 1970s when he started his ethnographic research in the Lao PDR. Personal communication.

[12] Quoted in turn from John Fineberg (ed.), *Marxism and the National and Colonial Question* (1936).

[13] I use here the term "minorities" instead of "groups" for it is evident that the civilizing project was not applied to the political majority that is also an "ethnic group" according to the Stalinist definition.

[14] Patricia M. Pelley has recently shown, however, that ethnic classification in Post-war Vietnam also resulted from a complex and often arbitrary exercise of fixing ethnic identities yet chiefly characterized by their fluidity. As a matter of fact, it was not until that the General Department of Statistics issued Decision 121 on the "nomenclature of Vietnamese ethnic groups" in March 1979 that the number of precisely fifty-four ethnic groups was officially and permanently adopted, while just a year before official sources were still commonly referring to the "more than sixty" ethnic groups in Vietnam (Pelley 2002, pp. 104–5).

[15] The five areas were the South (Champassak, Saravane, Sekong and Attapeu); the Centre (Savannakhet, Khammuan and Bolikhamsai); the North-West (Udomxay, Phongsaly, Luang Namtha and Bokeo); the North-East (Luang Prabang, Huaphan, Xieng Khuang and Saysombun); and an area including Vientiane, its prefecture and the adjacent province of Saignabouli.

[16] Kado, Kanai, Tong, In, Yàng, Meuang, Kàyong, Thai Rat/Lat, Summa, Bri/Labri, King, Thai Neua, Thaen.

[17] Phongsaly, Luang Namtha and Bokeo. As for the Thaen (separated from the Kmmu), I can only make suppositions. As Sisouk disagrees with the idea of granting them the status of "ethnic group", the other reason could be that they are influential enough to have gained visibility themselves.

[18] The Lahu ethnic group is also listed in the Thai and Vietnamese population censuses.

[19] A third group, the Khir, was simply suppressed for an unknown reason.

[20] The "correct" ethnic groups are as follows, with their former names in parentheses: Kmmu (Khammu), Y'ru (Lavaen), Tlieng/Trieng (Talieng), Blao/Brao (Lavè), Krieng (Ngae), Rarak/Lalak (Alak), Iumien (Yao), Akha (Kor), Singsili (Phounoy), Lahu (Kui and Mousseu), Sila (Sida).

 The four Vietnamese ethnic groups are: Kho-mu (Khmmu), Brâu (Brao), La Hu (Lahu), Si Là (Sila).

[21] Likewise, the Katu or Kantu, another Austro-Asiatic ethnic group that can be found both in Laos and Vietnam, were among their highland neighbours known as the "people who live in the mountains" (Le Pichon 1938, p. 363).

[22] These 8 ethnic groups are: Kàtang, Màkong, T'ri/T'li, Tà-Oy, Pàkò, Suay, Kàtu, Tlieng/Trieng. Sisouk also includes the sub-categories Kanay, In, Tong, Kàdu.

[23] Makong, Pàkò, Tri, Kàtang, Ngae, Katu, Tà-Oy, Suay.

[24] I thank an anonymous informant for the telling account.

[25] I would like to thank Vanina Bouté for this information.

[26] Kaysone translated the word *sat* as "nation". However, the term "nationality", in its cultural sense, seems to be a more appropriate translation in the light of his definition that follows; all the more so as, in the next paragraph, he refers again to the concept of nation, but this time using the term *pàthet sat, pàthet* meaning "country".

[27] Kaysone Phomvihane, *Rapport sur la situation de l'an dernier, les orientations et les tâches révolutionaires dans la nouvelle étape et les orientations pour 1977*, quoted from Amphay Doré (1982, p. 106).

[28] Sisouk told me about an intriguing conversation he had with his friend, who is himself (in Sisouk's words) a high-ranking "Bru" official. His friend apparently told him that there was a "Bru" association in France. Sisouk, then, asked him jokingly if he wanted to set up a similar association in Laos as well, which prompted his friend to retort: "Are you mad? Do you want us to get arrested?"

7

From Inclusion to
Re-marginalization[1]

According to the accepted wisdom, political, economic, social and cultural globalization in the late twentieth century brought about structural changes, most visibly, the decrease in the nation–state's capacity to fulfil its missions (for instance, the diminution of welfare in the case of Western European countries) and the erosion of national cultures once perceived as homogenous — that has in turn led to the fragmentation of identities (Tambini 2002). In essence, some analysts proclaim, national identity is in a state of crisis. In so-called postmodern societies, as McCrone advises, one should no longer assume "that there is much fixed, essential or immutable about identity, but that individuals assume different identities at different times which may not even be centred around a coherent self" (McCrone 1998, p. 32). Hence, from the proclaimed death of the idea of a "stable" identity has emerged the notion of "dislocation or de-centring of the subject" (Hall 1994, p. 275).

In this chapter, I would like to explore not so much the processes of globalization as this idea of fluidity and plurality of identities within the context of ideological, cultural and economic change in today's Lao society.

I have tried in the previous chapter to show the political mechanisms by which the Lao authorities attempt to forge an orderly and bounded representation of the country's culturally and linguistically diverse population with the support of state-controlled ethnographic research and the census. I intend now to discuss the notion of different coexisting (and perhaps conflicting) identities among the members of ethnic minorities whom I encountered in the course of my fieldwork, by examining their own perceptions of their ethnicity, national identity and citizenship in post-communist Laos. More specifically, how do these people take on a national identity that is increasingly essentialized? Likewise, how do they handle an ethnic labelling over which they have little, if any, control? It is paradoxically in the rural areas of southern Laos that I met veterans of the "Vietnam Wars" for whom the notion of citizenship was still quite compelling. The ties that bound them to the state anchored their identities to a larger community than their village or ethnic group. They felt a sense of belonging to, and being active participants in, a political community that, however, seemed no longer to recognize them.

Infra-politics in Ban Paktai

On my first visit to Ban Paktai, I wrongly assumed that Khamsing, a very tall and well-built man whom I understood was a direct descendant of Ong Keo (though at the time I did not know what his kinship tie was with his ancestor), was the head of the village, so authoritative was he with the other villagers and so at ease with the Lao official who accompanied me. Conversely, the real head of the village was so discreet that I was unable to confirm his identity until my second visit. Khamsing offered us a meal after we finished our work and then spent most of the rest of the evening talking with Sisouk after they realized that they had some common friends back in Savannakhet, where Khamsing fought in the 1970s. They even started talking in Vietnamese, as both of them had studied in Hanoi. Khamsing and Phumi, the Communist Party's village representative, were actually the only two men who directly addressed

Sisouk. They solemnly asked him for permission to talk, then bent down to the wooden floor with their palms joined over their heads. Thus, Khamsing and Phumi displayed signs of allegiance before Sisouk (the high-ranking official who had travelled a long distance from the central level especially to come to the village) and in front of myself (vaguely perceived as his protégée). The contrast between Khamsing and Phumi, on the one hand, and the rest of the villagers present during the meeting, who mostly remained quietly in the background unless they were asked a question, on the other, was quite striking.

It would take me several visits over a period of a year and a half to make sense of the power relations and political organization of the village. Several people (all of whom were men) would insist with me that it was he who was, or ought to be, the legitimate powerholder to rule the village and its inhabitants. To put it roughly, the tensions and disputes over the "ownership" (*chao khong*) of the village opposed the "civilians" (*pasason*) (i.e. those who did not join the Revolution) to the "revolutionaries" (*khon pativat*), such as Khamsing and Phumi. Yet, despite their military credentials, their status-role as "revolutionaries" had lost its aura in the village. The "civilians" dismissed their pasts and ignored their claims to have fought "for the Nation". The revolutionaries' own guilt furthermore deepened their sense of loss. They were ashamed of their condition, their final return to the village after years of fighting, studying and travelling (sometimes abroad). My following analysis will focus on three former revolutionaries in the village, two men and one woman. They shared a similar background, left their village during their adolescence in the 1960s to study in northern Laos and in Vietnam, then enrolled in the army and worked in the socialist administration. They settled back in the village after retiring early in the late 1980s and early 1990s. The three of them were more or less ostracized in the village because of the fear and contempt they inspired. They were also outcast, I argue, because of the "hidden transcript" employed by those same people who looked remarkably submissive in front of Sisouk, the high-ranking official from Vientiane, during his visit a few months ago. My suggestion is that in this village the public transcript of the Revolution (the former revolutionaries being the voice of the "public transcript", that is, the official discourse of the state) was battered by the contrapuntal discourse of the peasants — those who did not become soldiers or civil servants under the Revolution.

I returned alone to the village about a month and a half later. While heading to the house of the village chief, I saw Khamsing's tall silhouette slightly hidden between two houses a few metres away. He was wearing what seemed to be a worn-out red bathrobe. He looked scruffy as if he had just woken up and still recovering from a hangover. He saw me, too. As I was pondering whether it would be wise to go and talk to him at that particular time, the village chief and his wife came to meet me and took me to their house. They immediately warned me against him: "Don't get close to Khamsing! He's lost his mind; one of the nerves in his brain's burst!". They then explained that his present condition was the pathetic result of too many drinking sessions. The contrast between the man wandering aimlessly in the village that morning and the former revolutionary visibly delighted and proud to confide his war memories to Sisouk a few weeks earlier left me intrigued and perplexed.

Khamsing left the village in 1961 for Vieng Xai, Sam Neua, following the advice of his father who wanted him to go and study in Hanoi. Accordingly, the following year he went to the then capital of the DRV to study what he called "culture" courses (that were part of a general curriculum). "There were one thousand people, Lao people. From all over the country, all the provinces!" he told me, obviously moved by memories that were still vivid. He returned to Sam Neua in 1965 and was rapidly integrated into a battalion. He then was sent successively, with return trips to Sam Neua between each mission, to: Meuang Hiem, Luang Prabang Province (1965–66); Meuang Kham, Xieng Kouang Province (1967–69); Savannakhet Province (1971–73), and was then finally transferred to Vientiane in 1974. He went to Vietnam for a second time in 1982 for a year, until his wife asked him to come back to Laos, arguing that she could no longer bring up their family on her own. He finally retired in 1987 and returned to Ban Paktai in 1991.

Over the following weeks, I asked other villagers about Khamsing and his "madness": the story was more complicated than a simple diagnosis of excessive drinking. The son of the head of the LFNC and his wife told me that there was a period when Khamsing used to roam around the village waving an axe and accusing whomever was in his way to have cast a spell on him. They obviously thought that Khamsing was not only mad but also dangerous and unpredictable. During my next visit I noticed his absence and was told that he had gone to "the hospital" because of his detoriating mental health. Later on, I had the opportunity to ask Khamsing about his "hospitalization", however, and found out that the word was most likely a euphemistic and convenient way to explain Khamsing's absence and distancing from the village. He lowered his voice and replied that he never went to the hospital but instead stayed in a nearby village for several weeks to obtain a cure and to recover from the illness, which the people from his own village had inflicted upon him and which had paralysed the entire lower half of his body. The man visibly appeared to be paranoid. Why then would he come back to a place where he believed his life was at risk? It was not impossible for him to move to another village, as Thongkham had. My conversations with Khamsing and the villagers left me with no answers.

Meanwhile, the village was preparing for the election of the next village chief. The current head made clear that he would step down after holding the position for the past six years. A few days later, Khamsing declared during a village meeting his wish to become the next village chief. His candidature was received in silence by the crowd, though, and when I asked an elderly woman her opinion about it, she replied with little hesitation that it was Tone, the oldest son of the head of the LFNC, who would be "elected". Her assertive guess was confirmed by other villagers, including the wife of the present village chief and Khamsing himself! The man's attitude made even less sense to me now, unless I was willing to believe that he had truly lost his mind and in consequence, there was no logic or coherence to be sought behind his actions and words. My perception and understanding of the situation changed again when I met

Thongkham who was visiting the village during the New Year's celebrations in late February. We were all drinking in Khamsing's house. I had not mentioned either his "hospitalization" nor his candidature when the war veteran suddenly claimed that Khamsing was the true legitimate head of the village: "Nieung, Bounmak, Thongdi, they all look down on him now that they're rich; now they've gained some social status (*thana*)!", he complained. "But it is Khamsing who should be in their position because he's the heir of the oldest lineage in the village. His father, my oldest brother, taught me how to fight!". Khamsing nodded but said nothing. The three men whom Thongkham named were the oldest and the most well-off in the village, but more importantly in his eyes they did not have any revolutionary credentials to show: they did not spend their adult life (and part of their teenage years), unlike Khamsing, his father and himself, fighting against "the French and the Americans". In other words, they have usurped the power that Khamsing deserved to hold in the village. The reason why Khamsing came back to the village and volunteered for the position of village chief became suddenly clear: he believed that he was the true "owner" of the place.

Thongkham referred to a lineage which he and Khamsing belonged to and which he claimed was the oldest; however, according to the rest of the village, Nieung's lineage was the older of the two. I rapidly realized upon my second visit to Ban Paktai that the true head of the village was Nieung, the representative of the LFNC, as he was the most senior member of the dominant lineage of the main ethnic group, the *Ngè* as they call themselves, in Ban Paktai. It was he who in the following days guided me in my research on Ong Keo. The least poor villagers also happen to be those who did not "join the revolution" (*huam kan pàtìvàt*). Nieung told me briefly in his interview with me that he had been neither on "the enemy's side nor with the French nor with the Lao Issala": "I didn't go anywhere. I didn't fight on anybody's side". In fact, he was among the first ones to return to the village after the end of the war. He came back in 1977 after having fled to a village 25 km outside Pakse, the capital of Champassak Province, where he stayed for the next 20 years. As for Bounmak, a man in his sixties

and Nieung's cousin and assistant in his LFNC duties, he and his family
were the only household who never left the village. They stayed in the
forest nearby during the periods of most intense fighting. As a matter of
fact, he served both under the "French/American" army and under the
Issara troops. He thus told me, laconically: "it depended on the sides. They
were swapping all the time. All we did was to follow". He is now the head
of one of the least poor households in the village. His extended family (his
household includes his two daughters and their husbands, his son and
daughter-in-law and one grandchild) is among the few who possess a wet
rice field (see Table 1 in footnotes)[2] and they were planning to dig a joint
irrigation canal with Bounmak's brother (who also lives in the village) in
2001. One evening, a stormy argument erupted between Nieung, Khamsing
and Bounmak. The three men had already drunk a sizeable amount of
alcohol. They were shouting in Nieung's house. The rest of the family (his
son and daughter-in-law, his youngest daughter) and me had already
gone to sleep. But we were soon woken up by the violent dispute. Bounmak
began by accusing Khamsing of laziness, of spending his time drinking
and waking up late while the others were already at work. Khamsing
retorted that he was a "revolutionary" who had helped the country, unlike
him and Nieung. Bounmak then abruptly replied that the "Party-State did
not feed the people". In their houses, outside the public view and when
government officials are gone, the villagers speak words of defiance and
self-assertion. I have already shown in a previous chapter the villagers'
divergent version of Ong Keo's rebellion against the colonial authorities;
they told me their narrative of their ancestor's past when I came back
without the high-ranking official who was unable to accompany me for
my second visit. It is immodest to claim that my presence alone inspired
the villagers to expose their dissident views. Rather I would suggest that
I was the mere witness of a "hidden transcript"; in James C. Scott's words,
"a critique of power spoken behind the back of the dominant" (Scott 1990,
p. xii). Yet, their narrative of Ong Keo as a local hero was not a subversive
discourse in its fullest sense; the villagers suscribed to the official view

that Ong Keo was an anti-colonialist and anti-imperialist leader, too. The hidden transcript as the "privileged site for nonhegemonic discourse" (Scott 1990, p. 25) was located elsewhere, at the heart of the village's political life.

The reasons for Khamsing's accusations of sorcery and his apparent madness was to be sought in the economy and power relations of the village. Khamsing, as well as Phumi, endure the loss of their status, being reduced now in their own words to plain *pàsasòn* ("ordinary person"), as a form of punishment mixed with sentiments of guilt and shame. Moreover, their families were among the poorest households in the village. Individuals, like Khamsing and Phumi, had to accept what land was left when they quit the Army and came back to the village years later. But they bitterly resented, especially Khamsing, their condition and the domination of the hierarchy by the "civilians", i.e. Nieung, Bounmak, Thongdi. Every year they failed to grow enough rice to be self-sufficient. During my fieldwork, I heard that Khamsing had offered his labour in exchange for rice, but his offer was refused because the harvest season was long over (which was true). Phumi also lacked rice every year. As a result, their debts kept increasing and provoked scorn among the other villagers. Their poor harvests were interpreted as being a result of their laziness and heavy drinking. The other villagers thought that they had themselves to blame for their poor condition; it was their own fault if they had an "irresponsible way of living". However, Khamsing, unlike Phumi, believed that his misfortunes were caused by external forces. It was clear to him that the reason why he was unable to efficiently perform the daily activities that were demanded in an agricultural, peasant and subsistence economy was because he had been bewitched: the illness caused by the spell had left him physically weakened. In other words, an evil spell was responsible for his failure to secure his household's economic survival. More crucially, Khamsing believed that the curse sought to keep him away from the village and to stop him from claiming back his "ownership" of it. I never knew if he suspected anyone in particular of being the sorcerer; but he visibly resented the village as a whole for his unfortunate condition. Likewise, the villagers had little trust and respect for him. His "madness", or the perception of it, was in effect a convenient way for them to dismiss his accusations of sorcery and whatever else he claimed, including the "ownership" of the village.

The mechanisms of marginalization of the "revolutionaries" took other forms in the village. There was also Nok, a woman who was strongly feared. I was told that she could cast spells of ill-health on people. On the other hand, she also possessed the capacity to cure unmentionable "diseases" that mostly affected women who did not care about their reputations. In brief, I was advised not to listen to her and not to go to her house, because she was "powerful" and "insane" — a fearful combination indeed. Her external appearance was also distinctive. She wore her hair short, which was very unusual for a woman (at least in the countryside) and always wore an army shirt that covered the upper half of her sarong. She walked fast and talked loudly and abruptly. In addition, she mixed more often with men than women, and felt equally comfortable with both genders. In fact, she was considered to be an immoral woman. Each of her trips outside the village was interpreted, especially by the women, as a device to enable her to spend time with men, which was considered to be all the more immoral since she was married and had two boys from previous marriages. I also heard that she sometimes beat her husand up (he was a frail 70 year-old) and did not care much about her children's upbringing. In brief, she fit almost perfectly the stereotype of a witch: an independent adult woman who does not conform to the male (and female) idea of proper female behaviour:

> ... she is assertive; she does not require or give love...; she does not nurture men or children, nor care for the weak. She has the power of words — to defend herself or to curse. In addition, she may have other, more mysterious powers which do not derive from the established order (Larner 2002, p. 273).

Nok certainly did not conform to the village's patriarchal social structure — even Nieung was afraid of her and advised me against visiting her house. Her identification as a witch was the villagers' translation of her nonconformism and unspoken disturbance to the village's social order.

Above all, Nok was educated and was aware of it. She was a "revolutionary", as she introduced herself. Born in 1947 in Thateng district (Sekong Province), at around the age of 13, she went up to Huaphan Province, and in 1967 travelled on to Vietnam to take up courses in radio-communication for three years. From 1970 to 1980, she worked in the Department of Telecommunications in the "liberated zones": first in Phapilang district in Khammuan Province, then in the districts of Phine and Nong in Savannakhet Province. Finally, she was transferred to Kalum, in the eastern part of present-day Sekong Province. However, following an adulterous liaison, she was forced to quit her position. According to her, this was the reason why she ended up in Ban Paktai two years ago. She obviously still bitterly resented the sanction: "I became a *pasàsòn*, with no right to a pension", she complained to me. She strongly felt her loss of status as a disgrace, but at the same time kept repeating: "it is my fault, my punishment, my fate (*vatsàna*)". Feelings of guilt and shame emerged from the account when she confessed: "It's not the Party-Government's fault. It's me and only me who misbehaved, who is the sinner (*khòn bap*)". She often expressed nostalgia when recalling the war: "People were as united as if they came from the same mother's womb!" But she then carried on with a bitter tone in her voice: "Now, it's no longer the case. Nobody cares for each other; it's only for oneself!"

One evening, in a moment of sobriety, Phumi, playing down his pride at being the most educated person in the village, bitterly confessed to me that "despite my education, my experience, I've come back to square one. But that's my fate (*vatsàna*) to end up living in poverty". Khamsing, on the other hand, used the term "to abandon" (*pàthim*) (the Party-State) to explain his present situation: "It is not because the central level expelled me. I myself abandoned the Party-State", he said in his interview in a lifeless voice. The bodies of these war veterans show testimonies of the conflict. Their scars are not only performative. Phumi was wounded during his service in the army: he received a bullet in his leg (which has not yet been extracted), in addition to developing a cyst in his abdomen that he cut out himself. The messy scars were still visible. Phumi was convinced that he would die soon, but he seemed at times to suggest that his misfortune was not to have died during the war and "sacrificed his life" for the Revolution. His death would have brought closure to his narrative in a "heroic" style; instead of which he had to carry the burden of the present with little to heal his physical and psychological wounds. "[T]heir bodies are those of survivors", wrote Marita Sturken speaking of the Vietnam veterans in the United States (Sturken 1991, p. 132). Likewise, the war veterans in this village in southern Laos carry in their flesh the memories of the war; in a way, they embody an unfinished past.

Individual narratives do not necessarily produce coherence out of chaos, or meaning out of discordance, though. Indeed, narratives of self may be marked by confusion. Sentiments of loss dominate the stories of Phumi, Khamsing and Nok. For instance, the reasons behind the departure of the two men from the army will always remain a mystery to me. Both of them retired at a relatively young age (Phumi was in his early forties and Khamsing in his late forties). They explained their early retirement on the grounds of various reasons: homesickness, the desire for "peace and rest", or the wish to "raise a family". These causes are not totally convincing, though. In his interview, Khamsing became confused while trying to justify his resignation from the army:

> My father had died a long time ago, in 1977. And then my uncle died, too. There was nobody, except my mother, to look after my younger brothers and sisters. I said to my bosses that I wanted to go and have a rest, that I wanted to quit my work. So, I suggested to my boss that I become a policeman because low-level employees didn't do their job properly, didn't follow the Party's line. But I changed my mind, because I said I was getting old and felt pity for my wife who raised the family all by herself. So, I stayed. It's not because the central level sacked me. I never had any troubles with my bosses during those 25 years of army life. I never committed anything wrong against the Party. I never went through disciplinary examination. I wasn't good. I was average, enough to get along with, to work with my mates.

The brutal end to these exemplary trajectories, from exhilarating youth to an undignified return to their home village (which they accept, albeit bitterly), cannot alone explain their marginalization. The wide gap that has opened between these individuals and their society must be viewed in the larger context of structural changes in the country. I recall the time Phumi expressed his grievances to Sisouk. Before he died, he said, he wanted to know what his duties were as a Party member, and how he could convince people to become Party members because they did not listen to him. Sisouk then gave a vague answer, to the effect that people were allowed now to make profits, to trade what they grew; however, it was strictly forbidden to lie to "the people" (pasàsòn) and to infringe upon their welfare. Phumi, however, hardly reacted to these pieces of advice and kept saying that the people were not listening to him: "I eventually will have to let them do what they wish, and choose whomever, an ordinary person, to be a Party member". The transcript of individuals like Phumi, Khamsing and Nok, have drifted away from the new mantra promoted by the government and its agents; the individual search for material comfort is superseding the socialist rhetoric of equality and solidarity, though officially the regime still pretends it is not. Their discourses are no longer attuned: Sisouk enthusiastically gave them tips on investment and profit while they asked for the Party's line. The transcript has gone wrong and the "revolutionaries" of Ban Paktai do not understand why, as they somehow still believe in a status that has lost its substance. A few days before I left the village to return to Vientiane, Phumi received a letter from the district; they invited him to attend a meeting on the inflation of the kip — the national currency[3] — a rather dry topic for a district gathering I thought. But Phumi looked overjoyed when he showed me the letter: "Does this not prove that I'm an important person?", he bragged. "They're inviting *me* to this meeting!". He even had me read his name and his title on the piece of paper, and boasted again: "you see, it's me, really me: Phumi, the Party's Secretary!". My next encounter in the town of Pakse further reveals the increasing disjuncture between the views of the state and those citizens whose vision of their place in state–society relations is becoming obsolete.

Duality of being

A Lao family

In Pakse, I stayed with a family whose parents were both permanent members of political mass organizations. The father, Somchit, was in charge of Minority Affairs at the local LFNC office, and his wife, Manivong, worked in the Department of Propaganda at the Lao Women's Union (LWU). The couple had different ethnic origins: Somchit belongs to an ethnic group whose official ethnonym is "Oy", a group that falls under the Austro-Asiatic ethno-linguistic category, and Manivong introduced herself as "Phu Thai", officially classified under the Lao category according to the 1995 Lao census. Lao is their first language, though they can fluently speak their respective ethnic groups' languages, Oy and Phuthai. Both are relatively well educated, as they had been teachers. Manivong met her husband in 1975 during a "summer political seminar" near her home area, in Champhone District (formerly a province), Savannakhet Province. This district was located in the then "zone 5" that had been recently "liberated" by the Pathet Lao. She was a primary school teacher, and like all the civil servants who had been educated under the old regime, she went through the so-called "seminars of political re-education". As she was a low-ranking employee, she attended the seminars for one month and a half, during which time she was lectured on "Political Theory" (*Titssadee kan meuang*). Somchit was actually supervising the classes. Following this experience, she carried on her teaching, became the deputy head of the LWU at the district level in Champassak Province, and finally got promoted to the LWU provincial headquarters in 1993.

Somchit and Manivong have a fairly active social life. In early March 2000, a month that is considered to be a propitious time for getting married, Somchit and Manivong were invited to five weddings within two weeks. They subsequently had to split the *sukhuan* ceremonies and the dinner parties so as to cope with all the invitations. On two occasions, Manivong went to help the bride's family to prepare the dinner party while her husband went to assist at a *sukhuan* ceremony at another house. They also carefully calculated the sum of money to be given to the bride and groom, the traditional form of wedding gift. They only earned the standard civil servant's salary — between 100,000 kip and 150,000 kip a month (at that time, one US dollar was equivalent to approximately 8,000–9,000 kip). Their budget therefore was tight. Still, they went to all the weddings and spent nearly a month's salary on them. Manivong's favourite expression in March was "helping the house, helping the community".

One of Somchit's favourite conversations with me was to explain to the *farang Lao* (the "foreign Lao" or "white Lao") who I was in his eyes, what "being Lao" (*khwam pen lao*) meant. For instance, one evening on our way back home after one of the wedding parties, he considered it useful to define the "Lao"[4] way of entertaining. In his words, this was to "be able to drink, to sing, to dance, to eat and to talk"! Somchit's wish is to promote relationships between the Lao community abroad and the LFNC because, as he declares, "all the Lao people, even those abroad, remain Lao: if they eat sticky rice and *padaek*, and play *khaen*, then they're Lao!" He even tries to forbid his children to listen to Thai or Western songs, but with no great success. Like most urban teenagers, they like listening to Lao, Thai and foreign music and watching Thai programmes on TV, though they usually promptly switch to the Lao channel when their father comes back home. Somchit has also suggested several times that I should wear *pha sin* (the Lao sarong) more often so as to look like a "real Lao girl". Somchit insisted on the most distinctive, if not stereotyped, characteristics of the Majority culture. He liked boasting about his knowledge of it. In other words, he over-communicated his Lao-ness to mark his sameness with the ethnic Lao and to legitimate his membership of the majority group.

Living in Pakse, one of the biggest and most populous towns of the country, Manivong and Somchit's children — four girls and one boy who were between 24 and 14 years old in the year 2000 — had easier access to education than most Lao children of their age, all the more so since their parents strongly encouraged them to pursue their schooling. All five were still at school. Three of them studied at the Teachers' Training School in Pakse. The eldest daughter had married an ethnic Lao businessman in January 2000, but still continued her studies while working part-time for the Department of Information and Culture as a radio broadcaster. The second daughter had just finished a pre-university degree in pharmaceutical studies in Vientiane and was debating whether to carry on at school and therefore to return to the capital, or to look for a job in her hometown.

Despite both their parents being non-ethnic Lao, these young people felt unambiguously Lao. One evening, Tik, the third daughter, 20, witty and tomboyish, made this comment to me:

– Mixed-race people are said to be clever… like you, Lao-Thai!

I then remarked in turn:

– But you too, you're mixed-race people!

Nou, her elder sister, 22, looked surprised and asked, perplexed:

– What do you mean mixed-race? Lao-Lao?

– No… I mean…mixed-race Phuthai and…

But before I finished my sentence, the two sisters burst out laughing:

– That's right, we're mixed-race inside Laos!

My remark obviously sounded like a good joke. Nou insisted:

– It doesn't matter: our nationality is Lao.

And Tik added:

– Our race is Lao, our blood is Lao, and our nationality is Lao! Not like the Viet, their race is Viet and their nationality, Lao.

This conversation clearly shows the conflation between race, nationality and ethnicity with regard to the term "Lao" in the minds of Tik and Nou. These children were aware of their parents' ethnic origins, though in unclear terms, especially as regards their father's. His ethnicity was an alien element, from which they clearly distanced themselves. Here is another conversation I had with Tik. She wished to become a teacher for ethnic peoples at the Boarding School for Ethnic Minorities in Pakse, or in the "mountainous areas" (*khet phudoi*), as she described it. Despite her motivation and enthusiasm, she was apprehensive about the task she will have to face. She thus told me:

- These children don't have the same way of thinking as we do. They think differently. And, if you shout at them or get upset, they may put a curse on you or poison you.

I then asked her about the occasion upon which her father ate their pet dog, when his relatives came to visit from his native village. She immediately burst out:

- My father has a dark heart (*chai dam*)! He's got a dark heart; he's an ethnic person (*khòn chai dam, khòn sòn phaw*)!

Being One and the Other

Somchit does not hide his ethnic identity, but keeps it within a restricted sphere that does not even include his own family. Neither Somchit nor Manivong encourage their children to learn their native languages. None of their children can speak them, though the two eldest daughters can understand Phuthai, which they learnt with their maternal grandmother in their early childhood in Savannakhet, their mother's native province. Lao is the only language used at home. While I was staying with them, I never heard Manivong or Somchit using their native vocabulary, even in an interjection. The Lao and non-Lao milieus seem to be hermetically separated.

On a few occasions, people from his native village in Attapeu came to visit Somchit and sometimes stayed overnight. They spoke in both Oy and Lao, and once cooked the pet dog, to the great horror of the children. The children and their mother displayed a polite but distant attitude with them. Manivong rarely stayed in the evening to take part in the conversation, which was anyway mostly conducted in Oy when Somchit and his visitors were on their own. The first time these visitors came during my stay, Manivong whispered to me as if it were a secret that they came from "Somchit's village, Ban Tok of Attapeu. They are Oy"; while her eldest daughter, intrigued and amused, would observe that "Father and they are speaking in an ethnic language (*phasa sòn phaw*). Last night, I heard Father talking to them in that language".

Paradoxically, Somchit, who seemed to be well integrated into ethnic Lao culture and society, was not ashamed to declare himself non-Buddhist. Somchit made no effort to hide his scorn for the religion when he was with me. It was mid-October and we were waiting for the bus that would take me further east to Sekong Province. I promised him I would try to come back to Pakse for the end of Buddhist Lent, during which time an even larger number of believers than normal make merit by offering food to the groups of monks who walk the streets just after dawn. His answer was abrupt and like a piece of communist rhetoric:

– Don't bother! If you can't make it on time, it doesn't matter. Buddhist rituals are a legacy from feudal times. But the religion is too popular for the government to abolish it. Ninety per cent of the population follow it. But, if we could suppress it, we would.

He then added contemptuously:

– The monks are like beggars in the morning when they go along the streets asking for food.

Yet his wife and children are openly Buddhist. Moreover, his eldest daughter's religious wedding ceremony was organized according to Buddhist rituals.

Somchit is neither an "authentic" member of the Oy ethnic minority group nor a "true" ethnic Lao person. On the one hand, he shares *almost* all the mainstream cultural features: he speaks in Lao (most of the time), eats ethnic Lao food (most of the time) and respects ethnic Lao customs (most of the time), including Buddhist traditions as a social activity. To put it another way, there are no cultural or physical[5] traits that can distinguish him from the ethnic Lao people. However, as an individual, he says that he is not Buddhist (while in public he conceals this trait, or to be precise, he lets himself slip into the cultural mainstream). Yet his "intermittent" non-Buddhist attitude shows that he deviates somewhat from stereotypical "Lao-ness", with the potential to possess a split cultural identity. Or, to put it differently, he does not possess all the attributes for a full cultural membership of the Majority.

On the other hand, Somchit never had a culture of origin, or to put it another way, a cultural point of attachment: his Other ethnicity has no stable cultural content but only the consciousness of being different (though he tries to conform with the state's minority representation). But Somchit got it all wrong when trying to explain the Oy traditions to me, in particular their funeral ceremony. To his great surprise (as well as to mine), he was promptly contradicted by his fellow male villagers who said that they no longer practised these "backward" rituals!

> –   Oh, you no longer collect the bones and chop the head? [Somchit asked, looking confused.]
> One of the villagers shook his head and replied:
> –   No, we no longer do that. Now, we use the coffin. It's cleaner now. We stopped the backward rituals. We've evolved now.
> I intervened in the conversation by asking the following question:
> –   Do you not regret the disappearance of the rituals of your ethnic group?
> It was Somchit who promptly answered, with the silent approbation of his fellow men:
> –   No, no, these practices were backward. We regret nothing. The ethnic groups come closer. Like circles following a concentric movement.
> But all of a sudden, that same evening, Somchit expressed regret that the history of ethnic groups (*pavàt sònphaw*) was neglected, because of the lack of funding.
> –   We need people like you to be able to conduct research. But it depends on the leaders...

Somchit then had this intriguing comment: "The flag of three colours [i.e. the Lao flag] is in the grasp of the leaders (*thùng sam si yu nai kam phunam*)".

I did not ask him to explain his remark, but the expression of resignation on his face suggested he was referring to his sense of powerlessness before the authorities.

Individuals like Somchit locate themselves in both cultural spheres, ethnic and non-ethnic Lao. To put it differently, they are exhibiting a dual ethnicity, the Majority's and the Minority's. More precisely, the state's discourse of "multi-ethnic ethnicity", increasingly centred on the cultural (national) (ethnic Lao) Majority, leads them to position themselves in a dual manner within the regime of representation. Consequently, it may be the "duality of being"[6] that can best characterize men such as Sisouk and Somchit; that is, the experience of being *partially* One (members of the Majority) and *partially* the Other (members of the minorities) in post-socialist Lao urban society. I would argue that this dual display of ethnicity has been heightened by the "loss of a stable 'sense of self'" (Hall 1994, p. 275). From their childhood, their ethnicity has been subsumed within a social and political identity. These members of ethnic groups certainly show loyalty to a leadership whose project, in their perception, has blended ethnicity and socialist ideals. But, today, their world is progressively eroding under post-socialist transformations; subsequently, what has constituted the values and meanings of their identity is being shaken.

Post-socialist loss of a stable "sense of self"

A Status-Role

Benoît de Tréglodé has argued in his study of "revolutionary heroes" in northern Vietnam that the promotion of such values as loyalty and patriotism has contributed to the social transformation of traditionally subordinated people (Tréglodé 1999, p. 27). When I first met Manivong, perhaps eager to make me feel at home, she promptly told me that she and her husband, Somchit, understood my work because, as she explained: "We have the same intellectual culture. We are civil servants (*phànàkngan*). We know what it's like to conduct research when one is a student, unlike the merchants who wouldn't understand". My presence, as a young female foreign scholar, possibly gave her the opportunity to assert their social rank, which she clearly placed above the rich but ignorant and despised traders. In fact, Manivong explicitly reckoned that "civil servants are a distinctive category [because] they are better educated, better aware". In the 1991 Constitution of the LPDR — the first one promulgated since 1975 — "workers, farmers and intellectuals" are defined as "the key components" of the "multiethnic people", while all references to other social groups are omitted (Article 2). Manivong obviously classifies herself and her husband as "intellectuals". The hierarchical differential between "civil servant" and "trader" thus clearly does not so much denote professional classification as embody feelings of having a status, or to be exact, a status-role. I borrow here Marshall's definition of "status":

> ... The main argument for the merger [between status and role] is that a status, conceived as a position in a social system, can be imagined only in terms of relationships, and the substance of social relationships is expected behaviour. [...] It can be argued, therefore, that if the dynamic aspect of status is removed, nothing is left except a fallacious conception of a position in social system as a static objective thing (Marshall 2000 [1977], pp. 305–6).

Accordingly, Manivong's and Somchit's high self-esteem are induced not by their rank (civil servant above merchant), nor by their social status (i.e. their position in the hierarchy of social prestige within the community (Marshall 2000, p. 308) — which is anyhow difficult to assess) but by the pedagogical role made possible by their education and attached to their position as members of political mass organizations, i.e. the LFNC and LWU. As Marshall summed up, "status emphasizes the position, as conceived by the group or society that sustains it, and role emphasizes the person who occupies the position" (ibid., p. 306). Nevertheless, since the mid-1980s, the expectations associated with their position have become more and more blurred, especially for Somchit. Whereas he initially steadily climbed the career ladder and improved his social status, he had not been promoted for the past thirteen years. Clearly, his status, i.e. his social role, has changed along with the structural transformations that have affected the post-socialist regime. I recount below Somchit's interrupted social and political "trajectory".

The end of an exemplary trajectory

The narrative that follows is constructed from Somchit's own oral accounts of his activities as a "revolutionary". The episodes of his life represent the introduction to my reflections. First, I will transcribe the original linear narration; then, I will point out the contradictions. Somchit told his story spontaneously, as he was free to structure his "plot" as he wished. I started my interview with an opening question and thereafter rarely intervened. However, I am aware that by translating and writing down his story I have already disturbed it, although I am using his own words whenever I (again) consider it relevant to do so.

Somchit left his native village, Ban Tok, in Meuang Sanamsay,[7] Attapeu Province, at the age of 12 to "join the revolution" (*huam kan pàtìvàt*). His mother was killed by the "enemy" (*sàttu*) because his father and his uncles and aunts, whom his father "recruited" (*làdòm*), were "revolutionaries". She was shot in the evening, after having spent her day looking after the cattle in a rice-field hut. The "enemy" entrapped her on her way back home. In fact, they confused her with Somchit's uncle and killed her by mistake. This murder was the main cause of Somchit's involvement in the revolution.

Somchit also joined the revolution because his village was in the "middle of an intensely disputed zone (*khet nyadnyaeng*) between the Neo Lao Hak Sat (NLHS) and the "troops from Meuang May, Attapeu (or from Vientiane in Meuang May, Attapeu)".[8] Somchit therefore decided to leave; as he said, "As I saw there was no peace, I escaped (*bor sàgnòp, cheung ni*)". Furthermore, the Army officials of the "enemy", "the colonels Ketmany and Khoumki", were forcing people to work as "coolies" to serve and to enhance the power of the authorities in Meuang May. These three causes led Somchit to "sacrifice" (*sàlà*) his birthplace to join the NLHX: "In brief, I left because of feelings of resentment and revenge (*khuam khietkhaen*) against the "enemy", because I felt "injustice" (*bor nyùtitham*)". His uncles and aunt, also involved in the revolution, then took him with them to join the resistance activities.

Somchit's recollection of the beginning of his "revolutionary activities" (*khieunvai pàtìvàt*) interweaves the personal story with the historical context, with the addition of ulterior ideological motivations. The way in which he presented the death of his mother showed that the loss clearly represented the turning point of his life. She was killed because of her relatives' involvement in the revolution when the "enemy" mistakenly retaliated against her. Consequently, by dying involuntarily and brutally as an innocent victim of the "enemy's" barbarism, but (indirectly) for a just cause, she has become, for Somchit, a symbol of both injustice and the Revolution. Furthermore, these fierce emotions are reinforced by such figures as the "colonels Ketmany and Khoumki", the "enemy", presented in counterpoint as despotic rulers enslaving the population to be their "coolies". The vocabulary used clearly denotes the anti-colonial rhetoric he probably learnt during his political classes.

As a matter of fact, Somchit's initial participation in the revolution appears to have followed a less straightforward path. Upon being questioned in the aftermath of the interview, a process that disrupted his reconstruction of his life, some faults inevitably appeared and disclosed a rather more complex picture. When I asked him to tell me more about his experience as a soldier, his narration suddenly lost its linearity. Below is an extract from the interview in which Somchit recounts an episode of his life that he had previously omitted:

- So, you said that you were a soldier for three months. Can you tell me more about it?
- At the age of 16, the young men were forced to become *commando* soldiers, *maquis* soldiers,[9] or militiamen. I had been a soldier for three months. Then, I realized that it wasn't right, that we were badly treated, so I refused and escaped from the village, and joined the revolutionary action.
- So, it was the "enemy", who was forcing people [to become soldiers]?
- Yes, it was them who forced the men to become *maquis* soldiers. Then, those who were the most promising ones became *commando* soldiers. But, I didn't reach that level. I was just a *maquis* soldier. I didn't have the possibility (*bor mi ngern khai*) of becoming a *commando*. I saw that there was no justice, so I left.

The "American War" started in Attapeu in 1964, and some battles occurred in the late 1960s in the district of Sanamxay. Like most of the districts in Attapeu, Sanamxay was first controlled by the Royal Lao Army (RLA), who progressively withdrew westwards as the Pathet Lao and the Vietnamese troops gained territory. As Somchit himself explained, the tactical situation around his village was confusing: there were no clear-cut zones of influence belonging to either the RLA or the Pathet Lao. It was not uncommon, in effect, for a village in Attapeu or elsewhere to have been controlled alternately by the two sides; hence, the villagers were often caught between the RLA and the Pathet Lao troops. Somchit was recruited by the RLA because his village was temporarily under their control. The death of his mother may have well been the turning point of his life, but other circumstances also influenced his decision to "join the revolution". For instance, Somchit stressed the role of his uncle, Bounmy, in his involvement in the "struggle" (*kan tor su*); his repeated use of the verb "to escape" (*ni*) might also suggest that his choice of side was dictated mainly by random external factors, which forced him into making certain choices in order to survive. However, the constant theme was that his choice of allegiance was a result of deeply-held convictions and ideological beliefs. They reflected the re-presentation of *his* past. He embroiders his individual story with the patriotic discourse: they merge to form only one collective memory. To put it another way, his story was sensible and coherent in his mind — its composition drew heterogeneous events of his lived experience into "wholeness and shapeliness" (Miller 1987, p. 1104). More importantly, the structuring of action led to the "acquisition of an identity through inscribing oneself into a role in the world" (Clark 1990, p. 168). In other words, his reappropriation of the events produced meaning in his existence.

After he fled his village, Somchit started cooking for the staff of the Pathet Lao administration in Ban Mae Mork Namkong, in the district of Sanamxay. His father's youngest brother, Bounmy, was then the head of the administration, and along with the head of the province, Khamkhieng, they supported him. In 1964, he became a soldier in Sanamxay, and after just three months he was wounded — Somchit showed me the scar twice during one interview. He did not return to battle but was sent instead to a one-year training course in Ban May Hinlaat, in Sanamxay, to become a primary teacher. After the completion of his education in 1965, he started his career: "it was the beginning of my service" (*kan sàpsorn*). Indeed, year after year, his geographical movements went hand-in-hand with his promotion within the Pathet Lao system, and then within the Party-State's administrative apparatuses.

First, he was sent as a primary teacher to Ban Khanmaknao, in Sanamxay. Then, a few months later, the staff of the "Southern zone" administration located in Ban Mae Mork Namkong were transferred to the "Eastern Province" (now, Sekong Province), then called "Lao Tai zone". Somchit left his native province to work in the education administration in the "Lao Tai zone", the headquarters of which were in Meuang Bualapha, then in Savannakhet Province.[10] In 1969, however, the "Lao Tai zone" was dissolved by the Pathet Lao administration. Its staff were then dispatched to three different areas: some returned to the former "Southern zone" in Attapeu Province, while others were sent to the central level, in Huaphan Province. The rest left for Vietnam to study. Somchit was among those who had been selected to go and study in Vietnam, but, for reasons that remain unclear, conditions were not yet ripe: Hanoi could not receive the students yet. Instead, he went up to the province of Huaphan, to Vieng Xai (formerly called Nakai), then the headquarters of the Pathet Lao administration. He attended some upgrade courses during the next few years to become a secondary school teacher. Finally, in 1972, he was sent to Vietnam to attend courses in political theory. He went along with 24 others, including "the wife of Uncle Kaysone". Two years later, he came back to Laos and got promoted to the position of head of the administration of the Education Service of the Neo Lao Hak Sat (NLHS or Lao Patriotic Front) in Huaphan Province. The following year, he was appointed to supervise a seminar for Education officials in the newly "liberated zones" in Savannakhet Province (then called "Zone 5"), for a month and a half. Then, he taught the Party's policies in the same area for another month. In 1976, he came back to Vieng Xai and again got promoted, this time to the position of head of the Teacher Training Course at Dong Dok University in the prefecture of Vientiane. He stayed there for four years. In the early 1980s, the Ministry of Education sent him down to Pakse to administer the Teacher Training School. He carried on teaching political theory there. In 1983, he went to Vietnam for the second time, again to study. He stayed another two years. When he returned to Laos, he was nominated as a member of the Teacher Training School's management board in Pakse. Finally, in 1988, the first general assembly of the LFNC of Champassak Province appointed him as a permanent member of the mass organization. He was ranked seventh out of fifty-one senior members, and included in the permanent committee at the next general assembly. Since then, he has moved up to the third-ranking position.

Somchit's narrative, recorded on tape and for which he got prepared well in advance, appears as an uninterrupted flow, imprinting a logical, quasi-bureaucratic pattern upon the story. I heard different people talk in the same manner on several occasions. Bourdieu, in a short and compelling essay, has condemned the illusion of a "life history" that makes life falsely appear as "a whole, a coherent and finalized whole, which can and must be seen as the unitary expression of a subjective and objective 'intention' of a project" (Bourdieu 2000 [1986], p. 297). I do not disagree with him about the fact that the series of events Somchit recounted to me are to a certain extent structurally selected and ordered (consciously or unconsciously) to form an ascendant trajectory. These people, who became the cadres of the "revolution", went through the same educational system and ideological circuit. Their individual lives were absorbed by the bureaucratic and political machinery to such an extent that it seems that private and public spheres have merged in their personal identity. As Paul du Gay comments, Bourdieu's argument reflects "the ways in which humans' capacities, including the capacity for self-consciousness and self-reflection, depend upon definite forms of discourse and definite sets of activities and techniques in which they are trained and implicated as agents" (du Gay 2000, p. 280).

It is precisely the "biographical illusion" (Bourdieu 2000 [1986]), however, that gives meaning to these peoples' existence. The revolutionary period of their lives has transformed them. These moments were experienced very intensely. Victor Turner stressed the importance of the disruptions (such as war, or more mundane events like marriage) that are extracted from their everyday life by individuals and expressed in various forms such as narratives and plays. Turner saw experience as isolated sequences of events marked by beginnings, middles, and endings, as ways in which people told what was most meaningful about their lives (Turner 1986, p. 36). Somchit's upward route through the '"revolutionary" bureaucracy is one case among many. From childhood to adulthood, members of ethnic peoples were indeed educated and trained within a geographical space, i.e. the Pathet Lao "liberated zones", which also crossed the "national" borders into the Democratic Republic of Vietnam. In his interview, Khamdaeng, an official of the LFNC of Sekong Province, defined himself as a "fighting civil servant". His account of his "life/history" is almost identical to Somchit's. He left his Katu native village in Kalum district in 1963 and went to study in Nakai. He was then 17. He stayed in Vieng Xai (or Nakai) for seven years until he graduated as a schoolteacher. After a few years working in the provincial administration of the former "Eastern Province", he also was sent to Vietnam in 1983 for one year for further political training. Upon his return, he was appointed head of Kalum district.

Recruits from minority groups recount similar experiences or breaks in their early life, i.e. the outbreak of war and separation from their birthplace, which were concomitant with their "entry" into the "revolution". During one of my informal conversations with a woman called Keothong — when I was not working with her husband, a high-ranking LFNC official — I found out that she also had been educated under the Pathet Lao administration. As a matter of fact, Keothong called herself a "child of the war" (*dàek sòngkham*). She left her village when she was seven — she was born in 1954 — and went to the primary school in Viengsai (Huaphan Province), then later to Vietnam to continue her studies. She stayed in Vietnam in a boarding school, "only for children like me who came from Laos. We were hundreds, almost a thousand!" she said proudly. In 1972, most of them returned to Laos. Only a minority did not come back. She herself stayed in Vietnam from 1968 to 1978 to study irrigation systems. She met her husband in Nakai, during one of her return trips from Vietnam, and gave up her career to raise their children.

By these narratives of self, these people are expressing the desire to delineate and to retain a conception of cultural identity that is immutable and homogenous. Their stories follow the same pattern, composed of a series of identical events which is "organized as a history, and unfolds according to a chronological order which is also a logical order, with a beginning, an origin (both in the sense of a starting point and of a principle, a *raison d'être*, a primal force), and a termination, which is also a goal" (Bourdieu 2000 [1986], p. 298). In brief, they are conceptualizing their identity as One (Hall 1990, p. 223). Changes that have occurred since the late 1980s, however, have cracked the unified narration. As Kobena Mercer notes, "identity only becomes an issue when it is in crisis, when something assumed to be fixed, coherent and stable is displaced by the experience of doubt and uncertainty" (Mercer 1990, p. 43).

The loss of a stable sense of self

After several months, Somchit and Manivong could no longer hide their frustration at their situation in my presence. I have decided to transcribe in full the following conversation to try to render its tone of heightened emotions and sincerity. The couple deserves close attention. Somchit was seated in the armchair. He looked tired and gloomy. I had just come back for lunch. He asked me if I had brought back the report of the LFNC's 1998–99 activities that he had given me that very morning.

- Who wrote the document, Uncle Somchit? [I asked him]
- I wrote the report. But to be approved, it had to be sent to the districts and villages. It took two weeks! But they removed some portions out of my text... a big section, in fact.

I then asked him what this section contained, and he answered:

- I'd written a long section about the ways of solving problems and the way of behaving. It was me who wrote the document, but somebody else signed it. I, myself, can't. I don't have the authority to sign. In fact, those who decide are Phetsamay, Ketmany, Kamsing.... They are old people but newcomers, while Vanphone and I may be young but we were here before them.

Very intrigued, I asked again:

- But were they in the office? I never saw them.
- Of course, they are... somewhere... [Somchit replied elusively.]
- But Phetsamay and Ketmany, what do they do? [I insisted.]
- Nothing.

Manivong suddenly irrupted into the conversation:

- You're talking nonsense! Of course, they do have responsibilities!

Her husband burst out in turn and retorted:

- Can you tell me which ones? Phonchay does nothing but scratch his balls all day!

He then turned his head towards me and said in a quieter but still bitter tone:

- You're in touch with the central level, so please go and ask them why they've [i.e. Phetsamay and Ketmany] been nominated, while I remain in the same position. Because I'm from an ethnic group? Because I'm not a womaniser (bo lin phusao)?

Somchit enunciated these two questions in a voice loaded with bitterness and irony. I did not know how to answer and silence ensued. Then, Manivong decided that they should give me a fuller explanation:

- When Uncle Khampheng [the former head of the LFNC of Champassak Province] retired, he had to find someone else to replace him. Instead of choosing your Uncle Somchit who has worked at the Front for nearly 9 years now, Uncle Many went far away to choose Phonchay from the district of Champassak. Someone who wasn't particularly competent, whereas your Uncle has finished 'high level' in political theory, and Phonchay was only a district-grade Party member.

She then finally expressed her anger:
— Let me tell you, my niece, those who've got the power don't care about
the ethnic peoples! It's all for the Lao Lum, and only for the Lao Lum.
But, we are honest people (*sàtseu*), we don't benefit from favouritism
(*lin phàkphuak*). It's not the Party-State's fault, but the fault of those who
apply the doctrine!

I was surprised by the unexpected outburst from the couple who
over all the preceding months had been presenting an image of a model
pair of "revolutionaries". Obviously, there were some cracks in this
representation, which they were no longer able to conceal before me.
Somchit and Manivong's accusations were very explicit. They said they
were discriminated against because of their ethnicity. They expressed a
fierce criticism of favouritism (*lin phàkphuak*) along ethnic lines. As such,
they implicitly referred to themselves as the "minority", in terms of
power and status, versus the "majority", i.e. the "Lao Lum", who are
here accused of monopolizing political power, or in other words, of
nepotism.

Consequently, the obvious first analysis would be to refer to that
"Janus face of nationalism", Nairn's seminal expression (Nairn 1977),
which Eriksen has defined as "a nationalist ideology of the hegemonic
group that underlies a particularist ideology rather than a universalist
one, where the mechanisms of exclusion and ethnic discrimination are
more obvious than the mechanisms of inclusion and formal justice" (Eriksen
1993, p. 119). However, I argue that the concept of a vertical ethnic
differentiation in which, to put it simply, one ethnic group is subordinated
to another (Mason 1992) is too limited to comprehend the scope of variation
of these people's identities. In reality, categorization can be deceptive and
even problematic: as we have seen, Somchit feels both Lao and non-ethnic
Lao. The fact is that Somchit's social and political identity is being
challenged in the post-socialist era. His sentiments of social and political
exclusion lead to the emergence of negative ethnicity. The quality of
"being an ethnic person" (*pen khòn sòn phaw*) has at present negative
connotations, while under wartime conditions it was promoted. "Being an

ethnic person" during wartime and the revolutionary period embodied social and political values, such as equality between all individuals, respect for cultural diversity, equality of opportunity, unity in the form of struggle against a common enemy. However, these values seem to progressively be losing their aura under the current regime. What the revolutionary years gave them — a social and political identity — the post-revolutionary era dilutes: the community and ideals with which they used to identify are no longer there. As their values are being undermined, the quality of "being an ethnic person" itself is turning into a stigmatized identity. In other words, Somchit's identity is becoming overwhelmed by his ethnicity, as his status-role is losing its meaning. The following study of the work of the LFNC in the provinces shows the increasing disjunction between the functions of the political mass organization and the new objectives of the government.

Discourse of lack

From approximately 1935 to 1945, the Lao nationalist movement was known as the Lao pen Lao ("the Lao are Lao"). Just prior to the surrender of the Japanese in August 1945, the Lao Issara or Neo Lao Issara ("the Front for Lao Independence") was formed and replaced the Lao pen Lao until approximately 1954. From this time until 1979 the organization was known as the Neo Lao Hak Sat ("the Lao Patriotic Front"), and following the cessation of hostilities in 1975, the name was finally changed to one which would reflect the peacetime role of development — that is, Neo Lao Sang Sat or Lao Front for National Construction (LFNC) — during its Fourth Congress in 1979. Until 1975 the organization had indeed served as the public face of the LPRP. The need for a legal political partner, with which the Pathet Lao's adversaries could negotiate under "respectable" terms, had evaporated. Consequently, the LPRP came out onto the official political scene.

The organizational structure of the LFNC consists of a President, three Vice Presidents and a Permanent Committee of three persons. There is also a Secretariat and three Departments: Ethnic Minorities, Religion and Information. Each of the three members of the Permanent Committee acts as an advisor to one of the departments. In addition, the LFNC has a representative at each administrative level: provincial, district and village. The mass organization operates under an official directive as an arm of the government and has the mandate to provide socio-cultural support (i.e. local knowledge) in the planning and implementation phases of development projects. In other words, its role is to coordinate socioeconomic development projects with all partners, whether they are state-controlled institutions, NGOs or from the private sector (Khampheuye 1999, p. 3). On a political level, as Khampheuye Chantasouk, the vice-president of the LFNC, bluntly explains in an interview, the mission of the LFNC is to guide people's minds in the right direction: it instructs them about the Party's policies as well as about the Government's laws and rules. It is the interface that links the Party-State and the "masses", defined as "people of all ethnic groups, social backgrounds and religions" (Ibid., p. 3).

However, the LFNC's field of responsibilities is as vast and vague as its power of decision-making at the central level is limited. In 1950, 1956, 1959 and 1964, membership of the LFNC Central Committee consistently reflected the Party leadership's composition. Those who held power covertly, such as Kaysone Phomvihane, Nuhak Phumsavan, Khamtay Siphandon, Phumi Vongvichit or Prince Souphanouvong, were also enlisted in the LFNC.[11] The situation changed in 1979 when the LFNC called its first congress since 1975. Only one member of the LFNC Central Committee belonged to the Party's Politburo: Prince Souphanouvong, who was also the president of the newly formulated LFNC. The other leaders had already left and joined the real decision-making organ, the Politburo. The Sixth Congress of the LPRP and the Third Congress of the Front, which were held in the same year (1996), reflected the same political realities. The then LFNC President, Udom Khattigna, who died in December 1999, was ranked number four in the Politburo hierarchy (Stuart-Fox 1998, p. 1).[12] The latest government reshuffle in March 2001 confirmed the lack of influence of the LFNC. The deposed prime minister, Sisavath Keobunphanh (at present politically marginalized) was appointed as its new president and fell from second to seventh position in the composition of the 2001 Politburo, which now includes 11 members.

While I was working with the LFNC officials in different provinces, I heard a recurrent comment, often expressed in a weary tone. The remark was: "We're taking care of everything. We must be everywhere". Sentiments of frustration were eminently perceptible among the members of the mass organization. First, there was a striking contrast between, on the one hand, the immense scope of their role and on the other, their material and financial deprivation. For instance, among the eight provincial LFNC offices I visited,[13] only two — in Savannakhet and Champassak — had a car with the others having motorbikes or bicycles. LFNC members, especially outside the capital, sincerely felt that they were neglected both by their government and foreign aid donors, whereas in principle they should have been the principal vector of the country's development. In Savannakhet, for example, they complained about their undervalued status (with a salary that rarely exceeded US$15 a month), their lack of means and the absence of projects. I describe below the kind of situation I often came across in the course of my countless visits to LFNC offices in the provinces.

The LFNC office in Sekong — three rooms rented from the provincial National Assembly, two Japanese motorbikes, one Russian typewriter and no phone line — looked particularly deserted when I visited in late March 2000. The atmosphere of boredom and apathy contrasted sharply with the frenetic activities at the Department of Information and Culture whose premises were located a few metres away. The latter department was preparing the ceremony for the Year of Tourism in Sekong, which was scheduled to take place over three days. But the LFNC played no part in it. Subsequently, the office was as lethargic as ever. In addition, the LFNC head was sick. He asked the organization for some financial support to help cover his hospital expenses in Pakse, but, because of the financial crisis, he could only have his petrol costs refunded. The head of the Religious Affairs section, an ethnic Lao, the only official present that day, shook his head while telling me the story. Fortunately, the province had just received a godsend from the central level: 11 million kip to support programmes against HIV-AIDS. A special bureau, supervised by the vice-governor of the province, had been created to fight the pandemic disease, and the LFNC would receive some funding. Their role would mainly be to inform the population by gathering together the heads of the LFNC at the district level, who in turn would call in the heads of the LFNC at the village level within their respective administrative areas. The head of the Religious Affairs section once more shrugged his shoulders: "That's the way it is. We can't do anything more", he concluded.

Resentment was even greater when comparing their situation with the other mass organizations, the Youth Union and the LWU. The case of Champassak offered a good example of the gap between them. Below is a synthesis of the 1998–99 budgets of the LFNC and the LWU:

LFNC	LWU
Budget: 14 million kip	Budget: 114 million kip
Three offices rented from the provincial National Assembly (shared charges)	Own premises
Three motorbikes	Several motorbikes
A car — exclusively reserved for the LFNC president's use	Two cars, of which one is shared by all the members
Petrol and maintenance charges refunded	Petrol and maintenance charges refunded

Source: personal communication (LFNC Champassak).

In the following year, the LFNC budget was over twice as high. They received 40 million kip (excluding salaries) from the province; but, it was still the smallest amount distributed by the provincial authorities to any of the State organs. By comparison, the 1999–2000 LWU budget again exceeded 100 million kip, of which 70 million was assigned by the province and the rest provided by NGOs and international organizations' programmes. By contrast, the LFNC did not get any external aid. One of their members admitted that the public image of the LFNC was too politically connected; consequently, foreign organizations were reluctant to have their name attached to it. During my fieldwork, the then president of the LFNC, Sihot Banavong, was touring the country to meet staff at LFNC provincial and district headquarters. In February 2000, he came to Champassak and among the new projects he announced to its members was a change of name of the LFNC, following the example of the Vietnamese who had already modified the name of their equivalent. According to the LFNC president of Champassak Province, there thus existed the idea of reverting to the former name, the Lao Patriotic Front, or simply the Lao Front, which would sound ideologically more neutral and less "narrow"; hence, more attractive to foreign investors and donors.[14] In summary, the LFNC seems outdated and defined by a discourse of lack: lack of means, projects and authority.[15]

Concluding remarks

To analyse different aspects of ethnicity, Banks has proposed three pictorial perspectives on the "location of ethnicity": "ethnicity in the people's heart" (the primordialist approach), "ethnicity in the people's head" (the instrumentalist approach) and "ethnicity in the analyst's head" (Banks 1997, pp. 185–86). I will focus in particular on the third perspective, defined by Banks as follows: "[ethnicity] is an analytical tool devised and utilized by academics to make sense of or explain the actions and feelings of the people studied" (Banks 1997, p. 186). Through this perspective, Banks in fact tells us that ethnicity is not always relevant in making sense of people's actions. This was my impression when I was recording my informants' accounts of their pasts. I had to accept that the concept of ethnicity did not encompass all the contradictory aspects of their identity. Likewise, Eriksen asks

> if it [is] still analytically fruitful to think about the social world in terms of ethnicity". And he observes that "[p]erhaps a wider term, such 'social identity', would be more true to the flux and complexity of social processes, and would allow us to study group formation and alignments along a greater variety of axes than a single-minded focus on 'ethnicity' would (Eriksen 1993, p. 157).

Actions of individuals such as Somchit, Khamsing, Phumi and Nok cannot be encompassed within one analytical tool, i.e. the concept of ethnicity. Their identities have been shaped by history and war: they are proud to introduce themselves as "revolutionaries" (*khòn pàtìvàt*), an identity that is connected to a status-role invested with entrenched meaning. What is more their shared consciousness of being "One", i.e. members of the nation, is based on the awareness of their ethnic origins, enhanced by their education and socialization under the communist administration. But structural changes within the post-socialist society have upset this social and political identity: their position within the society lies within a grey zone, with uncertainty surrounding their role. In addition, the state's newly reformulated project of a national culture exacerbates the destabilizing experience for these individuals, who somehow feel that they are progressively coming to play the role of the Other in their own society.

In the now familiar phrase, Stuart Hall has pointed out the discursive character of the "narrative of the nation": it is, he writes,

> told and retold in national histories, literatures, the media and popular culture. These provide a set of stories, images, landscapes, scenarios, historical events, national symbols and rituals which stand for, or represent, the shared experiences, sorrows, and triumphs and disasters which give meaning to the nation (Hall 1994, p. 293).

Forms of communication that connect people on a national scale contribute to the imagining of, and sentiments of belonging to, a community and common destiny, yet the state cannot always impose "the national story" on the individuals. A more precise view is that nations are not mere constructions or representations performed in the public arena, stuffed with symbols, rituals and myths, and deployed by the state to brainwash its population. Nations do not only exist through a "set of stories" told and retold to their members, from one generation to another, above and outside individuals; they also need to make sense to their members in their everyday life. People who live within the territorial boundaries of a nation–state are not mere members of an "imagined community"; equally — and perhaps more — importantly, they (or a vast majority of them) are the citizens of a polity. If myths are necessary to maintain national identities, they cannot do the job alone: the pertinence of the modern nation–state as the most legitimate form of modern polity is also founded on its capacity to give its members access to resources, whether they be political, socio-economic or cultural. A national citizen as a member of a political community has rights and obligations. Likewise, a more prosaic function of national identities, besides forging cultural cohesion out of a diverse population, is that they are expected to provide social solidarity. The political authorities in Laos hoped during the socialist period to form "new socialist men" whose identities would no longer be defined by ethnic or religious loyalties, but by equality in social position. The post-war nation–state is no longer capable of fulfilling its promises of social advancement among its citizens, however. The programme of social citizenship as planned and (to some extent) executed over the past decades by the regime appears as an archaic fragment in the new economic mechanisms.

Notes

[1]   I thank Paul Cunnington for suggesting the title of this chapter.

[2]

Table: Agricultural practices in Ban Paktai

Rice sufficiency — always	0 houses
Rice sufficiency — sometimes	50 houses
Rice sufficiency — never	6 houses
Rotational swiddening cultivation (alone)	45 houses
Pioneering swiddening cultivation (alone)	0 houses
Rice-field cultivation (alone)	0 houses
Rotational swiddening and own rice-field	11 houses
Irrigation scheme	Yes
Number of families with irrigation scheme	4 families
Number of hectares irrigated	3.5 hectares

Source: *Province of Sekong, Meuang Thateng*, Integrated Rural Accessibility Planning (IRAP), Accessibility Data, Ministry of Communications, Transport, Posts and Construction, June 1997.

There are two categories of swidden cultivation in Laos, pioneering and rotational: Pioneering swidden cultivation involves the periodic movement of a group or village into a new location, usually one that is densely forested. The area is then completely cleared of trees and cropped until the soil fertility is depleted. At this point the villagers either continue to clear more land nearby or relocate the village. The area is left in a condition where regeneration of forest and soils would take many years.

Rotational swidden cultivation is carried out by sedentary villages that rotate the cultivation of fields. The land is partially cleared of brush, scrub and (small) trees. This plot may be then cropped for one to three seasons, depending upon soil fertility. Some rotating shifting cultivation systems have fallow periods that may be as long as 12–20 years.

3   The 1997 regional financial crisis sent a brutal signal to the Lao leadership on their over-dependence on the Thai economy, then badly shaken by the financial turmoil. The impacts were severe for the Lao economy.

4   I use quotation marks here to emphasize the conflation, in my informant's mind, between nationality and ethnicity with regard to the term "Lao".

5   Perhaps their skin is sometimes slightly darker, but in any case people (be they ethnic Lao or not) from southern Laos are known for having a darker than average complexion.

6   Anagnost (1997) defines the experience of a "duality of being" as being that which is experienced by a subject who is forced to play a role or occupy a status imposed by the spinning of power's own fictions, so that it is experienced by the subject as alien or "inauthentic". She uses this framework in a radically different context, i.e. Chinese society during the tumultuous years of the Cultural revolution, which forced people to learn how to disguise and to manipulate their identities. While keeping the notion of multiplicity, I, however, contest the idea of falsity or inauthenticity in the case of my informants.

7   Sanamxay is located on the western side of Attapeu. It is bordered by Champassak Province to the West, and by Cambodia to the South.

8   To put it differently, his village was controlled in turn by the communist Pathet Lao and the rightist Royal Lao Government (based in Vientiane), respectively.

9   The French term, *maquis*, historically refers to the French Resistance that fought against the German forces during the Second World War. The term refers more generally to organized underground armed resistance.

[10] Meuang Bualapha is at the present time located in Khammuan Province. It is bordered by two districts (Vilabuly and Sepon) of Savannakhet to the South; and it shares a boundary with Vietnam to the East. Meuang Bualapha was created in 1967 (along with Meuang Langkhang) from areas previously belonging to Meuang Mahasay, also in Khammuan Province. In 1975, they were all unified under the present Meuang Bualapha administration. The eastern part of Khammuan was a stronghold of the Pathet Lao from the 1950s onwards. The Ho Chi Minh trail also ran through that area, and Meuang Bualapha was the main entry point into Laos for Vietnamese trucks. (Handicap International 1997, p. 11).

[11] Norindr (1980, p. 990) and Kooyman and Stuart-Fox (1992, p. 247).

[12] The other 1996 Politburo members by ranking order were: Khamtai Siphandon, Saman Vinyaket (President of the National Assembly), Chummali Xainyason (Commander-in-Chief and Defence Minister), Thongsing Thammavong, Osakan Thammatheva (Minister of Information and Culture), Bunnyang Vorachit (Mayor of Vientiane), Sisavath Keobunphanh and Axang Laoli (Minister of Interior).

[13] From the North to the South: Luang Namtha, Udomsai, Sam Neua, Savannakhet, Champassak, Saravane, Sekong and Attapeu.

[14] At the time of writing, the mass organization still bears the name LFNC.

[15] I recall a conversation with Khamdaeng, the head of the Minority Affairs section of the LFNC of Sekong Province. He had just came back from Vientiane where he had attended a meeting about the government's campaign for preventing AIDS, which had gathered the leading members of the provincial Fronts. When we met, he promptly asked me if I knew a Hmong named Tuamua, a former LFNC official. The man, whom he saw in the capital, was now "a successful businessman with five houses and three cars" (Among his new projects, Khamdaeng told me, was the construction of a 50 km-road in Udomsai, in the North, which would lead directly to a Hmong village)! Khamdaeng looked to be full of admiration. With his meagre salary as a civil servant (less than US$12 a month), he spent more of his time in his rice-field than in the office.

8

Conclusion

The Lao Front for National Construction's loss of influence within the regime is perhaps the most revealing symptom of the end of the socialist project. As the country progressively opens itself to the market economy and to regional and international tourism, anti-capitalist and anti-Western imperialist rhetoric is no longer appropriate for galvanizing the population behind the leadership. The discourse of struggle is being replaced by a discourse of lack. The regime now calls for modernity. The education of the masses echoes the impetus to attain economic competitiveness in the world economy. In other words, the question of identity and culture is closely tied to the issue of overcoming "backwardness". On the other hand, members of ethnic minority groups, among those who were educated during the revolutionary period, show a desire to demonstrate individual agency. Through a divergent narrative of the national past or the assertion of an ethnicity that is not officially recognized, they in effect defy their nation–state's representation. The efforts of Sisouk, until recently a senior LFNC official, to create an official ethnic category, the Bru, outside the regime's enforced categorization — but within the nation–state's ethnic classification system — may epitomize this micro-level struggle for the legitimation of a self-defined identity, despite the low probability of his succeeding at the present time.

My specific intention in this research was to go beyond the apparent immutability of these two oppositional figures, the Majority and the ethnic minorities. In other words, I have tried to show that these two entities are dynamic. The Majority — or normality, to use the Foucaldian term — is not yet convincingly hegemonic, while the ethnic minorities — or deviant identity — cannot always be represented solely as the ethnic Other, either by the government or by academic researchers. There is no complete hegemony, as the newly reformulated nationalist discourse is itself unstable and still in the process of development. Neither is there an absence of autonomy on the part of those being represented. Simultaneously, they display openly a loyalty to the Party-State and feel they have the right to claim full membership of the nation. In a departure from Foucault's theory on power, interactions (rather than unilateral or asymmetric action) may perhaps better define the relations between the discourse and technologies of power, on the one hand, and agency and consciousness, on the other. To put it another way, normality (membership of the nation/the Majority) and deviancy (being an outcast of the nation/being an Ethnic Minority) still remain two inchoate representations in post-socialist Laos. To paraphrase Williams (1989), in the conception of the nation held by some "minority" members, those *outside* the mainstream are defined as ethnic Lao, politically stigmatized because of the civil war, as opposed to members of ethnic minority groups who claim a historical legitimacy for their political membership of the nation.

This project started with my observation of a modern phenomenon: the process of transformation of some upland people in French Indochina, who not so long ago were described as "savages" and "primitives", into "revolutionaries" and "patriots" during the Indochina Wars. I focus on the narratives of a number of these individuals, members of ethnic minority groups who fought in the Lao People's Liberation Army and/or were educated within the revolutionary administration. Their personal narratives reveal another narrative of the nation, born of specific historical, political and ideological contexts: during wartime when the "enemy", i.e. the rightist Royal Lao Government and the United States, served as the contrastive and defining figure of the Other; and when "being an ethnic person" (*pen khòn sòn phaw*) had the positive connotation of being attached to the ideals of revolutionary fraternity. The current tendency to revise the national history of struggle, i.e. to play down the participation and role of ethnic minority people during the war, progressively challenges their unified narration, however. As a consequence, these individuals may be coming to identify themselves less and less with the present representation of the national past. The narrative of the Nation in post-socialist Laos is gradually changing its tone and may challenge the political loyalty that emerged and was built up, especially during the American/Vietnam War, between the Pathet Lao and its ethnic minority fighters. This is, however, only a hypothesis that will certainly need further research. Likewise, the somewhat passive picture of early Lao communist recruits of ethnic minority origins (which represents their revolutionary motivations as being pervaded by a kind of political backwardness) needs reassessing. The memory of the Kommandans' struggle against the French authorities is still vivid among some highland groups in southern Laos. Much therefore remains to be investigated before the military, political and social history of the borderlands of Indochina gets satisfyingly mapped.

The writing of national histories by professional nationalists is guided by two key principles: continuity and homogeneity — the history of the nation is a linear, progressive history and the history of the national people is the history of the awakening of a race. Lao-language nationalist historiographies struggle with these interrelated cornerstones of perennialist historiography; in other words, they have failed to impose a standard and single narrative of the *origins* of *the national people*. As shown in my analysis of current Lao-language historiographies focused on the early period (prehistory and protohistory), the racially-based, China-located, historiography is not correct in the eyes of Marxist-Leninist professional historians swift to rebuff any suggestion of ethnic Lao chauvinism. While the versions of collective autochthonous origins uneasily balance between a highly discursive representation of a past mélange of races within the present-day borders of the national territory, on the one hand, and a search for a local, non-derivative, ancient civilization transcending the modern national boundaries, on the other. Lao amateur and professional historians, like their Vietnamese counterparts, therefore resort to emotionally-charged themes, of which the most constant one has been the "tradition of resistance against foreign aggression". The thread of continuity in those revolutionary historiographies lies in the mantra-like theme of popular resistance to foreign domination, epitomizing the liberation struggle of "the national people" of all ethnicities against a succession of exploitative political elites — feudal, imperial and colonial. In sum, the whole (Marxist) historiography of the Lao (or Vietnamese, Cambodian, Chinese, etc.) "nation" and "national people" proclaims to be a several-thousand-year secular struggle for independence and liberty.

The issue is as much about the loss of resonance of the narrative of the "Struggle for Independence" among some minority people, as about the lessening of its meaning among a population of whom more than half were born after 1975. To put it differently, the blanket theme of "the Struggle for Independence" that gives to the standard narration a thin thread of continuity is no longer able to mobilize affective reactions; hence, it can be challenged in terms of its ability to provide an adequate basis for a national history that can appeal to all the Lao people. On the other hand, one should welcome this gap between the regime's standard historiography and the past as represented and narrated by individuals. The objective of professional nationalists is to produce a "national identity" that encompasses and overrides all other forms of identification. In contrast, the study of the narratives and life stories among members of ethnic minority groups and former Pathet Lao fighters reveals different "nation-views", different ways in which the "nation is imagined, viewed and voiced"; as Prasenjit Duara illuminatingly suggests: "[i]n place of the harmonized, monologic voice of the Nation, we find a polyphony of voices, overlapping and criss-crossing; contradictory and ambiguous;

opposing, affirming, and negotiating their views of the nation" (Duara 1996, pp. 161–62). It is a commonplace in the study of nationalism that the construction of national identity necessarily relies on the creation and use of narratives — part history, part myth — that imbue nations and nationalist projects with coherence and rationale. However, the connection between the collective discourse and the personal narrative is often missing. Works on nations and nationalism tend to neglect to address individual interpretation. This book shows that the double process of simultaneity and homogeneity (of knowledge, thoughts and emotions) that define Benedict Anderson's political imagined communities is overridden in the fluid context of the politics of history, culture and identity in post-war Laos.

The identity politics of the "peripheral" ethnic minority population will continue to develop, both in the countryside and in urban areas, and within the context of increasing exposure to global discourses. The internationalization of minority issues through the work of NGOs, international organizations and academics inside and outside Laos, for instance, is starting, albeit very slowly and at an uneven pace, to affect the government's discourse and policies towards minority groups. The legacy of pre-colonial Buddhist ideologies of ethnic hierarchy, combined with the current regime's obsession with state control of ethnic identity and its approach to national development and national identity, do not provide propitious conditions for the emergence of a liberal conception of multiculturalism. The global discourse of cultural diversity is slowly beginning to circulate in Laos, nonetheless, and it may grow stronger if (or, when) Laos democratizes. What form a liberal politics of recognition would take in Laos, however, and whether its effects would necessarily be beneficial, remains to be seen.

Appendices

Appendix 1
Ethnic Composition of the Population of Laos, 1911–55

	1911	%	1921	%	1931	%	1936	%	1942	%	1955	%
Lao	276,801	45	429,000	52	485,000	50	565,000	56	441,450	43.6 / 60.9	856,000–865,000 (Lao-Tai)	77–74
Tai	124,238	19	122,000	15	113,000	12	100,000	10	175,170	17.3	210,000–	19–22
Kha	195,996	32	221,000	27	268,000	28	247,000	24	300,138	29.6	258,000[b]	
Meo-Yao	15,205	2	25,000	3	39,000	4	47,000	5	49,240	4.9	52,300–52,900	4
Vietnamese	4,109	0.7	9,000		19,000	2	27,000	2.7	39,470	3.9	8,000[c]	
Chinese	486		353		3,000	0.3			6,100	0.6	32,350[c]	
European	226[d] / 163[e]		8[f]		1,000	0.1			900	0.1	8,000	
Cambodian	1,270		1,300				2,000					
Indian and Pakistani	6										500	
Total	618,500	98.7	807,653	97	964,000	96.4	988,000	97.7	1,012,468	100	1,291,951–1,320,402	100

Sources: Lao Ministry of the Interior, 1955 figures; *Annuaire Statistique du Laos* 1913–22; *Annuaire Statistique de l'Indochine* 1930–31, 1936–37, Gouvernement Général de l'Indochine; *Bulletin de l'Office Colonial* 1911, No. 62, Février 1913; Direction des Affaires économiques, Service de la Statistique Général (Hanoi), 1927; *Plan de développement économique et social, Royaume du Laos,* Mars 1959, quoted from Halpern (1961: 19).

b Kha underestimated due to the exclusion of provinces that contain few Lao
c 1959 estimates; 41,121 non-Lao Asians were registered in Laos in 1959
c *Idem.*
d French
e Mixed-race
f Other Europeans

Appendix 2

Ethnic composition of Laos, 1954–55, by percentage of ethnic groups in each province[a]

Province	Total population	Lao & Tai[b]	%	Kha	%	Meo & Yao	%	Total %
Nam Tha	46,809	17,104	36.54	26,798	57.25	2,907	6.21	100
Luang Prabang	136,821	66,687	48.74	63,416	46.35	6,718	4.91	100
Sayaboury	98,516	86,389	87.69	8,167	8.29	3,960	4.02	100
Xieng Khouang	93,609	44,090	47.10	12,178	13.01	37,341	39.89	100
Vientiane	186,269	183,978	98.77	317	0.17	1,974	1.06	100
Khammouane	108,603	99,785	91.88	8,818	8.12			100
Savannakhet	214,974	171,743	79.89	42,231	19.64			99.5
Saravane	125,957	65,498	52.0	60,459	48.0			100
Champassak	122,078	117,769	96.47	4,309	3.53			100
Attopeu	43,315	12,865	29.70	30,450	70.30			100
Phong Saly[c]	50,000							
Sam Neua[c]	65,000							
Total	1,291,951	865,908		258,143		52,900		

Sources: Unpublished records of Ministry of Interior of the Government of Laos, Vientiane, quoted from Halpern (1961: 18).

a exclusive of Chinese, Vietnamese and European population

b includes Lu, Tai Dam and other tribal Tai groups; does not include Thai

c data incomplete since most of the area was under Pathet Lao Control during this period

Appendix 3
"Assessment of the ethnic groups' names in the Lao PDR accepted
during the LFNC meeting on 13–14th August 2000"

Lao-Thai : 8 ethnic groups
ລາວ Lao
ຜູ້ໄທ Phuthai
ໄຕ Tai
ລື້ Lue
ຍວນ Yuan
ແຊກ Saek
ຢັ້ງ Yàng
ໄທເໜືອ Thai Neua

Hmong-Mien : 2 ethnic groups
ມົ້ງ Hmong
ອິວມຽນ Iumien

Sino-Tibetan : 7 ethnic groups
ອາຄາ Akha
ສິງສິລິ Sìngsili
ລາຮູ Lahu
ສິລາ Sila
ຮາຢີ Hayi
ໂລໂລ Lolo
ຫໍ້ Hor

Mon-Khmer : 32 ethnic groups
ກັມມຸ Kmmu
ໄປຣ Plai/Prai
ຊິງມູນ Sìngmun
ຜົອງ Phong
ແທນ Thaen
ອິດູ Idu
ບິດ Bìt
ລະເມດ Làmet
ສາມຕ່າວ Samtao
ກະຕາງ Kàtang
ມະກອງ Màkong
ຕຣີ T'li/T'ri
ຕະໂອ້ຍ Tà-Oy
ຢຣຸ Y'lù/Y'rù
ຕຣຽງ Tlieng/Trieng
ແຢະ Yàe
ລະວີ Làvi
ເບຣົາ Blao/Brao
ກະຕູ Kàtu
ໂອຍ Oy
ກຣຽງ Klieng/Krieng
ສະດາງ Sàdang
ຣາຣັກ Lalàk/Raràk
ຊ່ວຍ Suay
ຂະແມ Khmer
ປະໂກະ Pàkò
ຕຸ້ມ Tùm
ງວນ Nguan
ມອນ Mon
ກຣີ K'li/K'ri
ເຈັ້ງ Chéng

Source: Table reproduced from Sisouk (2000), "Meeting's Report on the Research and Study on the Ethnic Groups' Names in the Lao PDR", 16 November, Xerox Copy.

Appendix 4
"Assessment of the provincial LFNC censuses 1999-2000 (list of 55 ethnic groups)"

1) ລາວ Lao
2) ຜູ້ໄທ Phuthai
3) ກົມມຸ Kmmu
4) ມົ້ງ Hmong
5) ລື້ Lue
6) ກະຕາງ Kàtang
7) ມະກອງ Màkong
8) ກໍ Kor
9) ຊ່ວຍ Suay
10) ຍວນ Yuan
11) ຍຣຸ Y'rù
12) ຕະໂອຍ Tà-Oy
13) ຕະຮຽງ Tàrieng/Tàlieng
14) ພູນ້ອຍ Phunoy
15) ຕຣີ T'ri
16) ພົ້ອງ Phong
17) ຍ້າວ Yao
18) ເບຣົ້າ Blao/Brao
19) ກະຕູ Kàtu
20) ລະເມດ Làmet
21) ໄປຣ Plai/Prai
22) ຣາຣັກ Lalàk/Raràk
(ອາລັກ) (Alak/Arak)
23) ປະໂກະ Pàko
24) ກາໂດ Kado
25) ກາໄນ Kanai
26) ຕົງ Tong
27) ອິນ In
28) ໂອຍ Oy
29) ມູເຊິ Musser

30) ກຣຽງ Klieng/Krieng
(ແງະ) (Ngae)
31) ກຸຍ Kuy
32) ຫໍ Hor
33) ເຈັງ chéng
34) ເຮີນ໌ Herne,
(ຍາເຫີນ) (yaherne)
35) ຢັ້ງ Yàng
36) ແຍະ Yàe
37) ສາມຕ່າວ Samtao
38) ຊິງມູນ Sìngmun
39) ຕຸ້ມ Tùm
40) ແຊກ Saek
41) ເມື້ອງ Meuang
42) ບິດ Bìt
43) ງ່ວນ Nguan
44) ໂລໂລ Lolo
45) ລະວີ Làvi
46) ສະດາງ Sàdang
47) ກະຍ້ອງ Kàyong
48) ຂະແມ Khmer
49) ແທນ Thaen
50) ໄທເຫນືອ Thai Neua
51) ໄທຣາດ Thai Rat/Lat
52) ຊຸມມາ Summa
(ກົ້ງສາດ) (Kòngsat)
53) ກຣີ K'li/K'ri
54) ບຣີ B'li/B'ri (ຄົນ ປ່າ) Khòn Pa
("man of the forest")
55) ກົງ Kìng (ຫວຽດ Viet)

Source: Table reproduced from Sisouk (2000), "Meeting's Report on the Research and Study on the Ethnic Groups' Names in the Lao PDR", 16 November, Xerox Copy.

Appendix 5
"Assessment of the names of the 34 ethnic groups"

1) ລາວ Lao
2) ຜູ້ໄທ Phuthai
3) ກັມມຸ Kmmu, including Thaen (ແທນ)
4) ມົ້ງ Hmong
5) ລື້ Lue
6) ບຣູ B'lù/B'rù (ກະຕາງ Kàtang, ມະກອງ Màkong, ຕຣີ T'li/T'ri, ຕະໂອ້ຍ Tà-Oy,
    ປະໂກະ Pako, ກາໄນ Kanai, ອິນ In, ຕົງ Tong, ຊວ່ຍ Suay, ກະຕຸ Kàtu,
    ກລຽງ Klieng/Krieng)
7) ກໍ Kor (ຊຸມມາ Summa, ກົງສາດ Kòngsat)
8) ຍວນ Yuan
9) ຍຣຸ Y'rù
10) ຕຣຽງ Tlieng/Trieng
11) ພູນ້ອຍ Phunoy
12) ພົ້ອງ Phong
13) ຢ້າວ Yao
14) ເບຣົາ Blao/Brao
15) ລະເມດ Làmet
16) ໄປຣ Plai/Prai
17) ຣາຣັກ Lalàk/Raràk
18) ໂອຍ Oy
19) ລາຮູ Lahu
20) ຫໍ Hor
21) ເຮີມ໌ຍ Herne
22) ຢ້າງ Yàng
23) ແຊກ Saek
24) ສາມຕ່າວ Samtao
25) ຊິງມູນ Sìngmun
26) ຕຸ້ມ Tùm
27) ເມື້ອງ Meuang
28) ບິດ Bìt
29) ຫງ່ວນ Nguan
30) ໂລໂລ Lolo
31) ຂະແມ Khmer
32) ກຣີ K'li/K'ri
33) ລາບຣີ Labri
34) ກິງ King (ຫວຽດ Viet)

Source: Table reproduced from Sisouk (2000), "Meeting's Report on the Research and Study on the
         Ethnic Groups' Names in the Lao PDR", 16 November, Xerox Copy.

References

References in English, French and Thai

Ahmad Abu Talib and Tan Liok Ee, eds. *New Terrains in Southeast Asian History*. Singapore: Singapore University Press, 2003.

Aijmer, Goran. "Reconciling Power with Authority: An Aspect of Statecraft in Traditional Laos". *Man* 14, no. 2 (1979): 734–49.

Alonso, Ana Maria. "The effects of Truth: Re-presentations of the Past and the Imagining of Community". *Journal of Historical Sociology* 1, no. 1 (1988): 33–57.

―――. "The Politics of Space, Time and Substance: State Formation, Nationalism, and Ethnicity". *Annual Review of Anthropology* 23 (1994): 379–405.

Amselle, Jean-Louis and Elikia M'Bokolo, eds. *Au cœur de l'ethnie. Ethnie, tribalisme et État en Afrique*. Paris: La Découverte, 1999 (1985).

Anagnost, Ann. *National Past-Times. Narrative, Representation and Power in Modern China*. Durham and London: Duke University Press, 1997.

Anderson, Benedict. *Imagined Communities: Reflections on the Origins and Spread of Nationalism*. London: Verso, 1991 (1983).

Archaimbault Charles. *Structures religieuses lao (rites et mythes)*. Vientiane: Éditions Vithagna, 1973.

Ardener, Edwin. "Language, Ethnicity and Population". In *The Voice of Prophecy and Other Essays*, edited by Malcom Chapman, pp. 65–71. Oxford: Blackwell, 1989 (1972).

Baker, Chris. "Afterwords: Autonomy's Meanings". In *Recalling Local Pasts. Autonomous History in Southeast Asia*, edited by Sunait Chutintarinond and Chris Baker, pp. 167–82. Chiang Mai: Silkworm Books, 2002.

Balibar, Etienne. "La forme nation: histoire et idéologie". In *Race, nation, classe. Les identités ambiguës*, edited by E. Balibar and I. Wallerstein, pp. 117–43. Paris: La Découverte, 1997 (1988).

Bank, Marcus. *Ethnicity: Anthropological Constructions*. London and New York: Routledge, 1996.

Barth, Frederik. "Introduction". In *Ethnic Groups and Boundaries: The Social Organization of Culture Difference*, edited by Frederik Barth, pp. 9–38. Bergen/Oslo: Universitetsforlaget (Scandinavian University Press), 1969.

Bentley, Carter G. "Indigenous States of Southeast Asia". *Annual Review of Anthropology* 15 (1986): 275–305.

Bhabha, Homi K. "DissemiNation: Time, Narrative, and the Margins of the Modern Nation". In *Nation and Narration*, edited by Homi K. Bhabha, pp. 291–322, London and New York: Routledge, 1995 (1990).

Bounthavy Sisouphanthong and Christian Taillard. *Atlas de la république démocratique populaire lao. Les structures territoriales du développement économique et social*. Paris: CNRS-GDR Libergéo-La Documentation française, 2000.

Bourdieu, Pierre. "The Biographical Illusion". In *Identity: A Reader*, edited by P. du Gay, J. Evans and P. Redman, pp. 297–303. London, Thousand Oaks, New Delhi: Sage Publications, 2000 (1986).

Branfman, Fred. "Presidential War in Laos, 1964–1970". In *Laos: War and Revolution*, edited by N.S. Adams and A.W. McCoy, pp. 213–80. New York, Evanston and London: Harper Colophon Books, 1970.

Brocheux, Pierre and Daniel Hémery. *Indochine, la colonisation ambiguë*. Paris: Editions La Découverte, 1994.

Brown, MacAlister and Joseph J. Zasloff. *Apprentice Revolutionaries: The Communist Movement in Laos, 1930–1985*. Stanford University, Stanford, California: Hoover Institution Press, 1986.

Bruner, Edward M. "Ethnography as Narrative". In *The Anthropology of Experience*, edited by V.W. Turner and E.M. Bruner, pp. 139–55. Urbana and Chicago: University of Illinois Press, 1986.

———. "Experience and Its Expressions". In *The Anthropology of Experience*, edited by V.W. Turner and E.M. Bruner, pp. 3–30. Urbana and Chicago: University of Illinois Press, 1986.

Burchett, Wilfred G. *Mekong Upstream*. Hanoi: Red River Publishing House, 1957.

Chamberlain, James R. "The Origin of the Southwestern Tai". *Bulletin des amis du royaume Lao*, no. 7–8 (1972): 233–44.

Chamberlain, James R., Charles Alton and A.G. Crisfield. *Indigenous Peoples Profile: Lao People's Democratic Republic*. Vientiane: CARE International, 1995.

Chatterjee, Partha. *Nationalist Thought and the Colonial World: A Derivative Discourse*. London: Zed Books, 1993a (1986).

————. *The Nation and Its Fragments: Colonial and Postcolonial Histories*. Princeton, New Jersey: Princeton University Press, 1993.

Chou Norindr. Le 'Néo Lao Hak Xat' ou le Front patriotique lao et la révolution laotienne. Unpublished thesis, Université de Paris III, Sorbonne nouvelle, 1980.

Christie, Clive J. *Ideology and Revolution in Southeast Asia 1900–1980. Political Ideas of the Anti-Colonial Era*. Richmond, Surrey: Curzon Press, 2001.

————. "Marxism and the History of the Nationalist Movements in Laos". *Journal of Southeast Asian Studies* 10, no. 1 (1979): 146–58.

————. *Race and Nation: A Reader*. London, New York: I.B. Tauris, 1998.

Clark, Steve H. *Paul Ricoeur*. London and New York: Routledge, 1990.

Clifford, James. "Introduction: Partial Truths". In *Writing Culture: The Poetics and Politics of Ethnography*, edited by J. Clifford and G.E. Marcus, pp. 1–26. Berkeley, Los Angeles, London: University of California Press, 1986.

Cohn, Bernard S. "The Census, Social Structure and Objectification in South Asia". In *An Anthropologist among the Historians and Other Essays*. Oxford, New York: Oxford University Press, pp. 224–54, 1987.

Cohn, Bernard S. and Nicholas B. Dirks. "Beyond the Fringe: The Nation State, Colonialism, and the Technologies of Power". *Journal of Historical Sociology* 1, no. 2 (1988): 224–29.

Comaroff, John L. "Ethnicity, Nationalism, and the Politics of Difference in an Age of Revolution". In *The Politics of Difference: Ethnic Premises in a World of Power*, edited by E.N. Wilmsen and P. McAllister, pp. 162–83. Chicago and London: University of Chicago Press, 1996.

Condominas, Georges. *L'espace social à propos de l'Asie du sud-est*. Paris: Flammarion, 1980.

Connerton, Paul. *How Societies Remember*. Cambridge: Cambridge University Press, 1995 (1989).

Connor, Walker. *The National Question in Marxist-Leninist Theory and Strategy*. Princeton, New Jersey: Princeton University Press, 1984.

Constitution de la République démocratique populaire lao. Vientiane: Assemblée populaire suprême, 1991.

Constitution du Royaume du Laos, du 11 mai 1947, révisée en 1949 et 1952. In Katay Don Sasorith, *Le Laos. Son évolution politique, sa place dans l'Union française.* Éditions Berger-Levrault: Paris, 1953, pp. 98–110.

Constitutions of Vietnam (The): 1946–1959–1980–1992. Hanoi: Thê Gioi Publishers, 2003 (1995).

Culas, Christian and Jean Michaud. "A Contribution to the Study of Hmong (Miao) Migrations and History". *Bijdragen tot der Taal-, Land-en Volkerkunde* 153, no. 2 (1997): 211–43.

Dauplay, Jean-Jacques. *Les terres rouges du plateau des Boloven.* Saigon: Bibliothèque documentaire Extrême-Orientale, Chambre d'agriculture de la Cochinchine, 1929.

Delannoi, Gil. *Sociologie de la nation: Fondements théoriques et expériences historiques.* Paris: Armand Colin, 1999.

Dikötter, Frank. "Group Definition and the Idea of 'Race' in Modern China (1793–1949)". *Ethnic and Racial Studies* 13, no. 3 (1990): 420–32.

Doré, Amphay. "The Three Revolutions in Laos". In *Contemporary Laos: Studies in the Politics and Society of the Lao People's Democratic Republic,* edited by Martin Stuart-Fox, pp. 101–15. St Lucia, London: University of Queensland Press, 1982.

Dreyfus, Hubert L. and Paul Rabinow. *Michel Foucault: Beyond Structuralism and Hermeneutics.* Brighton: Harvester Press, 1982.

Duara, Prasenjit. "Historicizing National Identity, or Who Imagines What and When". In *Becoming National: A Reader,* edited by Geoff Eley and Ronald Grigor Suny, pp. 151–77. New York, Oxford: Oxford University Press, 1996.

Elias, Norbert. *The Civilizing Process.* Oxford: Basil Blackwell, 1982 (1939).

Eriksen, Thomas H. *Ethnicity and Nationalism: Anthropological Perspectives.* London: Pluto Press, 1993.

Evans, Grant. "Laos. Minorities". In *Ethnicity in Asia,* edited by Colin Mackerras, pp. 210–24. New York: RoutledgeCurzon, 2003.

———. *The Politics of Ritual and Remembrance: Laos Since 1975.* Chiang Mai: Silkworm Books, 1998.

———. "Buddhism and Economic Action in Socialist Laos". In *Socialism: Ideals, Ideologies, and Local Practices,* edited by in C.M. Hann. London and New York: Routledge, 1993.

———. *A Short History of Laos: The Land in Between.* Allen & Unwin, 2002.

————. *Lao Peasants under Socialism and Post-Socialism*. Chiang Mai: Silkworm Books, 1995 (1990).

————. "Apprentice Ethnographers: Vietnam and the Study of Lao Minorities". In *Laos: Culture and Society*, edited by G. Evans, pp. 161–90. Chiang Mai: Silkworm Books, 1999.

————. *Laos: Culture and Society*. Chiang Mai: Silkworm Books, 1999.

————. "Different Paths: Lao Historiography in Historical Perspective". In *Contesting Visions of the Lao Past*, edited by Christopher Goscha and Søren Ivarsson, pp. 97–110. Copenhagen: NIAS Press, 2004.

Fabian, Johannes. "Time and Writing About the Other". In *Time and the Other: How Anthropology Makes its Object*, pp. 71–104. New York: Columbia Press, 1983.

Fall, Bernard. "The Pathet Lao. A "Liberation" Party". In *The Communist Revolution in Asia: Tactics, Goals, and Achievements*, edited by R.A. Scalapino, pp. 173–97. New Jersey: Englewoods Cliffs, 1965.

Forbes, Andrew D.W., "The 'Čīn-Hŏ̌ (Yunnanese Chinese) Caravan Trade with North Thailand during the Late Nineteenth and Early Twentieth Centuries". *Journal of Asian History* 21, no. 2 (1987): 1–47.

Foster, Robert F. "Making National Cultures in the Global Ecumene". *Annual Review of Anthropology* 20 (1991): 235–60.

Foucault, Michel. "Nietszche, Genealogy, History". *The Foucault Reader*, edited by P. Rabinow, pp. 76–100. London: Penguin Books, 1991 (1984).

————. "Two Lectures". In *Power/Knowledge, Selected Interviews and Other Writings 1972–1977*, edited by C. Gordon, pp. 78–108. Brighton: Harvester Press, 1980.

————. "Afterword. The Subject and Power". In *Michel Foucault: Beyond Structuralism and Hermeneutics*, edited by H.L. Dreyfus and P. Rabinow, pp. 208–26. Brighton: Harvester Press, 1982.

Fox, Richard G. "Introduction". In *Nationalist Ideologies and the Production of National Cultures*, edited by R.G. Fox, pp. 1–14. Washington D.C.: American Anthropological Association, 1990.

Gillis, John R. *Commemorations: The Politics of National Identity*. Princeton and New Jersey: Princeton University Press, 1994.

Giteau, Madeleine. *Art et archéologie du Laos*. Paris: Éditions A.&J. Picard, 2001.

Gladney, Dru C. "Salman Rushdie in China: Religion, Ethnicity and State Definition in The People's Republic". In *Asian Visions of Authority: Religion and the Modern*

States of East and South East Asia, edited by C.F. Keyes, L. Kendall and H. Hardacre, pp. 255–78. Honolulu: University of Hawaii Press, 1994.

———. "Clash of Civilizations? Muslim and Chinese Identities in the PRC". In *Making Majorities. Constituting the Nation in Japan, Korea, China, Malaysia, Fiji, Turkey, and the United States*, edited by D.C. Gladney, pp. 106–31. Stanford, California: Stanford University Press, 1998.

———. ed. *Making Majorities: Constituting the Nation in Japan, Korea, China, Malaysia, Fiji, Turkey, and the United States*. Stanford, California: Stanford University Press, 1998.

Goscha, Christopher E. *Vietnam or Indochina? Contesting Concepts of Space in Vietnamese Nationalism, 1887–1954*. Copenhagen: NIAS (Nordic Institute of Asian Studies) Reports Series, No. 28, 1995.

———. "Vietnam and the World Outside. The Case of Vietnamese Communist Advisers in Laos (1948–62). *South East Asia Research* 12, no. 2 (June 2004): 141–85.

Goudineau, Yves, ed. *Resettlement & Social Characteristics of New Villages: Basic Needs for Resettled Communities in the Lao PDR. An Orstom Survey*. Vientiane: UNESCO (2 volumes), 1997.

———. "Ethnicité et déterritorialisation dans la péninsule indochinoise: considérations à partir du Laos". In *Logiques identitaires, logiques territoriales*, edited by Marie-José Jolivet, pp. 17–31. Cahier des sciences humaines, Éditions de l'Aube, IRD (Institut de recherche pour le développement, ex-Orstom), 2000.

———, ed. *Cultures minoritaires du Laos: valorisation d'un patrimoine*. Paris: Editions UNESCO, 2003.

Grabowsky, Volker. "The Isan up to its Integration into the Siamese State". In *Regions and National Integration in Thailand 1892–1992*, edited by Volker Grabowsky, pp. 107–29. Wiesbaden: Harrassowitz Verlag, 1995.

Gunn, Geoffrey C. "A Scandal in Colonial Laos: The Death of Bac My and the Wounding of Kommadan Revisited". *Journal of the Siam Society* 75, no. 1 and 2 (1985): 42–59.

———. *Political Struggles in Laos (1930–1954)*. Bangkok: Editions Duang Kamol, 1988.

———. *Rebellion in Laos: Peasant and Politics in a Colonial Backwater*. Boulder, San Francisco, Oxford: Westview Press, 1990.

————. "People's War in Laos: a New Guerrilla Model ?". *Journal of Contemporary Asia* 21 no. 4 (1991): 529–36.

Hall, Stuart. "Cultural Identity and Diaspora". In *Identity. Community, Culture, Difference*, edited by J. Rutherford, pp. 222–37. London: Lawrence and Wishart, 1990.

————. "The Question of Cultural Identity". In *Modernity and its Futures*, edited by S. Hall, D. Held and T. McGrew, pp. 273–325. Cambridge: Polity Press, 1994 (1992).

Halpern, Joel M. *Economy and Society of Laos: A Brief Survey*. Yale University Monograph Series No. 5, South-East Asian Studies, 1964.

Handler, Richard. *Nationalism and the Politics of Culture in Quebec*. Madison: University of Wisconsin Press, 1988.

Harrell, Stevan. "Introduction: Civilizing Projects and the Reaction to Them". In *Cultural Encounters on China's Ethnic Frontiers*, edited by S. Harrell, pp. 3–36. Seattle and London: University of Washington Press, 1995.

Hearn, Jonathan. "Narrative, Agency, and Mood: On the Social Construction of National History in Scotland". *Comparative Studies in Society and History* 44, no. 4 (2002): 745–69.

Hickey, Gerald. *Sons of the Mountains: Ethnohistory of the Vietnamese Central Highlands to 1954*. New Haven and London: Yale University Press, 1982.

Higham Charles. *The Archaeology of Mainland Southeast Asia: From 10,000 B.C. to the Fall of Angkor*. Cambridge: Cambridge University Press, 1989.

Hirschman, Charles. "The Making of Race in Colonial Malaysia: Political Economy and Racial Ideology". *Sociological Forum* 1&2 (1986): 330–62.

————. "The Meaning and Measurement of Ethnicity in Malaysia: An Analysis of Census Classifications". *Journal of Asian Studies* 46, no. 3 (1987): 555–82.

Hobsbawn, Eric. "Introduction: Inventing Traditions" In *The Invention of Tradition*, edited by E. Hobsbawn and T. Ranger, pp. 1–14. Cambridge: Cambridge University Press, 1983.

Hoskins, Janet. "The Headhunter as Hero: Local Traditions and their Reinterpretation in National History". *American Anthropologist* 14, no. 4 (1987): 605–22.

Ho Tai, Hue-Tam. "Situating Memory". In *The Country of Memory: Remaking the Past in Late Socialist Vietnam*, edited by Hue-Tam Ho Tai, pp. 1–17. Berkeley, Los Angeles, London: University of California Press, 2001.

Houmphanh Rattanavong. *On the Way to the Lolopho Land*. Vientiane: Institute for Cultural Research, Ministry of Information and Culture, 1997.

———. "Regarding What One Calls the 'Thai' ". In *Proceedings of the 4th International Conference on Thai Studies*. Kumming, China, 11–13 May 1990, pp. 162–75.

Hutchinson, John and Anthony D. Smith. *Nationalism*. Oxford: Oxford University Press, 1994.

International Labour Office (ILO). *Policy Study on Ethnic Minority Issues in Rural Development*. Project to Promote ILO Policy on Indigenous and Tribal Peoples, Geneva: ILO, 2000.

———. "Sustainable Development of Ethnic Minorities in Lao PDR under the INDISCO Approach". Project Document, ILO multi-bilateral programme of technical co-operation, 2000.

Institute for Cultural Research. *1997–1998 Vientiane Social Survey Project*. Vientiane: Ministry of Information and Culture, 1998.

Ireson, Carol J. and W. Randall Ireson. "Ethnicity and Development in Laos". *Asian Survey* 31, no. 10 (1991): 920–37.

Ivarsson, Søren. "Towards a New Laos: *Lao Nhay* and the Campaign for National 'Reawakening' in Laos, 1941–45". In *Laos: Culture and Society*, edited by Grant Evans, pp. 61–78. Chiang Mai: Silkworm Books, 1999.

Izikowitz, Karl Gustav. *Lamet: Hill Peasants in French Indochina*. Göteborg: Elanders Boktryckni Aktiebolag, 1951.

Jenkins, Richard. *Rethinking Ethnicity. Arguments and Explorations*. London, Thousand Oaks, New Delhi: Sage Publications, 1998 (1997).

Jory, Patrick. "Problems in Contemporary Thai Nationalist Historiography". *Kyoto Review of Southeast Asia* 3, March 2003, website visited on 21 May 2003.

Kapferer, Bruce. *Legends of People, Myths of State: Violence, Intolerance, and Political Culture in Sri Lanka and Australia*. Washington and London: Smithsonian Institution Press, 1988.

Katay Don Sasorith. *Le Laos. Son évolution politique. Sa place dans l'Union française*. Paris: Editions Berger-Levrault, 1953.

Kaysone Phomvihane. "Political Reports presented by Mr Kaysone Phomvihane at the National Congress of the People's Representative in Laos (December 1, 1975, condensed). *Journal of Contemporary Asia* 6, no. 1 (1976): 110–19.

———. "Strategy of Bypasssing to Socialism". Vientiane Home service,

10–17 March 1982, *Summary of World Broadcasts*, (SWB) of BBC, April 5, Part 3, The Far East, 1982.

———. *La Révolution Lao*. Moscow: Edition du Progrès, 1980.

Kertzer, David. *Ritual, Politics and Power*. New Haven and London: Yale University Press, 1988.

Keyes, Charles F. "Who are the Tai? Reflections on the Invention of Identities". In *Ethnic Identity: Creation, Conflict and Accommodation*, edited by Lola Romanucci-Ross and George DeVos, pp. 136–60. Walnut Creek, London, New Delhi: Altamina Press, 1995 (1975).

———. *The Golden Peninsula: Culture and Adaptation in Mainland Southeast Asia*. Honolulu: School of Hawaiian, Asian and Pacific Studies, University of Hawai'i Press, 1995 (1977).

———. "Cultural Diversity and National Identity in Thailand". In *Government Policies and Ethnic Relations in Asia and the Pacific*, edited by Michael E. Brown and Sumit Ganguly, pp. 197–231. Cambridge, Mass. and London: MIT Press, 1997.

———. "Presidential Address: "The Peoples of Asia" — Science and Politics of Classification of Ethnic Groups in Thailand, China, and Vietnam". *Journal of Asian Studies* 61, no. 4 (November 2002): 1163–203.

Keyes, Charles F., Helen Hardacre and Laurel Kendall, eds. *Asian Visions of Authority: Religion and the Modern States of East and South East Asia*. Honolulu: University of Hawaii Press, 1994.

Khamphao Phonekèo. "La religion et le régime politique. Le Bouddhisme, le Marxisme et le développement national". *Le Rénovateur* 77, 18 May 2000.

Kohl, Philip L. and Clare Fawcett. "Archaeology in the Service of the State: Theoretical Considerations". In *Nationalism, Politics, and the Practice of Archaelogy*, edited by Philip L. Kohl and Clare Fawcett, pp. 3–18. Cambridge: Cambridge University Press, 1995.

Kohl, Philip L. "Nationalism and Archaeology: On the Constructions of Nations and the Reconstructions of the Remote Past". *Annual Review of Anthropology* 27 (1998): 223–46.

Langer, Paul F. and Joseph J. Zasloff. *North Vietnam and the Pathet Lao: Partners in the Struggle for Laos*. Cambridge, Mass.: Harvard University Press, 1970.

Larner, Christina. "Was Witch-Hunting Woman-Hunting?" In *The Witchcraft Reader*, edited by Darren Oldridge, pp. 273–75. London and New York: Routledge, 2002.

Le Boulanger, Paul. *Histoire du Laos français: essai d'une étude chronologique des principautés laotiennes*. Paris: Librairie Plon, 1931.

Le Goff, Jacques. *Histoire et mémoire*. Paris: Gallimard, 1988 (1977).

Leach, Edmund. "The Frontiers of Burma". *Comparative Studies in Society and History* III (1960–61): 49–68.

LeBar, Frank M., Gerald C. Hickey and John K. Musgrave. *Ethnic Groups of Mainland Southeast Asia*. New Haven: Human Relations Area Files Press, 1964.

Lefèvre-Pontalis, Pierre. *Mission Pavie Indo-Chine 1879–1895. Géographie et voyages. Voyages dans le Haut Laos (et sur les frontières de Chine et de Birmanie)*. Paris: Ernest Leroux, 1902.

Litzinger, Ralph A. *Other Chinas: The Yao and the Politics of National Belonging*. Durham and London: Duke University Press, 2000.

Lockhart, Bruce M. "Education in Laos in Historical Perspective". Unpublished Paper.

Maha Sila Viravong. *History of Laos*. Paragon Book Reprint Corp.: New York, 1964 (1959).

Malarney, Shaun Kingsley. "'The Fatherland Remembers Your Sacrifice'". Commemorating War Dead in North Vietnam. In *The Country of Memory: Remaking the Past in Late Socialist Vietnam*, edited by Hue-Tam Ho Tai, pp. 46–76. Los Angeles, London: University of California Press: Berkeley, 2001.

Marcus, George E. and Michael M.J. Fischer. *Anthropology as Cultural Critique: An Experimental Moment in the Human Sciences*. Chicago and London: University of Chicago Press, 1986.

Marcus, George E. "Ethnography in/of the World System: The Emergence of Multi-Sited Ethnography". *Annual Review of Anthropology* 24 (1995): 95–117.

Marr, David G. *Vietnamese Tradition on Trial, 1920–1945*. University of California Press: Berkeley, 1981.

Marshall, T.H. "A Note on 'Status'". In *Identity: A Reader*, edited by P. du Gay, J. Evans and P. Redman, pp. 304–10. London, Thousand Oaks, New Delhi: Sage Publications, 2000 (1977).

Mason, David T. "Ethnicity and Politics". In *Encyclopedia of Government and Politics* 1. London: Routledge, 1992, pp. 568–85.

Maspéro, Henri. "Mœurs et coutumes des populations sauvages". In *Un empire colonial français, l'Indochine*, edited by G. Maspéro, pp. 233–55. Paris, Bruxelles: Les Editions G.Van Oest (Publications de l'Ecôle Française d'Extrême-Orient), Tome 1, 1929.

Mayoury and Pheuiphanh Ngaosyvathn. *Kith and Kin Politics: The Relationship between Laos and Thailand*. Manila: Journal of Contemporary Asia Publishers, 1994.

McCoy, Alfred W. "French Colonialism in Laos, 1893–1945". In *War and Revolution*, edited by N.S. Adams and A.W. McCoy, pp. 67–99. New York, Evanston, and London: Harper Colophon Books, 1970.

McCrone, David. *The Sociology of Nationalism: Tomorrow's Ancestors*. London and New York: Routledge, 1998.

Mercer, Kobena. "Welcome to the Jungle: Identity and Diversity in Postmodern Politics". In *Identity: Community, Culture, Difference*, edited by J. Rutherford, pp. 43–71. London: Lawrence and Wishart, 1990.

Michaud, Jean. "The Montagnards and the State in Northern Vietnam from 1802 to 1975: A Historical Overview". *Ethnohistory* 47, no. 2 (2000): 333–68.

Miller, J.H. "But are Things as We Think They are?". *Times Literary Supplement*, 9–15 October 1987, pp. 1104–5.

Ministry of Communications, Transport, Posts and Construction. *Province of Sekong, Muang Thateng*, Integrated Rural Accessibility Planning (IRAP), Accessibility Data, 1997.

Moppert, François. Mouvement de résistance au pouvoir colonial français de la minorité protoindochinoise du plateau des Bolovens dans le sud Laos: 1901–1936. Unpublished Thesis, Université de Paris VII, 1978.

———. "La révolte des Bolovens (1901–1936)". In *Histoire de l'Asie du Sud-Est: révoltes, réformes et révolutions*, edited by P. Brocheux, pp. 47–62. Presses universitaires de Lille, 1981.

Murdoch, John B. "The 1901–1902 "Holy Man's" Rebellion". *Siam Society Journal* 62 (1974): 47–66.

Nairn, Tom. "The Modern Janus". In *The Break-Up of Britain: Crisis and Neo-Nationalism*. London: NLB, 1977: 329–63.

Nation (The) (Bangkok). "Thai TV Gets Mixed Review in Laos". 28 January 2001.

National Statistical Centre/State Planning Committee. *Results from the Population Census 1995*, Vientiane, Lao PDR, 1997.

Nora, Pierre. "Between Memory and History: Les Lieux de Mémoire". *Representations* 26, Special Issue: Memory and Counter-Memory, Spring 1989: 7–24.

Okely, Judith. "The Self and Scientism". In *Own or other Culture*, pp. 27–44. London and New York: Routledge, 1996 (1975).

Ovesen, Jan. "All Lao? Minorities in the Lao People's Democratic Republic". In *Civilizing the Margins. Southeast Asian Government Policies for the Development of Minorities*, edited by Christopher R. Duncan, pp. 214–40. Ithaca and London: Cornell University Press, 2004.

Party Central Committee's Administrative Commission. "Concerning Cultural Activities in the New Era", Directive of the ninth meeting of the Party Central Committee's Administrative Commission, Fifth Party Congress, Vientiane, 9 October 1994.

Pelley, Patricia M. " "Barbarians" and "Younger Brothers": The Remaking of Race in Postcolonial Vietnam". *Journal of Southeast Asian Studies* 29, no. 2 (1998): 374–91.

———. *Postcolonial Vietnam: New Histories of the National Past*. Duke University Press, 2002.

———. "The History of Resistance and the Resistance to History in Post-Colonial Constructions of the Past". In *Essays into Vietnamese Pasts*, edited by K.W. Taylor and J.K. Whitmore, pp. 232–45. Ithaca, New York: Cornell University Press, 1995.

Phongsavath Boupha. *The Evolution of the Lao State*. New Delhi: Konark Publishers, 2002.

Pietrantoni, E. "La population du Laos de 1912 à 1945". *Bulletin de la Société des Etudes Indochinoises* 27, no. 1 (1953): 25–38.

———. "La population du Laos en 1943 dans son milieu géographique". *Bulletin de la Société des Etudes Indochinoises* 32, no. 3 (1957): 222–43.

———. Le problème politique du Laos. Unpublished paper, Vientiane, 1943.

Proschan, Frank. " 'We are all Kmhmu, just the same': Ethnonyms, Ethnic Identities, and Ethnic Groups". *American Ethnologist* 24, no. 1 (1997): 91–113.

Rabinow, Paul. *The Foucault Reader*. London: Penguin Books, 1991 (1984).

Rajah, Ananda. "Orientalism, Commensurability, and the Construction of Identity: A Comment on the Notion of Lao Identity". *Sojourn* 5, no. 2 (1990): 308–33.

Reinach, Lucien (de). *Le Laos*. Paris: E. Guilmoto, 1911.

Renan, Ernest. *Qu'est-ce qu'une nation?* Paris: Éditions Mille et une nuits, 1997 (1882).

Reynolds, Craig J. "A New Look at Old Southeast Asia". *Journal of Asian Studies* 54, no. 2 (May 1995): 419–46.

Ricoeur, Paul. "Can There be a Scientific Concept of Ideology?". In *Phenomenology* and the Social Sciences: A Dialogue, edited by J. Bien, pp. 44–59. The Hague, Boston, London: Martinus Nijhoff, 1978.

———. "Narrative Time". Critical Inquiry 7 (1980): 169–90.

———. Temps et récit. Tome I, Paris: Seuil, 1983.

———. "Dialogues with Paul Ricoeur". In Dialogues with Contemporary Continental Thinkers, edited by R. Kearney, pp. 15–46. Manchester: Manchester University Press, 1986 (1984).

Said, Edward W. Orientalism: Western Conceptions of the Orient. Penguin Books, 1995 (1978).

Salemink, Oscar. "Primitive Partisans: French Strategy and the Construction of a Montagnard Ethnic Identity in Indochina". In Imperial Policy and Southeast Asian Nationalism, 1930–1957, edited by H. Antlöv and S. Tønnesson, pp. 262–93. Richmond, Surrey: Curzon Press, 1995.

Savèng Phinit. "La frontière entre le Laos et le Viêtnam (des origines à l'instauration du protectorat français) vue à travers les manuscrits Lao". In Les frontières du Vietnam, edited by P-B. Lafont, pp. 194–203. Paris: L'Harmattan, 1989.

Schein, Louisa. "Gender and Internal Orientalism in China". Modern China 23, no. 1 (1997): 68–98.

———. Minority Rules: The Miao and the Feminine in China's Cultural Politics. Durham and London: Duke University Press, 2000.

Scott, James C. Domination and the Arts of Resistance: Hidden Transcripts. Yale University Press: New Haven and London, 1990.

Smail, John R.W. "On the Possibility of an Autonomous History of Modern Southeast Asia". In Autonomous Histories, Particular Truths: Essays in Honor of John R.W. Smail, edited by Laurie J. Sears, pp. 39–70. University of Wisconsin, Centre for Southeast Asian Studies, Monograph no. 11, 1993.

Smith, Anthony D. Myths and Memories of the Nation. Oxford and New York: Oxford University Press, 1999.

———. Nationalism and Modernism: A Critical Survey of Recent Theories of Nations and Nationalism. London and New York: Routledge, 1998.

——— The Nation in History: Historiographical Debates about Ethnicity and Nationalism. Cambridge: Polity Press, 2000.

Souneth Photisane. "A New Trend in Researching the Ancient History of Laos". In Studies of History and Litterature of Tai Ethnic Groups, edited by Sarasawadee Ongsakul and Yoshiyuki Masuhara, pp. 57–79, 2003 (in Thai).

Stalin, Joseph. *Marxism and the National Question: A Collection of Articles and Speeches.* Lawrence and Wishart: London, 1936.

State Planning Committee. *National Rural Development Programme 1996–2000, Lao PDR*, Vol. 1 (Main Document), 1998.

———. *Report on the Round Table Meeting on Human Resource Development and Rural Development.* Vientiane, 11–13 May, 1998.

———. *The Rural Development Programme 1998–2002: The 'Focal Site' Strategy.* Government Document, Sixth Round Table Follow-Up Meeting, Vientiane, 13 May 1998.

Steenbergen, Bart van, ed. *The Condition of Citizenship.* London, Thousand Oaks, New Delhi: Sage, 1994.

Streckfuss, David. "The Mixed Colonial Legacy in Siam: Origins of Thai Racialist Thought, 1890–1910". In *Autonomous Histories: Particular Truths. Essays in Honour of John Smail*, edited by Laurie Sears, pp. 123–53. University of Wisconsin, Center for Southeast East Asian Studies, Monograph No. 2, 1993.

Stuart-Fox, Martin. "Socialist Construction and National Security in Laos". *Bulletin of Concerned Asian Scholars* 13, no. 1 (1981): 61–71.

———. "The First Ten Years of Communist Rule in Laos". *Asia Pacific Community* 31, no. 1 (1986): 55–81.

———. "On the Writing of Lao History: Continuities and Discontinuities". *Journal of Southeast Asian Studies* 24, no. 1 (March 1993): 106–21.

———. "The French in Laos, 1887–1945". *Modern Asian Studies* 29, no. 1 (1995): 111–39.

———. *Buddhist Kingdom, Marxist State: The Making of Modern Laos.* Bangkok: White Lotus, 1996.

———. *A History of Laos.* Cambridge: Cambridge University Press, 1997.

———. *The Lao Kingdom of Lan Xang: Rise and Decline.* Bangkok: White Lotus, 1998.

———. "Laos: from Buddhist Kingdom to Marxist State". In *Buddhism and Politics in Twentieth Century Asia*, edited by I. Harris, pp. 153–72. London and New York: Pinter, 1998b.

Sturken, Marita. "The Wall, the Screen, and the Image: The Vietnam Veterans Memorial". *Representations* 35, Special Issue: Monumental Histories (Summer, 1991): 118–42.

Taillard, Christian. "Les transformations de quelques politiques agricoles socialistes en Asie entre 1978 et 1982 (Chine, Vietnam, Cambodge, Laos)". *Etudes rurales*, 89–90–91, 1983: 111–43.

———. *Le Laos: stratégies d'un Etat-tampon*. Montpellier: Groupement d'Intérêts Publics Reclus, collection Territoires, 1989.

Tambini, Damian. "Post-national Citizenship". *Ethnic and Racial Studies* 24, no. 2 (March 2002): 195–217.

Terwiel, Barend J. "Civilising the Past: Nation and Knowledge in Thai Historiography". In *Time Matters. Global and Local Time in Asian Societies*, edited by Willem van Schendel and Henk Schulte Nordholt, pp. 97–111. Amsterdam: VU University Press, 2001.

———. "The Origin of the T'ai Peoples Reconsidered". In *Oriens Extremus* 25 (1978): 239–57.

Thongchai Winichakul. *Siam Mapped: A History of the Geo-Body of a Nation*. Chiang Mai: Silkworm Books, 1994.

———. "The Changing Landscape of the Past: New Histories in Thailand since 1973". *Journal of Southeast Asian Studies* 26, no. 1 (March 1995): 99–120.

———. "The Others Within: Travel and Ethno-Spatial Differentiation of Siamese Subjects 1885–1910". In *Civility and Savagery: Social Identity in Tai States*, edited by Andrew Turton, pp. 38–62. Richmond, Surrey: Curzon Press, 2000a.

———. "The Quest for "Siwilai": A Geographical Discourse of Civilizational Thinking in the Late Nineteenth and Early Twentieth-Century Siam". *Journal of Asian Studies* 59, no. 3 (August 2000b): 528–49.

———. "Writing at the Interstices. Southeast Asian Historians and Postnational Histories in Southeast Asia". In *New Terrains in Southeast Asian History*, edited by Abu Talib Ahmad and Tan Liok Ee, pp. 3–29. Singapore: Singapore University Press, 2003.

Tonkin, Elizabeth. *Narrating our Pasts: The Construction of Oral History*. Cambridge University Press, 1992.

Tønnesson, Stein and Hans Antlöv, eds. *Asian Forms of the Nation*. London: Curzon Press, 1996.

Trankell, Ing-Britt. "Royal Relics: Ritual and Social Memory in Louang Prabang". In *Laos: Culture and Society*, edited by G. Evans, pp. 191–213. Chiang Mai: Silkworm Books, 1999.

Trankell, Ing-Britt. and Laura Summers, eds. *Facets of Power and its Limitations:*

Political Culture in Southeast Asia. Acta Universitatis Upsaliensis: Uppsala Studies in Cultural Anthropology 24, 1998.

Tréglodé, Benoît de. Héros nouveau" et "Combattant d'émulation" en République démocratique du Viêt Nam, 1948–1964. Doctoral thesis, École des Hautes Études en Sciences Sociales, Doctorat d'histoire et de civilisation, Paris, 1999.

————. "Reflet d'une nation: la figure de Hô Chi Minh dans les biographies du "héros nouveau' ". Symposium paper, Institut d'études politiques de Paris, Groupe d'études sur le Viêt-Nam contemporain, "Le Viêt Nam depuis 1945: Etats, Marges et Constructions du Passé", 11–12 January 2001.

————. *Héros et Révolution au Viêt Nam, 1948–1964.* Paris : l'Harmattan, 2002.

Trigger, Bruce G. "Romanticism, Nationalism, and Archaeology". In *Nationalism, Politics, and the Practice of Archaelogy*, edited by Philip L. Kohl and Clare Fawcett, pp. 263–79. Cambridge: Cambridge University Press, 1995.

Turner, Bryan S. "Outline of a Theory of Citizenship". *Sociology* 24 (1990): 189–217.

Turner, Victor W. "Dewey, Dilthey, and Drama: An Essay in the Anthropology of Experience". In *The Anthropology of Experience*, edited by V.W. Turner and E.M. Bruner, pp. 33–44. Urbana and Chicago: University of Illinois Press, 1986.

UNESCO (1996). *Réunion internationale d'experts pour la sauvegarde et la protection du patrimoine culturel immatériel des groupes minoritaires de la République démocratique populaire du Laos*, Final Report, Vientiane, 7–11 October, 1996.

Vipha, Utthamachant, *Phonkratopkhongsanyawitanyoulaethorathatkhamphromdaenra wangthailao* [Impacts of cross-border radio and television transmissions between Thailand and Laos], Chulalongkorn University Press: Bangkok, 2001.

Walker, Andrew. *The Legend of the Golden Boat: Trade and Traders in the Borderlands of Laos,Thailand, China and Burma.* Surrey: Curzon Press, 1999.

Watson, Rubie S. "Memory, History, and Opposition under State Socialism: An Introduction". In *Memory, History and Opposition under State Socialism*, edited by Rubie S. Watson, pp. 1–20. Santa Fe, Mexico: School of American Research Press, 1994.

Wekkin, Gary D. "The Rewards of Revolution: Pathet Lao Policy towards the Hill Tribes since 1975". In *Contemporary Laos: Studies in the Politics and Society of the Lao PDR*, edited by M. Stuart-Fox, pp. 181–98. St Lucia and London: University of Queensland Press, 1982.

Williams, Brackette F. "A Class Act: Anthropology and the Race to Nation across Ethnic Terrain". *Annual Review of Anthropology* 18 (1989): 401–44.

Wolters, Oliver W. *History, Culture, and Region in Southeast Asian Perspectives.* Ithaca, New York: Southeast Asian Program Publications, Cornell University, 1999 (1982).

Wright, Susan. "The Politicization of 'Culture' ". *Anthropology Today* 14, no. 1 (1998): 7–15.

Wyatt, David K. *A Short History of Thailand.* New Haven: Yale University Press, 1984.

Zasloff, Joseph J. *The Pathet Lao: Leadership and Organization.* Lexington, Mass.: Lexington Books, 1973.

References in Lao

Bouaphan Thammavong, ປະຫວັດສາດລາວເຫລັ້ມນຶ່ງ : ສະໄໝບູຣານ ["History of Laos I : Ancient Epoch"], Committee in social sciences, History section, Ministry of Education, National University of Laos, Vientiane, 1998.

Bounhèng Bouasisèngpaseut, ປະຫວັດສາດສິນລະປະ ແລະ ສະຖາປັດຕະຍະກາໍສິນລາວ ["History of Arts and Lao Architectural Arts"], vol. 1, Vientiane, 1991.

Bounkhong Soukhavath, ປະເທດລາວໃນສັງຄົມນາໆຊາດ ["Laos within the international community"), Vientiane, 2002.

Department of Religion, ສາສະໜາກັບສັງຄົມມະນຸດ ("Religion and Society"), *Lao Sang Sat*, 1(1), 1998: 43 and 51–52.

Désanoulat Sèndouangdeth, ປະຫວັດສາດລາວເຫລັ້ມສາມ : ສະໄໝໃໝ່ ແລະ ປະຈຸບັນ ["History of Laos III: Modern and Contemporary Periods"], Committee in social sciences, History section, Ministry of Education, National University of Laos, Vientiane, 1998.

Douangsay Louangphasi, ອານາຈັກ ຂຸນເຈືອງ ["khunchiang kingdom"], Vientiane, 2001 (1996).

Douangsay Louangphasi, ພົງສາວະດານຄົນລາວແຜ່ນດົນຂອງລາວ ["History of Lao people, Lao people's territory"], Vientiane, 2001 (1995).

Houmpanh Rattanavong, ວັດທະນະທາໍ ແລະ ວັດທະນະທາໍລາວ ["Culture and Lao culture"], *Lanxang Heritage Journal*, 1(2), 1996: 149–70.

Institute of research in educational sciences, History Handbook for Teachers, ວິຫຍະຍາສາດສັງຄົມ ["Social Sciences"], First year secondary school, Ministry of education, Vientiane, 1996.

Institute of research in educational sciences, ວິຫຍະຍາສາດສັງຄົມ ["Social Sciences"]. Second year secondary school, Ministry of education, Vientiane, 1997.

Institute of research in educational sciences, ວິຫະຍາສາດສັງຄົມ ["Social Sciences"], Third year secondary school, Ministry of education, Vientiane, 1997.

Kaysone Phomvihane ເສີມຂະຫຍາຍມູນເຊື້ອແຫ່ງຄວາມສາມັກຄີລະຫວ່າງເຜົ່າຕ່າງໆໃນ ວົງຄະນາຍາດແຫ່ງຊາດລາວທີ່ເປັນເອກະພາບເດັດດ່ຽວປົກປັກຮັກສາປະເທດຊາດໄວ້ ໃຫ້ໝັ້ນຄົງແລະ ກໍ່ສ້າງສັງຄົມນິຍົມໃຫ້ສໍາເລັດຜົນ ("Enhancing solidarity's roots between the diverse ethnic groups within the Lao national community, united and determined to durably preserve the nation and to successfully build up socialism"), Vientiane, 15 June 1981, Xerox copy.

Khampheuye Chantasouk, ເສີມຂະຫຍາຍບຳໃຈຮັກຊາດລາວເອກະພາບໃຫ້ສູງ... ("Expanding love for the Lao nation to a high level... "), *Vientiane Mai*, 12 August 1999.

Lao Revolutionary People's Party's Central Committee ມະຕິຂອງຄະນະບໍລິຫານ: ສູນກາງພັກປະຊາຊົນປະຕິວັດລາວກ່ຽວກັບບັນຫາສາສະໜາ ("Resolution of the Lao Revolutionary People's Party's Central Committee related to Religious Issues"), Vientiane, 30 June 1992, Xerox copy.

Maha Sila Viravong, ປະຫວັດສາດລາວແຕ່ບູຮານເຖີງ 1946 ["History of Laos. From ancient epoch to 1946"] National Library, Vientiane, 2001 (1957).

Ministry of Education, Centre for Teachers' Training, Teaching Manual, ປະຫວັດ ສາດລາວສະໄໝບູຮານ ແລະ ສະໄໝກາງ ["History of Laos in Ancient and Middle Ages"], Vientiane, 1998.

Ministry of Education, Centre for Teachers' Training, Teaching Manual, ປະຫວັດ ສາດລາວເຫຼັ້ມສາມ : ສະໄໝໃໝ່ ແລະ ປະຈຸບັນ ["History of Laos, vol. 3: modern and contemporary periods"], Vientiane, 1998.

Ministry of Information and Culture, ປະຫວັດສາດລາວເຫຼັ້ມນຶ່ງ ["History of Laos, vol. 1"], Vientiane, 1996.

Ministry of Information and Culture, ປະຫວັດສາດ (ເດີກດໍ້ບັນ - ປະຈຸບັນ) ["History of Laos (Ancient Epoch-Contemporary Period)"], Vientiane, 2000.

Ministry of Education and Sport, Social Research and Institute, ປະຫວັດ ສາດລາວເຫຼັ້ມນຶ່ງ ("History of Laos, vol. 1"), Vientiane, 1995.

Ministry of Education, Centre for Teachers' Development, ວັດທະນະທໍາໃສັງຄົມລາວ ("Lao Culture and Society"), Vientiane, 1998.

Ministry of Information and Culture, ມາດຕະຖານຂອງການສ້າງຊີວິດວັດທະນະທໍາໃໝ່ ("Criteria/Guidelines for constructing life in the new cultural era"), Vientiane, 1998.

Ministry of Information and Culture, ແຈ້ງການ (ເລກທີ 848)/ຖວ (Notice. No. 848), *Vientiane Mai*, 21 March 2000.

Noychansamon Denchaleunsouk, ບັນຫາພື້ນຖານກ່ຽວກັບບັນຫາຊົນເຜົ່າ ("Fundamental questions concerning ethnic groups' issue") in [*Idem.*] ເອກະລັກຂອງ ບາງຊົນເຜົ່າຢູ່ແຂວງເຊກອງ ("Characteristics of some ethnic groups in Sekong Province"), 3 October, Xerox copy, 1999.

Saravane Provincial Administration Office, ປະຫວັດສາດແຂວງສາລະວັນ ["History of Saravane Province"], State Printing House, Vientiane, 2000.

Sinsai Keomanivong, ລັດຖະບານລາວອິດສະຫຼະ ແລະ ແນວລາວອິດສະຫຼະ ("Lao Issala Government and Neo Lao Issala"), *Lao Sang Sat*, 1(1), 1998: 23–27.

Sisouk ບັນດາບ່ອນອີງທລິມາດຕະຖານໃນການຄົ້ນຄວ້າເພື່ອຂຶ້ນບັນຊີຊົນເຜົ່າຕ່າງໆໃນທົ່ວ ປະເທດລາວບັນດາວິທີ ການຄົ້ນຄວ້າແບບວິທະຍາສາດລະອຽດແລະຮອບດ້ານກ່ຽວ ກັບເຜົ່າອ^ນໆ ("Criteria for Conducting Research on Ethnic Groups for Statistical Collection throughout the Country. Comprehensive Scientific Research Methodology"), Xerox Copy, 1999.

Sisouk ບົດສະຫຼຸບກອງປະຊຸມສຳມະນາຄົ້ນຄວ້າປິກສາທາງລິກກ່ຽວກັບຊື່ເອີ້ນເຜົ່າໃນສປ ປລາວ ("Meeting's Report on the Research and Study of the Ethnic Groups' Names in Lao PDR"), 16 November, Xerox Copy, 2000.

Souneth Photisan, ຄວາມສຳຄັນຂອງພື້ນຂຸນບູລົມຕໍ່ປະຫວັດສາດລາວ ("The Importance of the Khun Bulòm chronicle in Lao History"), *Lanxang Heritage Journal*, 1(1), 1996: 48–62.

Thongsa Sayvongkhamdi et al., ປະຫວັດສາດລາວແຕ່1893ເຖິງປະຈຸບັນ ["History of Laos 1893 until present time"], vol. 3. Institute of research in educational sciences, Ministry of education and sports, Vientiane, 1989.

Vientiane Mai, ເພື່ອສັກສິແມ່ຍິງລາວ.... ແผ່ນດົນລາວ ("For Lao Women's Dignity... Lao Territory"), 25 April 2000.

Index

About the Author

Vatthana Pholsena is an Assistant Professor at the Southeast Asian Studies Programme, National University of Singapore. A graduate of the Institut d'Etudes Politiques of Grenoble, France, with a PhD from the University of Hull, she is the author of several studies on politics, historiography and ethnicity in Laos and the co-author of *Le Laos au XXI° siècle. Les défis de l'intégration régionale* (Bangkok: IRASEC, 2004).